BRAND DRIVEN

THE ROUTE TO INTEGRATED BRANDING THROUGH GREAT LEADERSHIP

BY

F JOSEPH LEPLA
SUSAN V DAVIS
LYNN M PARKER

AuthorHouse™
1663 Liberty Drive, Suite 200
Bloomington, IN 47403
www.authorhouse.com
Phone: 1-800-839-8640

AuthorHouse™ UK Ltd.
500 Avebury Boulevard
Central Milton Keynes, MK9 2BE
www.authorhouse.co.uk
Phone: 08001974150

This book is a work of non-fiction. Unless otherwise noted, the author and the publisher make no explicit guarantees as to the accuracy of the information contained in this book and in some cases, names of people and places have been altered to protect their privacy.

First published by AuthorHouse 3/29/2007

ISBN: 978-1-4259-3706-5 (e)
ISBN: 978-1-4259-3708-9 (sc)

Printed in the United States of America
Bloomington, Indiana

This book is printed on acid-free paper.

Bloomington, IN Milton Keynes, UK

authorHOUSE

Acknowledgements

While every book is a team effort, this one is particularly so. First off, many of its ideas came from collaboration with team members at Parker LePla. Every team member at Parker LePla helped out in some way to further the theory and practice of integrated branding: thank you all for your efforts in this important endeavor.

There would be no reason for this book if not for our clients. It is in counseling these companies that our ideas have been tested. The real world is a harsh mistress, but an honest one, and we appreciate both the fodder for ongoing improvement and the successful case studies it offers.

Several colleagues contributed to this book, either with content, concepts or case studies. Of particular note were Cheryl Stumbo, Lisa Samuelson, Kerry Sturgill and Eric Nobis who researched, project managed, wrote and edited substantial portions of this book: it would not exist without them. Special mention goes to Briana Marrah, who wins the "can-do" award for valor with graphics. Thanks also go out to Dom Williamson for help with visuals.

Early readers of our manuscript also deserve special mention for their time, perseverance, feedback and overall good sense. Thanks go to Sally LePla, Jill LePla, Keneta Anderson, Betsy Edwards, Ronan O'Loan, John Rae-Grant, and Jamie Gier for their help in this regard. Cheryl Scott and Byron McCann need acknowledgement for their help on the healthcare and merger and acquisition chapters, respectively. Alan Gulick helped immensely with information about Washington Mutual.

All our families demonstrated their love and patience during the manuscript writing process: may we show as much graciousness and support to you as you have shown to us.

Thanks to my wife, Teresa Rodriguez for supporting me through this effort, you were a great source of ideas and feedback, and, as always, you encouraged me to do my best. Thanks also to my sisters Sally and Jill LePla for your above-and-beyond editing efforts, and to Chris Arlen and John Quinlan for kicking around ideas and directions and adding a fresh perspective to my writing. FJLP

Thank you Tim, Ethan, and Serena. Your confidence and support make my world go around. Additional thanks to my friends, colleagues, and clients past and present, especially at Microsoft. You allowed me to test out some ideas and continue to learn from your experience and passion for a productive workplace. SVD

Larry, Tristan, Rebecca and Calvin: I know I promised, after the first one, that there would be no further transgressions. I am in awe of your capacity for forgiveness. Thanks for letting me write a second book. LMP

PREFACE

This is a book about leadership – and about creating value throughout any company that wants customer loyalty and the bottom-line value of actions that create and maintain this type of loyalty. Many leaders mistakenly believe brand is a marketing problem, reserved for those companies that can afford Super Bowl ads or snazzy logos. But a brand is the sum total of every experience a customer has with a company or product – a sum total that customers begin to think of as the promise of the brand. The reality is if you want to create a strong brand, keeping the brand promise is every leader's responsibility. Brand value and customer loyalty come from smart and disciplined leaders who implement brand strategy and model brand action every day.

No matter what organization you lead, it is simply good business to invest in the people and strategies that engender deep customer relationships. Every successful organization – big or small, for profit or non-profit, business or consumer, high tech or low tech – thrives on such customer loyalty. Loyalty creates repeat business, a willingness to pay more, and a bond that transcends cynicism during tough times.

Chief among the actions that create and maintain customer loyalty is understanding how your brand promise creates a unique and compelling customer experience, and how to deliver it time and time again. Integrated branding is the process of revealing the brand promise, then aligning the entire organization to deliver on that promise.

Joe LePla's and Lynn Parker's first book, *Integrated Branding, Becoming Brand-driven Through Company-wide Action* (1999), answered the fundamental question, 'How do organizations reveal and build a strong brand that they can integrate throughout the organization?' That book explained that integrated branding means:

- the brand is built on the company's actual strengths;
- the brand is also built on what customers value;
- the brand needs to be implemented organization-wide through both words and deeds.

This book, *Brand Driven: The Route to Integrated Branding through Great Leadership*, takes the next step. It answers the question, 'How can I, as a leader, guide everyone throughout my organization to live our brand?' Unlike many other branding books, this one ventures inside the organization, taking the focus off external marketing communications and putting it on every leader. It demonstrates that successful leaders are those who pursue directions, decisions, strategies and actions to align a company's activities, employees, products, and services with the delivery of a consistently compelling customer experience.

Leaders of all types – from the mailroom to the boardroom – have tremendous potential to shape customer experience and impact the day-to-day execution of the brand. We call this living the integrated brand. It is every leader's journey. A leader, as used to in this book, is anyone who has the responsibility to guide others in a direction they deem successful. An individual contributor can be a leader of others without a formal management title. For clarity, where we are referencing leaders in formal positions, we have used the terms senior management or executive.

Living the integrated brand is the road to long-term business success and sustainability. It is something leaders carry with them as they face the day-to-day challenges of creating, selling and delivering their products or services in a very competitive world.

We've designed this book as a leader's travel guide for living an integrated brand. Each chapter of this guide includes the major milestones every leader should consider along their journey. Chapters 1-12 contain the meat of the journey. Each chapter concludes with a travelogue, recapping the chapter from the perspective of various leaders and how they would apply their leadership to the ideas provided. Chapters 13-17 contain milestones for leaders involved in specific types of situations: more mature organizations, start-ups, non-profits, healthcare and organizations facing mergers and acquisitions.

Having traveled this road themselves and with their clients, the authors and contributors have included navigational tools, points of interest and important clarifying questions in each chapter. They have pulled examples and case studies from their combined experience to help illustrate their points. Most of the examples and case studies are from larger, more recognizable companies. This is not to imply that integrated branding is only for large companies. Instead, these examples were used in an effort to illustrate points in ways that were quickly recognizable to a broad readership.

In living the integrated brand, each leader faces a personal, challenging role: Behaviors they can reinforce; decisions they can make; actions they can reward; functions they can influence. Not every milestone, tool or question will directly apply to every leader. At each milestone you need to ask yourself 'what's my role here? What can I do to enhance the customer experience, and in turn, reap their loyalty?'

For the purposes of this book, the term customer may mean your clients, constituents, dealers, partners, or even the general public (for example, if your organization serves everyone). A customer is anyone the organization sells to, sells with or serves. For simplicity, throughout the book, customer is a placeholder for all of these audiences. Don't be misled by the term company, either. Non-profits, schools, community groups and governmental organizations can also benefit from a strong brand that leads to client, constituent or customer loyalty.

These and other terms are explained in detail in the first few chapters.

So buckle up and get out your map. Get ready to travel down an exciting and rewarding road that will lead you to the heart of your compelling customer experience.

CONTENTS

INTRODUCTION

In 1991, when I started working for Starbucks Coffee Company in Vancouver, BC, there were only 112 stores in all of North America. The not-yet-public company had stores in Seattle, Portland, Chicago and Vancouver – period. Did any of us envision what it would become today – a global brand with 8,337 stores throughout North America and around the world? No. Did we believe in what we were doing? Yes. Did we think that we could change the world? Yes. Why did we think those things? Well, I'm not sure that we could have articulated it back then in exactly the same manner that it would be articulated today, but it really started with the Mission Statement and Guiding Principles of the organization and the whole notion of *integrated branding* – even if we didn't know what to call it back then. And it didn't start in the marketing department – but in the executive suite.

At Starbucks, we used to say *everything matters*, and it does. The people in the organization must *live the brand* one employee at a time; one transaction at a time and one customer at a time. In doing so they will, in effect, be *walking the talk* of the brand and providing brand-driven customer experiences that ultimately provide bottom-line benefits.

What LePla, Davis and Parker have accomplished in *Brand Driven* is to provide the quintessential guidebook for anyone who wants to instill their organization with *brand* and to do it in a very simple, clear and no-nonsense manner. There aren't any "silver bullets" to shaping the way in which organizations work and the impact that they have on the customers' experience – would that there were! As the authors lay out in detail in *Brand Driven*, it starts with leadership that has a very clear vision of who the brand is and what is possible and then aligns the people *and* the processes in the organization to support that vision internally and externally through consistent messaging. Becoming *brand driven* is not easy, but leaders and organizations that make the journey will be amply rewarded – as will their customers.

Roly Morris is the President & CEO of KremeKo Inc., the private Canadian company that makes and distributes Krispy Kreme doughnuts across Canada (excluding British Columbia). KremeKo Inc. is a joint venture partnership with Krispy Kreme Doughnuts Inc., one of the world's most admired brands.

WHY ALL LEADERS NEED TO BE BRAND DRIVEN

The journey is the reward.

–Taoist Saying

In a nutshell, the leader's task is to align people to deliver value. This book is about just that: leadership that focuses every employee's actions on delivering your organization's brand promise. But isn't branding solely a marketing function? No, the biggest myth in business today is that branding is just about marketing. If the marketing department is making promises to your customers, who is responsible for making sure that promise is delivered? Company leaders. And the way to deliver on your organization's promise is through integrated branding.

Integrated branding is a leadership practice that aligns all actions and messages with the core value an organization brings to its line of business. With integrated branding, a company carefully orchestrates everything it does to deliver a highly differentiated and consistent, positive experience. You could say integrated branding is the promise that you keep.

The goal of your integrated branding promise is to create unbreakable customer relationships through compelling customer experiences. Because a company's brand is the sum of a customer's experience with it and based on what the company does well, delivering on that brand becomes every leader's responsibility. When this responsibility is met, the result is a consistent customer experience with a positive bottom line impact.

According to B. Joseph Pine II and James H. Gilmore, products and services act as the stage for a memorable customer experience. And branded experiences are critical to creating a bond with customers:

'While prior economic offerings – commodities, goods and services – are external to the buyer, experiences are inherently personal, existing only in the mind of an individual who has been engaged on an emotional, physical, intellectual or even spiritual level.' [1]

By integrating everything from broad processes to employee actions in the service of building an integrated brand, a company is many times more likely to create deep, long lasting relationships with its best customers.

Contrary to some schools of thought, employee branding cannot be a separate activity if companies are going to walk their talk. Employees need to be taking action based on building a company's overall brand, in order for the company to realize the full benefits of brand integration. 'If we want to exceed the trust of our customers, then we first have to build trust with our people,' says Howard Schultz, Starbucks' chairman. Brand has to start with the culture and naturally extend to our customers.'[2]

Take the example of a retail-clothing brand. In a truly integrated brand, a customer experiences everything about a clothing store as a seamless experience, including its logo, its ads, its retail environment, its salespeople, its Web site, its customer service, its gift box and, of course, its clothes. Even things that happen behind the scenes – such as how a company manages inventory and order fulfillment – can contribute to the customer's experience. WalMart, for example, knows that the greeter at the door is as much a part of the brand as the logo. Strong brands are those that align all their activities to deliver on a compelling customer experience.

Just the opposite is true, also. Take, for example, the discount store that promises the lowest prices, but the cash register the checker uses cannot ring up a competitor's discount without having a manager's key to override the program. The checkers hesitate to involve the manager in customer transactions for fear they will be perceived as not doing their job competently. The customer, who found the competitor's discount, and expects to get it quickly, doesn't like waiting for the manager. The company has just failed to deliver on its brand experience for this customer. Without an understanding of how a brand must permeate the organization, down to supplying the necessary tools at a checkout counter, a company cannot deliver the expected customer experience.

FIGURE 1.1: THE TRULY INTEGRATED BRAND
The company brand is at the center of all actions and functions.

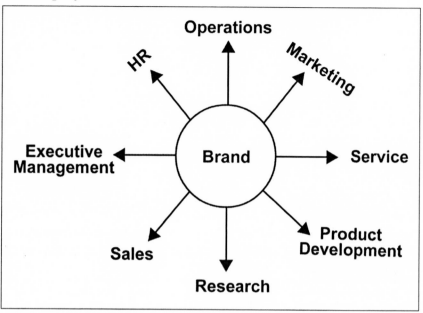

You might think that when Federal Express officially shortened its name to FedEx, it was solely the look and feel of the new company image that built it into the mega-brand it is today. While brand conveyors, such as a company's logo or colors, play an important role in public image and awareness, it would be a mistake to think that FedEx was able to grow from its humble roots in 1973 into the shipping giant it is today by just having the right 'look and feel.' FedEx's success is based on keeping promises. Shortly after FedEx began making promises about its revolutionary new business model, Xerox Corporation tested FedEx's system by shipping empty boxes for two weeks before entrusting the company with real documents. There isn't a 'look and feel' in existence that can help a company pass a test like that.

So why does branding usually live in the marketing department? Because many leaders are fundamentally confused about what branding is or is not. They think it's only a marketing or corporate identity function, rather than something that lives in every experience every customer has with the company. Wise leaders know unless they are communicating the truth, all their marketing efforts will come up short. Customers know when companies are not walking the talk. Employees know even quicker. When a company is paying lip service to a concept, rather than living it, employees are less loyal to and productive for that company. As J. Marriott Jr. of the Marriott hotel chain says about employees, 'Motivate them, train them, care about them and make winners out of them... we know that if we treat our employees correctly, they'll treat the customers right. And if customers are treated right, they'll come back.'

Integrated branding is the path to training every employee how to treat the customer right. To work, it must be the seed within the company that blooms in every department, creating a consistent customer experience. And good leaders will make guiding people on how to live the brand one of their chief aims. If your company has integrated its brand, every person knows and takes actions based on what the company is great at, its personality and its key promise to customers. Furthermore, they know how their job function directly or indirectly creates the customer's experience. When employees are living an integrated brand, they can:

- make decisions smarter and faster;
- consistently act in a way that customers appreciate;
- design products and services that emphasize the company's key promise;
- consistently act to increase the company's differentiation;
- hire the type of people and create a work environment that reflects the company's key values;
- budget the company's money in a way that builds the brand and reinforces key brand attributes.

And yes, they also will market the company's products and services in a way that reinforces the company's brand.

Do all companies need to live their integrated brand? In a word, yes. Yes, if they care about attracting and retaining loyal customers and employees. Yes, if they care about returning value to shareholders. And, yes, if they care about maximizing the company's investments and expenditures. You don't need to be a multimillion-dollar company with an astronomical marketing budget to reap the internal and external rewards of an integrated brand. You simply need the clarity of vision to understand the importance your customers' experience plays in your future success.

THE SECRET TO CREATING LOYAL CUSTOMERS

As we said, the goal of the integrated branding process is to create unbreakable customer relationships, compared to just gaining people's awareness, as the dotcoms did during the 2001 Super Bowl. You want customers ultimately bonded to your company in many deep ways, like a Starbucks experience, where it's not just the coffee taste, but how Starbucks grows it, what music you listen to while drinking it, the sense of place Starbucks creates and how well coffee servers know their stuff.

Figure 1.2 shows the progression of the customer experience using integrated branding: from awareness through preference to loyalty, and then on to commitment. How can having more loyal and committed customers help your company? Frederick F. Reichheld, author of *The Loyalty Effect: The Hidden Force behind Growth, Profits and Lasting Value*, has demonstrated that bringing just 5% more of your customers into the loyalty or commitment levels would lead to an average 25% to 100% increase in profit per customer.[3]

But loyalty and commitment won't result from increased awareness, great advertising or even customer willingness to sign on to 'loyalty programs.' According to a Gallup study of a major hotel chain's affinity club, members who were strongly attached to the brand gave the chain 32% more of their total lodging dollars – even though other club members received the same perks and benefits from the club.[4]

What can leaders do to create loyalty? There are several ways that you can use integrated branding to move your customers to loyalty and commitment. In the article 'Brand Zealots' by Horacio D. Rozanski, Allen G. Baum and Bradley T. Wolfsen in *Strategy + Business*, the authors cite work by Professor Susan Fournier of Harvard University, who has outlined three triggers to create an emotional tie with a brand:

1) congruence with deeply rooted life themes [values], such as personal freedom
2) helping in the accomplishment of life projects such as college graduation or parenting
3) resolution of current concerns, such as getting enough vitamins

According to Fournier, all three triggers can occur either through the customer's personal relationship with the brand – resulting in the customer seeing the brand as a friend or partner – or through a community of users – where the community becomes a significant part of the customer's life.

When these triggers result in either high levels of satisfaction or significant personal investment in the brand (either of emotions, time or money), customer loyalty increases. These customers will remain loyal, be vocal about your brand, and help your brand overcome any missteps.[5] In fact, companies that overcome missteps generate greater customer loyalty than those that never make a mistake. 'Southwest Airlines customers, for example, say the airline effectively deals with problems in 77% of cases, compared with less than 50% for the four largest carriers. As a result, nearly half of those who say they are loyal to an airline identify Southwest as their favorite.'[6]

FIGURE 1.2: BRAND EQUITY PYRAMID
Moving up the pyramid creates an unbreakable customer relationship.

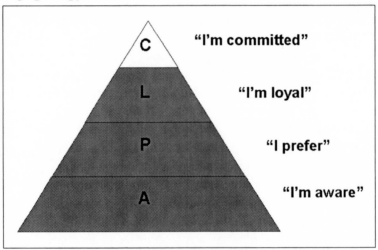

When customers understand and buy into the value of the experience employees create, they also develop a rationale for why they prefer your product or service and company. The combination of intellectual and emotional identification with your brand can move customers past loyalty to the commitment level where they often become customers for life. Harley-Davidson, for example, is known for the fanaticism of its customers. The company is not just selling motorcycles, but as stated in its mission, it is fulfilling 'dreams through the experience of motorcycling.' To that end, Harley-Davidson has created a community of highly committed users – there are 660,000 enthusiasts from 115 countries who pay U.S. $40 annually to be members of the Harley

Owner's Group (H.O.G.), to share in the experiences of motorcycling and be part of the Harley-Davidson family. The company also connects with its customers and creates an emotional bond in a myriad of other ways: open houses, cause-related rides, apparel and collectibles, parts and accessories to customize your motorcycle, Rider's Edge (the Harley -Davidson Academy of Motorcycling), *The Enthusiast* magazine, and H.O.G rallies worldwide.

The benefits of creating a strong brand also extend to increased profits. Companies with strong brands have measurable results:

- 5-7% higher stock price than others;[7]
- customers who are willing to pay up to 25% more than other brands for the same features/functions;[8]
- up to 289% earnings (before interest and taxes) growth over low-relevance brands;[9]

Harley-Davidson for example, has not only created a community of intensely loyal customers – who sometimes wait up to a year for their new bikes and pay U.S. $2,000 - $4,000 above the sticker price – it has, as a result, also enjoyed 16 consecutive years of record revenue and earnings, an annual earnings growth of 37% and a share price that is up 15,000% since 1986.[10]

If you move from a communications-only brand, like the drug store that advertises friendly, neighborhood service but comes off feeling sterile and impersonal to customers, to an integrated brand, you will also experience higher levels of growth – even in a mature market. That's because you will have successfully clarified a customer's emotional and intellectual reasons for buying from you rather than from the competition. Brands are assets that organizations can use to drive economic value above and beyond business infrastructure. Therefore, brands have a unique and powerful role in formulating business strategy.

Even during times of corporate distress, having a strong brand can be valuable. Brokerage firms have reported fondness for companies with powerful brands that have securities trading at low levels. In an article entitled 'Favorite Feasts: Good Brands Hit by Bad Luck' published in *The New York Times*, 21 January 2001, Riva Atlas suggests that these investors find 'the assets of these companies easier to value and, if necessary to sell off...(such as) the Vail ski resort; retailers like

Barneys, Bloomingdale's and Macy's; and Continental Airlines, to name a few.'

But the benefits of a strong brand accrue in direct proportion to the degree your brand is integrated.

FedEx is one company that makes bold promises – and keeps them. Founder and CEO Fred Smith is a leader who believes in the power of on-brand actions,

and is frequently quoted as being in support of 'living the brand.' The result is that when you think overnight delivery, you think FedEx. The brand is synonymous with quick, reliable delivery.[11]

So what does it look like to 'live' quick and reliable delivery? How do you apply it to every person, process and action throughout the company? 'As consumers, we're quick to form opinions about FedEx based on the emotions we feel when, for instance, we hear the drop box closing. Does it sound cheap and tinny? Secure and reassuring? Do we fear that it didn't quite shut all the way and someone will come and pour coffee all over our very valuable packages? These things matter to us.'[12] And so FedEx set about rethinking and redesigning everything from its customer centers to its drop boxes to the bags carried by its couriers. It even went so far as to redesign the electronic scanners carried by FedEx drivers so that they were quicker and more reliable.

FedEx's Smith clearly understands brand equity on a level that many companies do not. His ability to harness the FedEx brand by living it makes all the difference for the shipping giant as it moves into increasingly competitive times.

INTEGRATED BRAND DEFINED

An integrated brand is one in which every part contains the whole; where every action is based on the brand. Many companies, small and large, are doing this today. Their brands are powerful not because of the number of ads they run during televised sporting events but because of the customer loyalty they generate and maintain during good times and bad. In fact, communication alone doesn't even do a good job of generating awareness, let alone brand loyalty. According to a study of 80 online businesses performed by Copernicus, a marketing consulting firm in Newton, Massachusetts, these companies typically realized a .03% rise in awareness for each U.S. $1 million they put into advertising.[13]

Examples of large, international companies that do a good job of living their brand include Amazon.com, IBM, Volvo, Avis, FedEx, Nike, Ikea, Apple, Starbucks, Sony, and 3M. Smaller organizations that are doing it well include Group Health, Trendwest Resorts, Sakson & Taylor, Avanade and Seattle Children's Home. Each of these organizations has clearly defined the center of its brand's gravity, communicated that center, and is acting upon it. Each company's employees understand the meaning of their brands, and pull together in the same direction to build and sustain them.

The difference between integrated branding and what others may think is branding is that typical branding efforts are focused solely on communication tools to build awareness. For a company to start

---

Once there was a financial services company that thought branding would help it appeal to more customers. By coming up with a customer-friendly message and personality, reflected in the company's logo and ads, the company believed it could attract more customers and make them more loyal. So far, so good. The company went through a brand development exercise, where it decided that its customers would respond to a value of respectful. It created a corporate identity and a marketing campaign that showed respect through a strong-yet-not-brash logo and through advertisements that told customers they would be treated as partners, where their needs would be understood and honored.

Then things started to go wrong. Customers responded well to the advertising campaign and the company's new look, but found that the company wasn't delivering on its promises. The customers didn't come back. You see, the sales employees believed senior management team didn't truly respect them, much less worry about the customers. In turn, they grew cynical about their jobs, making the customers' experience of the brand even worse than it was prior to the brand exercise. Soon word got out in the company that branding doesn't work, and the company reverted to its previous way of doing things.

Why did this branding exercise go astray so badly? Because the company was fundamentally confused about branding, believing it was a marketing-only function. Saying that branding is just about marketing is like going to a restaurant that features great décor, advertising, service and a tantalizing menu, but serves inedible food.

---

seeing the results of an integrated brand, it must also be using brand attributes to guide actions within the company: in senior management; product and or service development; sales; human resources; operations; marketing; and customer service. Without company alignment and execution – living your brand – all branding efforts are doomed to fall short.

Your brand must be based on actual company strengths, rather than a pasted-on mask – no matter how pretty. Otherwise, your branding efforts will not create a sustainable advantage. Integrated branding is the way for organizations to achieve their vision. It does this by providing a clear map to making decisions: providing clarity on which actions to do more of to cement customer relationships.

THE INTEGRATED BRANDING PROCESS

For the integrated branding process (Figure 1.3) to work its full magic, there are three key areas that a company must explore and execute thoroughly:

1. brand clarity;
2. company activity alignment;
3. communications.

FIGURE 1.3: INTEGRATED BRANDING PROCESS
Integrating your brand is a three-part process: reveal it, ensure everyone throughout your company is living it, and communicate it to all audiences.

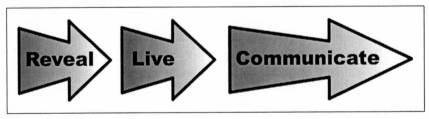

BRAND CLARITY

First, you have to know who you are. The key reason most branding efforts fail is that no one took the time to understand the brand's inherent meaning and then articulate it in a way that people could act on. To know what this inherent meaning is, you have to do research. This means asking customers, prospects, employees, partners, analysts, vendors, distributors and others, questions that get to the heart of what you bring to the party. Then, you need to sort through all that data to discover the brand assets of your company. A brand asset is any company activity that benefits customers such as unique customer experience, unique company approach, company reputation, industry leadership position, quality control systems, employee skill, company culture, employee compensation and rewards, and delivery systems. You also need to discover the personality people attribute to your company and the associations people have with your brand. Finally, you need to refine these assets and attributes into actionable brand tools.

The Volkswagen Beetle brand is a good example of how brand clarity creates brand value. While many people attribute the Beetle's success to the car's quality, low maintenance costs and unique look, Volkswagen was clear that the brand assets of a Beetle were around building special relationships with customers. 'Moreover, there are several things that VW itself did that seemed to reinforce its growing emotional segment (for example, quirky media campaigns, owner magazines in the 1960s, gold watch rewards for Beetle longevity and bonds for babies born in Beetles).'[14] According to James M. Flammang in his book *Volkswagen: Beetles, Buses & Beyond*, 'Life Magazine dubbed the Volkswagen "a member of the family" that just happens to live in the garage.'[15]

Some companies achieve brand clarity, only to stop there. Marketing may use the brand tools to drive communications, but if you ask other employees in such a company what their brand is, you'll get a blank stare or they'll point to the logo. Some companies take branding to the next level, where they ensure a consistent experience at every customer touchpoint, by training sales, marketing and customer service to live the brand. But the full benefit of integrated branding can't be achieved until *all* employees are living it.

COMPANY ACTIVITY ALIGNMENT

Second, you must have organizational alignment, or you can't achieve an integrated brand. For long-term success, you must create a company filled with leaders leading from the brand and employees executing upon it. This requires a whole new way of thinking, from getting leaders to be brand evangelists, to setting up employee compensation systems rewarding brand-based behavior, hiring based on branding, organizing company processes and designing products and services to reflect the brand. This is not a one-time event or program. It takes an ongoing commitment and effort from leaders at all levels to align the organization to execute on the brand.

Avis Rent a Car Systems focuses on how customers feel about every step of the rental car experience, and then applies that knowledge to the process of renting a car. Knowing that customers care most about a convenient, speedy process, Avis concentrates on aligning all company actions to create a customer experience of *stress-free transportation.* Recent brand changes include: training counter agents to observe and anticipate customers' needs, reducing perceived ambiguity by putting headphones on counter agents and providing Internet connections and posting flight information in its lounges and rental offices.[16]

COMMUNICATION TOOLS

Lastly, you have to tell the world who you are. Brand-based communications deliver the brand tools you'll learn how to develop in the next chapter, verbally and visually, via logos, ad campaigns, collateral, taglines, brand characters, colors, public relations, direct mail and Web sites. Rather than the place to focus all of your branding efforts, communications are the last step. Effective communication of brand messages will turbo-charge your marketing efforts, ensuring the message rings true to the customer and every communication conveys the same overall message and feeling. And if you kick off your brand in a big way, via enthusiastic communications to employees *and* clear, compelling communications to customers, you will have better luck at sustaining your brand efforts.

Outdoor consumer-cooperative retailer REI uses every opportunity to communicate its brand. Using a tagline of 'Get Outside Yourself ™,' REI focus its employees on communicating 'The Seven Summits of the REI Brand Experience,' a series of values with a big emphasis on giving customers a taste of the experience they will have using REI gear. For example, on the side of its shopping bags it features first-person testimonials such as the following:

'Almost there.' Fragile, crusty snow lingers in the high valley. We occasionally punch through to our thighs. So going is slow. My 5-year-old son gives in to exhaustion. I set down my pack, hoist him on my back and cautiously cover the last mile to camp, food and rest. He recovers. Then, as the sun's last rays turn the peaks to glowing orange snow cones. He says, 'That hike is longer than it sounds, isn't it?' 'Yes, it is.' 'Can we do it again soon?'

Many companies invest in brand clarity and communicate the brand externally, but don't actively attend to organization alignment and execution. Executing and delivering on your brand's promise doesn't just magically happen because the marketing department did some 'branding work.' Companies that execute well know that behind every strong brand is insight and commitment from company leaders. This type of brand leadership shows up every day in the choices leaders make within all functions and at all levels - especially those leaders closest to customers, leaders who are often not at the top of the organization chart. These choices shape key touchpoint experiences with customers and the impressions they walk away with.

In this book, we will focus on the company alignment and execution necessary for companies to live their brands. We will outline what leaders must do to live the brand, and how they can lead others to do the same. This is not a step-by-step handbook, but a framework for applying tested practices that are proven to increase company value and profitability. Whether you work for a start-up, a service company, a manufacturer, a large diversified corporation, a non-profit or a technology company, this framework will make your leadership more effective.

We will also address how to achieve brand clarity and how to communicate the brand. It is only through day-to-day actions that a company can truly say: 'We have integrated our brand into everything we do, and are living our promise to our customers.'

EVERY LEADER'S JOURNEY

According to *The New Rules of Branding*, by Court, Forsyth, Kelly and Loch, of McKinsey, 'A distinctive consumer experience that matches the brand promise requires consistent brand delivery. To make this happen, the brand leader must identify and prioritize key touchpoints, then translate the brand's meaning at those key touchpoints into guidelines that mobilize and inspire the people who are delivering the brand experience.'[17]

Brand leadership is a journey that uses tools, management and measurement to create distinctiveness despite inevitable changes in the market, employees and competition. The penalty for not exercising brand leadership is the loss of market position and brand assets, a defocused workforce, and the deploying of conflicting strategies that waste precious resources.

Living the integrated brand is a responsibility of every leader, at every level. That's what leading is all about: aligning employees behind company goals and doing so in a way that maximizes profitability and return on investment. But effective leadership is no accident. Effective leaders know what behaviors cause others to follow them. And regardless of your position, you are only a leader if others follow your lead. Being a great leader isn't the result of an extensive education or a powerhouse resume. Being a great brand leader is simultaneously holding and demonstrating your convictions about how to live your brand while maintaining your connection with others.

We designed this book as a guide to give company leaders the concepts; tools and processes they'll need to build powerful integrated brands.

TRAVEL GUIDE TO LIVING THE INTEGRATED BRAND

This book is a travel guide for leaders on how to live their company's integrated brand. It is divided into mile markers that will increase your ability to execute on your company's brand promise.

This is a travel guide, not a to-do list. Branding isn't something you do once and then it's done. As a leader, you will continuously improve your brand while adapting it to a changing world. *Brand Driven* suggests the most direct and cost-effective route to revealing and building your company's integrated brand. It will:

- give you the knowledge and direction necessary to create the right leadership strategies;
- show you effective ways to exercise leadership as you build the brand company-wide or in departments and work groups;
- save you from wasting your time, money and resources doing non-productive company activities.

Every leader can play a role in living the integrated brand. But the ideas and directions provided in each chapter will not apply to every leader in the same way. You'll need to determine how you can turn direction into action, given your current leadership circumstances. Each chapter is there to help you prepare for and deploy an integrated brand, while avoiding getting lost. Please note that Chapters 13-17 address specific audiences in living the integrated brand, such as non-profits, healthcare organizations and start-ups.

Ask yourself at each chapter *'Have I (and other leaders) done this yet? What's at risk if I (and other leaders) don't do this? What's the first step I should take, given my leadership role and function?'*

Enjoy the journey.

EXECUTIVE LEADER LOG

Interesting – since I've been at the helm, I've tightened our processes to be more efficient, I've instituted a performance-review system that no longer lets long-time employees who've been coasting get away with not working to their best abilities, and I've nailed our service and support department to the wall, after doing random customer surveys and finding out all the problems we create for our customers. Integrated branding – which sounds like it takes a more strengths-based approach to fixing problems – might be the next best thing I can initiate here. My VP of marketing's been trying to get on my calendar for months now to talk about a new logo and annual report design. That stuff's just fluff to me, but if I could wrap those things into a larger, more meaningful initiative that helps address serious, larger issues – threats and opportunities – it may be worth investing in a new look. It would certainly make a visual reminder of some major changes I'd be asking people here to make, for the sake of the company's long-term-future viability in the market.

HUMAN RESOURCES LEADER LOG

In exit interviews, departing employees have remarked that we 'believe our own BS.' Sounds like they're saying we don't always walk the talk, and that we don't face up to that like we should. Maybe the integrated branding process could help us face up to our words but also move us on quickly to making it right.

SALES LEADER LOG

We've had it hammered into us here that the salesperson 'owns' the experience with the customer. But this integrated branding theory says the customer experience needs to be owned by everyone in the company. This will be a big change for us, if we make it. How can we do it successfully without losing the benefits that holding salespeople fully accountable for customers' care bring us? Something to think about: what are our salespeople doing well that others in the company can start doing too? Going about it this way would be a good start to getting the salespeople to think of themselves as leaders.

NOTES

[1] Pine, B. Joseph II, and Gilmore, James H., 'Welcome to the Experience Economy', (July-August 1998), *Harvard Business Review*, pgs 98-99

[2] Khermouch, Gerry, (6 August 2001), 'The Best Global Brands,' *BusinessWeek,* p 57

[3] Appelbaum, Alec, (Summer 2001), 'The Constant Customer,' GMJ pgs 20-21

[4] Appelbaum, Alec, (Summer 2001), 'The Constant Customer,' GMJ pgs 20-21

[5] Rozanski, Horacio D.; Baum, Allen G.; Wolfsen, Bradley T. (Fourth quarter 1999). 'Brand Zealots: realizing the full value of emotional brand loyalty,' *Strategy + Business* pp 51-62

[6] Appelbaum, Alec, (Summer 2001), 'The Constant Customer', GMJ, p 24

[7] Corporate Branding, LLC website: www.corebrand.com

[8] Parker LePla 2002 customer survey

[9] Y&R (1995-1997 survey report) *Brand Asset Valuator*

[10] 2001 Harley Davidson Inc. Annual Report

[11] Iwanowychk, K., Lee, S. and Wells (5 December 1999), Cornell Equity Research

[12] Casey, S. (May 2001) 'Object Oriented: Federal Expressive', *eCompany Now*

[13] Freedman, David H., (May 2001), 'Last Guys Finish First,' *eCompanyNow*, p 96

[14] 'The Volkswagen Beetle: The Emotional Power of the Love Bug,' (Fourth Quarter '99), *Strategy + Business,* p 59

[15] 'The Volkswagen Beetle: The Emotional Power of the Love Bug,' (Fourth Quarter '99), *Strategy + Business,* p 59

[16] Mucha, Thomas, (August 2002), 'The Payoff For Trying Harder,' Business 2.0

[17] Court, D., Forsyth, J, Kelly, G and Loch, M, (2000), 'The New Rules of Branding,' *McKinsey Marketing Practice White Paper*, p 7

CHAPTER

BRING YOUR BRAND INTO FOCUS

*I may not have gone where I intended to go, but I
think I have ended up where I intended to be.*

–Douglas Adams

This chapter will help you determine your brand destination. With a defined brand, you'll know where you're heading and what success will look like when you get there. Of course, with integrated branding, the destination is a starting point for a new round of improvements. Using this and subsequent chapters, every leader can then start designing brand-based plans and strategies. You can lead others in a common direction and help them stay on track. The most valuable skill of any leader is the ability to show people the road to success.

You will also do your job better – whether you are in human resources, the corner office or on the factory floor – if you know the brand promise you are keeping with your customers, your co-workers and partners. For instance, if you as the receptionist can answer the phone in a way that reflects the brand, then you are building your company's customer relationships. If you are a product designer who knows your company's key strengths, then you can better create products that reflect those strengths. If you are an operations expert looking for ways to improve your company's efficiency, then learning what your firm's unique promise is will guide your efforts and tell you what procedures and costs are sacrosanct and should never be eliminated.

When you have articulated your brand's promise in all its glory, then you'll know what you are working toward. You'll have more reference points to guide your decisions. You'll know what kinds of partnerships to create. You'll know how to respond to change. You'll know what tone to strike in internal and external communications – and even what to say. And you'll know what types of people will find working for your company a rewarding experience.

Most importantly, by articulating your brand promise, you'll create the right customer experience, which is what drives company success.

A brand-driven customer experience achieves bottom line benefits: customer loyalty; market dominance; better stock valuations; higher profit margins and greater employee productivity. It also helps on the expense side of the equation by driving down the cost of acquiring (or winning back) customers and reducing ill-conceived product and service directions. And in the realm of less tangible benefits, it helps create healthier corporate cultures and leads to employees becoming more loyal. These benefits accrue because a clear promise that focuses on delivering your value:

- helps customers choose your products or services more quickly and builds more and deeper customer relationships;
- gives shareholders confidence that you know where you are heading;
- ensures you will create brand assets that differentiate you over the long-term, and leverages the effect of all marketing;
- enables up to 25% price-premiums over equivalent products or services;
- gives your employees clear direction for decision-making;
- means you take advantage of the right new opportunities because you understand your customer experience.

So the point is, brand clarity is *good*. Brand confusion is *bad*. Once you've accepted this premise, the question becomes, 'How do I achieve this nirvana that is brand clarity?' (And remember, it's just the first step; once you are clear on your promise, you must communicate and act on it.)

The road to establishing brand clarity is often, but not always, instigated by marketing or senior management. But even if you're not one of these people, you can alert your management team to the need for, and the benefits of, brand clarity, and make suggestions for how to get there.

We asked vacation ownership (where people purchase points that they can spend on resort time, cruises or guided vacation experiences) company Trendwest  Resorts' executive vice president, Al Schreiber, how he convinced his management team to tackle the integrated branding process. He said, 'I knew that if we were to be able to compete against larger established brands, such as Marriott and Disney, we needed to be clear about our brand strategy. I also knew we didn't have a brand strategy. Since we were poised on an expansion and could use some direction for our new ventures, we decided to embark on the integrated branding process. Not only did it deliver a clear plan and vision for our brand that is impacting all areas of the company, but it brought the various divisions of the company closer together because we developed the brand strategy as a team. It also gave us a way to measure our branding effectiveness.'

How you can help drive toward brand clarity depends on your role. If you're the brand manager, the answer is easy: you drive the process. If you are in senior management, then maybe your role is to lead the process, or be on the brand team, or be someone who is interviewed for input and perspective, or to advocate the necessity of integrated brand development within your company. If you are in middle management or an individual contributor, your role may be to advocate for brand clarity, or to help leaders reach their goals.

Keep in mind, whatever your leadership position in the company; your most important role comes once the brand is clearly identified. Making sure the brand promise is reflected in your actions and in those of others in your department and in all company activities is your most important role. Managing the brand must become part of your day-to-day responsibilities for branding to be successful.

A key leadership role in brand development is to ask the hard questions and challenge existing assumptions. What's the value in knowing your customer brand promise? What's the opportunity cost of not knowing your brand promise? What input can you give the brand development team from you department's or work group's perspective? Of all these, getting senior management to realize the necessity of achieving brand clarity is clearly job one.

Would a Clear Brand Have Made a Difference?

One way to measure the positive impact of integrated branding before you've done it is by re-engineering the past. Think back to three company or departmental decisions you've made in the past year and ask these questions of each one:

- *How long did it take to reach consensus or was consensus even reached?*

- *If not, who made the decision and how did they make it?*

- *Was the decision consistent with past company actions?*

- *How well executed were actions based on the decision?*

- *What were the results?*

- *If everyone making the decision understood what activities enhanced your customer experience, would the decision have been different?*

- *How different would the decision be if it had been made based on how it impacted the customer experience? How would that have impacted the company?*

CREATING YOUR BRAND AND BRAND STRUCTURE: THE NINE STEPS

Brand clarity is the result of a process that digs into the hearts and minds of your employees, customers and other important audiences, and then synthesizes that information into useful tools and a clearly defined customer experience. We've identified nine steps to revealing your brand promise. You may be intrinsically involved in every aspect, or be an observer of the process; but whatever your role, it's important to know the process so that you trust its results.

This is a point where departmental or divisional heads outside the marketing department or the executive office often abdicate brand development responsibility. Don't take a back seat in the process! Each leader's connection to the brand creation process will fall along a continuum, depending on specific roles and levels with the company. At the very least, leaders need to understand the value of integrated branding and how to live their company brand. At the other end of the spectrum are those managers who drive the process and are personally involved in every step. After describing the nine steps, we've included a case study for Amalgamated Play that demonstrates how its leaders specifically executed the nine steps to brand clarity.

FIGURE 2.1: THE LEADER INVOLVEMENT CONTINUUM
Leaders in every role have a part to play in living the integrated brand.

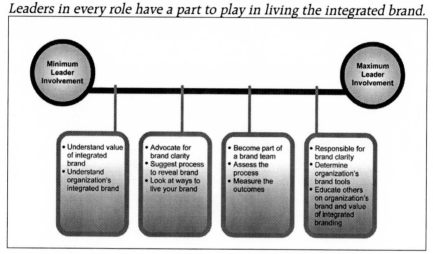

The nine steps are:

1. Sell your company on the integrated brand concept.

2. Set up a brand team and appoint a brand manager.

3. Conduct a brand environment audit.

4. Develop a brand environment report.

5. Determine a brand structure.

6. Create preliminary brand tools.

7. Facilitate brand team meetings to create final brand tools.

8. Determine your strategic role with customers.

9. Develop a brand strategy.

STEP 1: SELL THE INTEGRATED BRAND CONCEPT

To begin, senior management must buy into the concept that developing an integrated brand is a good idea. If the rationale of aligning company actions and messages with the company's greatest strengths' isn't enough, most executives can quickly buy into the higher profit margins and stock valuations strong brands create. Regardless, the practice of integrated branding must be embraced by senior management or the branding effort is doomed to failure. People follow the CEO's lead; if senior management doesn't believe in integrated branding, no one else will bother with it for very long.

Having said that, there is an important difference between buy-in to integrated branding and sponsorship of integrated branding. Buy-in is the first step. It's an agreement that integrated branding is a goal worth pursuing. However, we've found that buy-in is not enough; it doesn't require leaders to model new behavior. To 'walk the talk' so to say. The integrated branding process requires looking at nearly every practice in your company and aligning it behind delivery of your customer experience. For this to happen you need sponsorship, which is demonstrated leadership by senior management. We provide guidance on securing and demonstrating sponsorship in Chapter 4.

Getting sponsorship from senior management means leaders must be willing to first advocate for brand clarity. Advocacy is the art of influencing others when you don't have authority. This isn't easy, but it's another valuable skill for any aspiring leader. There are a number of ways to advocate for brand clarity:

- Support your claim that brand confusion exists.
- Identify customer scenarios where company actions created confusion; or where product or service initiatives failed because they were clearly outside the company's core competencies.
- Conduct marketing audits that reveal the company's lack of coherent messaging, low public awareness, and low brand equity.
- Show situations where low brand clarity had an adverse effect on employee decisions, practices and actions.
- Advocate to the right people, including senior management, your brand manager, department heads and division heads.
- Be clear and very specific about successful outcomes and measurements, including potential business results, and benefits to customers and employees, by department.
- Understand the impact of what you are asking in terms of cost, time required, and what the company will have to start, stop and continue to do.

- Demonstrate passion and stamina by sticking with it, fully addressing objections and adjusting your proposal based on new information.

Many leaders will feel the urge to skip this step and move right into a process that will reveal their brand. However, without senior management sponsorship you aren't likely to come out with consistent communications - let alone an integrated brand.

BRAND SELLING POINTS

Here are some brand selling points:

According to the Human Capital Index study conducted annually by Watson Wyatt, an international HR consulting firm, companies with high employee commitment versus low employee commitment (much of which is due to how well a company is living its brand), had 26-percent-higher three-year total returns to shareholders.[1]

This is what the McKinsey Group, one of the most respected researchers on the economic value of brand, has to say about stock value and branding:

'Strong branding can generate enormous shareholder value. Few would be surprised that a large share of Coca-Cola's market capitalization is accounted for by its intangible assets, mainly its brand. But few realize quite how much. On December 31, 1997, Coca-Cola's market capitalization was U.S. $165 billion, while its book value excluding goodwill was U.S. $16.2 billion – less than 10% of the total. That means that as much as 90% of Coca-Cola's value is intangible.' Much (but not all) of that intangible value derives from the brand.

Even at companies where marketing would not immediately be recognized as being at the heart of the business, brands are increasingly creating value. KeyCorp, one of the largest retail financial services companies in the United States, has seen its stock market value double in the past two years. Part of the reason for this growth is that it offers a common set of products and services nationwide, and positions itself clearly with an umbrella brand, Key: KeyBank, KeyCenters, Key Money Management Account.'[2]

According to McKinsey, on average, prices of the strongest brands are 19% higher than those of the weakest brands. In the same survey, the firm determined that brand is responsible for 18% of the total purchase decision.[3]

The auto industry provides one of the clearest examples of the role of brand in creating price-premiums. In a report entitled *Revving up Auto Branding,* by Anjan Chatterjee et al in *The McKinsey Quarterly,* 2002, Number 1, workers at the General Motors and Toyota joint venture plant in California built the same car under two different names - the Toyota Corolla and the Chevrolet Prizm.

> 'Toyota designed both models, and the differences in their components and trim are minor. Both vehicles receive high marks from *Consumer Reports,* and comparably equipped midrange models have similar price tags. Yet the Prizm requires up to U.S. $750 more in buyer incentives to support its sales. Even so, only one-quarter as many Prizms are sold, and their trade-in value depreciates much more quickly. Toyota's name on the Corolla attracts customers, while the Prizm is lost among the offerings on a Chevy dealer's lot.'[4]

STEP 2: SET UP A BRAND TEAM

Once your management team has agreed to sponsor integrated branding, the next step is to create the team that will reveal your brand. The brand team, including the brand manager, is responsible for brand management and measurement. It will be involved in every step, from revealing the brand to fine-tuning it over time. It assigns tasks and schedules, and finds help (either inside or outside the company) for key brand initiatives. It also prevents brand management from splintering into departmental or divisional efforts; it is the overseer making sure the customer experience is consistently delivered and communicated.

This team typically consists of six to 15 individuals, and participates in developing, revealing and educating around the brand. Senior management and representatives from operations, product or service development, marketing, sales, customer support and human resources need to be on the team. In addition, it's a good idea to include key influencers from other places in your organization, since the brand team will also be brand ambassadors.

We also recommend adding outside brand counsel to the team – independent brand strategists who have experience with multiple brand initiatives, and don't have a vested interest in seeing particular types of brand work done. For instance, if you hire a firm that does brand in conjunction with advertising, design or even HR services, you run the risk of your resulting brand strategy looking very like an ad campaign, a visual corporate identity or an employee-recruitment campaign. However, brand counsels should have existing relationships with all of these vendors and experiential knowledge with how all of these departments and practices support a brand.

STEP 3: CONDUCT THE BRAND AUDIT

A major step in the brand development process is to discover what's in people's heads and hearts about your company. This is the raw material that will shape your brand promise. Getting to this data demands some sleuthing – it's usually not going to be in a form that's clear, consistent or that people can easily act on. Your job is to find patterns leading to 'head and heart strengths' through interviews with many different audiences.

The integrated branding process distills the value you provide from the first-hand experiences of customers, vendors, partners, employees, legislators, competitors and industry analysts. You can talk directly with some groups; for others you must look to public information such as competitor's Web sites, industry analysts' reports and recent media articles.

You'll always want to use a third party to conduct in-depth interviews with internal audiences and your core customers. The benefit of in-depth research is that it features open-ended questions that allow people to describe your value to them in their own words. We recommend conducting supplementary quantitative research to provide greater statistical support for in-depth results. The questions your brand counsel asks should be designed to illuminate key strengths, your current customer experience (versus your hoped-for experience) and how you compare to the competition.

Any brand research is predicated on you knowing who your best, most loyal customers are. Understanding what these customers value will give you a blueprint for attracting prospects. The way to figure this out is to analyze your customer database for recurring purchasers, demographics, industry segments, titles and other shared traits.

DISCOVERING BRAND ASSETS

The brand audit will reveal your unique brand assets. Brand assets are the result of practices that your customers find valuable and are willing to pay more for. Assets can include the company's general reputation, values such as trustworthiness and product or service characteristics such as an excellent quality control system. One of the results of revealing your brand will be tools to help you determine which assets to invest in for the greatest return.

Here are some brand asset examples, which are as varied as each company's unique approach to its business. DoubleTree Hotels always gives guests a warm chocolate chip cookie upon arrival. Chico's clothing stores send frequent purchasers a percentage-off coupon every month. Newhall Land features lovely paved walking trails known as paseos throughout its planned-development communities.

Understanding what your brand assets are has three benefits. First, it will allow you to better invest in them. Second, assets serve as signposts pointing you to your compelling customer experience. Third, by identifying and managing your intangible assets, you'll build company valuation at a faster pace and be less likely to inadvertently reduce company value.

STEP 4: DEVELOP A BRAND ENVIRONMENT REPORT

The next step to creating your brand and brand structure is to analyze the raw data from a variety of angles:

- *What's the key benefit your company offers the marketplace? Has that remained consistent over time?*
- *How does the marketplace describe what your company does?*
- *What's your firm's compelling differentiator?*
- *Who are your best customers? Why?*
- *What does your customer experience look like? What about it is working best? Not working?*
- *What is your biggest opportunity? Your biggest threat?*

This analysis needs to be shared with others in a form they can understand. We call this a brand environment report, which reports interview results as quotes, patterns, conclusions and recommendations. The report provides senior management with a big-picture perspective through side-by-side comparisons of internal and external company perceptions, finding patterns among multiple answers and highlighting where management's perception doesn't match with reality.

STEP 5: UNDERSTAND YOUR BRAND STRUCTURE

Another step on the way to revealing your brand is to understand just how many brands you actually have, and how they relate to each other. It's very easy to end up with a confused jumble of brands because decisions about product naming, the number and types of offerings, and mergers and acquisitions tend not to be viewed from a customer-experience perspective. Management often gives more weight to short-term profitability or politics than to how their business could function most effectively. In addition, product brand managers seek to enhance the performance of their piece of the company by adding product variations – often without looking at the big picture.

As a leader in any department, you advocate to management to look at its brand structure from a customer experience point-of-view and then make any necessary changes. You can base brand structure changes on what would create a stronger head and heart connection with your customers. An example of one type of brand structure is the umbrella brand, where most of the equity is in the company name, such as K2 Skis. Another type of structure is the product brand, where the product name is where more of the equity and meaning lies. An example of this type of structure is Sierra Online, a computer gaming company known far more for its individual titles, such as Half Life and Tribes, than its corporate brand.

STEP 6: CREATE PRELIMINARY BRAND TOOLS

The integrated branding model includes a set of brand tools. These tools are used by employees and leaders inside brand-driven companies to create a consistent, compelling and unique customer experience. Tools include organization drivers of mission (the business you are in), values (shared beliefs that influence how you work), and story (what you say about the company's history and purpose). They also include the brand drivers of principle (the compass for actions and messages), the personality (the tone and manner of the brand), and associations (mental short cuts to what is valuable about the brand). If you have highly distinct product brands—such as Proctor and Gamble's Tide, Pringles, CoverGirl, Metamucil and Sunny Delight—you may have the need for different brand drivers to support each brand.

Of all the tools, the brand principle, personality, values and story will be the most important and useful on a daily basis for every leader living the integrated brand. These tools align company and employee actions with a branded customer experience.

The next chapter, 'Tools to Live Your Brand,' explains each tool in more detail. If your company already has some brand tools in place, such as a mission or values statement, you can use the brand environment report to see how well these tools are working for you and as a starting point for developing the other brand tools.

Preliminary brand tools are developed by identifying key concepts from the research. You can then create a first draft of each brand tool – typically in a facilitated group discussion. It's best to have your brand counsel create preliminary tools and facilitate final tools with your brand team to provide third-party objectivity. Creating preliminary tools for the brand team to discuss and change saves several hours of discussion by 'priming the pump.'

FIGURE 2.3: THE INTEGRATED BRANDING MODEL
This outlines the organization drivers, brand drivers, and brand conveyors necessary to live an integrated brand.

STEP 7: FACILITATE BRAND TEAM MEETINGS TO CREATE FINAL BRAND TOOLS

Step seven in the brand development process is to build brand team consensus for each of the brand tools, using the preliminary tools as a starting point. Consensus means not stopping until every participant on the brand team agrees that they can live with a particular tool. This is not always the same as agreeing that this is the best tool, because if you wait for that, one group member could hold the entire group hostage. The final tools need to be compelling, simple and able to be acted on by all employees. The next chapter, 'Tools to Live Your Brand,' provides many examples of brand tools.

This facilitated process, including the presentation of the brand environment report, can take several sessions, depending on group dynamics. In the final session, the group also decides how it will assign responsibilities for the next step – rolling out the brand tools to employees and aligning company activities with the brand.

People often ask if they should test their brand tools. The answer is that 'the test' happened up front in the form of researching audience opinions on what's valuable. What you can test is how using the tools impacts your customer experience, within customer touchpoints or company processes, such as a Web site. While you should test multiple ways of expressing the brand to see which works the best, the underlying brand direction would not change.

STEP 8: DETERMINE YOUR STRATEGIC ROLE WITH CUSTOMERS

Determining your strategic role - similar to an industry category - answers the question of *'what part do you want to play in your best customers' lives?'* Creating a role that is bigger than your current products or services will allow you to gain some emotional distance from your current products – while focusing your energy where it will do the most good – meeting your customers' needs. For example, a long time ago, IBM decided it wasn't in the business of manufacturing adding machines, but rather in the role of meeting customers' needs to manage data.

In the short term, this will help you justify the investments that will make your entire customer experience stand out – which is how you build valuable differentiation. If you don't view your work from a strategic role position, investments in training and in brand assets probably won't even make sense to your senior management team.

In the longer term, keeping your role in focus will keep your company flexible. You'll be open to new ways of meeting customer needs and not get stuck in some product backwater.

Your brand environment report is one place to look for the customer needs you are meeting. Another is through extrapolating up from your current products and services. Facilitated brand meetings are an effective forum for determining your strategic role.

STEP 9: DEVELOP A BRAND STRATEGY

The final step in the brand clarity process is to determine your first year's brand strategy, which is the plan you will use to get your company's practices, assets, culture and communications in better alignment with delivering your desired customer experience. The brand strategy is a core component of annual planning because it addresses your most important company asset – your customer experience. You can create a brand strategy by answering the following questions:

- *In terms of aligning company activities with your brand, what do you need to accomplish in the first year? Two years? Five years?*
- *At what point do you want to have employees and company activities aligned with the brand promise?*
- *What are acceptable benchmarks for brand awareness and equity over the same time periods?*
- *What is your target level and time period for creating or enhancing your product's or service's price premium? What percentage of annual revenue does it represent?*
- *What are the ways you will build your brand into company goals, objectives and compensation?*
- *What other products or services should you contemplate creating based on meeting the needs of your customers?*

The Integrated Branding Process
at Amalgamated Play, Inc.

The acquisition manager for fictitious toy company, Amalgamated Play, Inc., believed that the company needed to define its brand to find the right matches and reap the full value of acquisitions. The company believed its brand promise was delighting children, but its actions didn't always support that statement. Furthermore, the company didn't give employees examples of what *delighting children* meant or even if it was a long-term focus for the company.

While it was not the acquisition manager's job to clarify the company's brand, as a leader within one of the company's strategic departments, she was in an ideal position to begin to advocate brand clarity. First off, the acquisition manager compared recent successful acquisitions to less valuable ones. She couldn't find a correlation between the financial due diligence and successful acquisitions. There were clearly other factors that dictated success – and she suspected they had to do with the cultural, values and purpose fit between her company and those acquired.

The acquisition manager made her case to the VP of mergers and acquisitions. Together they advocated to the CEO, COO and VP of marketing, as well as other executives. The acquisition manager used past research to demonstrate Amalgamated Play's unaided brand awareness was 25% less than its peer group average. She also discovered that brand loyalty measurements for the company's two closest rivals were considerably higher than Amalgamated Play's.

The acquisition manager showed how brand clarity could have allowed the company to enhance its value through comparing specific brand tools, strategic roles, assets, practices and cultural norms from the three most recent acquisitions. By clarifying their own brand, the acquisition manager advocated that they could be much more strategic about how acquired company's assets, practices and cultural norms play into what the company is trying to achieve – hence reaping more value out of each acquisition. She also showed data demonstrating how integrated branding helps the bottom line directly through increased sales and profitability. For each department, she identified two or three benefits of branding.

The acquisition manager outlined the process for revealing her company's brand (based on the nine steps), the budget and time commitment necessary, and suggested a timeline and outside resources that would help.

After getting senior management sponsorship, the acquisition manager turned the project over to the brand team. This team conducted one-on-one in-depth research with customers, prospects, distributors and internal people, and created a brand environment report, which indicated to Amalgamated Play that customers valued some things that management never realized, such as the fact that distributors base the volume of purchases on how confident the CEO is in their bi-yearly face-to-face meetings with the company. Or, that customers feel that the company's products are particularly good at enhancing kids' creativity. Amalgamated Play decided to begin managing and investing in these heretofore unrecognized brand assets of enhancing creativity and personal attention. It also used these assets as part of the raw material for shaping its brand tools.

In facilitated sessions where its brand counsel presented preliminary brand tools, the Amalgamated Play team crafted the following final brand tools:

- Principle: encouraging creative play;
- Personality: kind, personal, grandmotherly and playful;
- Mission: bringing joy through play to curious children;
- Values: personal relationships, integrity, value and good role model;
- Association: a child's footsteps.

Amalgamated Play management knows that *encourage creative play* will test well because the research uncovered that customers valued it.

The company designated a subset of the brand team, which included progress reporting to and input from the CEO, to create its first-year strategy for living the brand. The agreed upon brand strategy was to focus on aligning distributor and end-customer touchpoints with its brand principle and values. The company used its principle of *encouraging creative play* to prioritize company activity alignment for the following year – including which companies to consider as acquisitions. It decided that its first goal was to realign its product development group to create toys that fulfilled the brand principle. Its second goal for the first year was to expand its ability to enhance personal relationships with distributors and end customers. Tactics to meet this goal included adding sales support people that provided more company touchpoints for distributors and *creative play coordinators* whose job was to create events for kids and parents in the U.S.'s eight largest metropolitan areas that demonstrated the fun and educational benefits of creative play.

EXECUTIVE LEADER LOG

Organizational alignment – where I deliver on the promise. But how can we align every company action with the customer experience if everyone doesn't know what the promise is? Have managers clarified our brand promise to their employees? What tools have we given them?

HUMAN RESOURCES LEADER LOG

How close is HR to understanding our customers' experiences? What can I learn about our customers – their experiences, their needs, who they are, what they're like – to make HR's role more relevant to our brand?

SALES LEADER LOG

Are our customers more informed than we give them credit for? Do we have enough respect for our customers? Is marketing over-promising? Is the rest of the company under-delivering? Both? Neither? Does sales know when we deliver as promised? When we don't? How can we create alignment on this? Can we tie financial incentives to delivering our promise?

Notes

[1] The Human Capital Index Survey report, (2000), Watson Wyatt, p 10

[2] Desmet, D et al (1998) 'The End of Voodoo Brand Management',
The McKinsey Quarterly, *3*, pp 106–117

[3] Court, D. et al (1996) 'Uncovering the value of brands', *The McKinsey Quarterly*, 4, pp 176-178

[4] Chatterjee, A. et al (2002) 'Revving up Auto Branding', *The McKinsey Quarterly*, 1

CHAPTER

TOOLS TO LIVE YOUR BRAND

*History is a guide to navigation in perilous times. History
is who we are and why we are the way we are.*

–David C. McCullough, historian, author

In your journey to create a compelling customer experience, you need
navigation tools to make sure you're traveling in the right direction. In
the previous chapter, we outlined nine steps to revealing your brand, the
outcome of which is a set of brand tools, a brand strategy and a *unique*
and *compelling* customer experience. This chapter will help leaders
understand the purpose of and how to use each brand tool to help the
company live its integrated brand. While it's not every leader's role to
be on the brand team and define the brand tools, it's imperative to know
what they are, and how to use them. We also recommend advocating
for the creation of any of these tools if you see they're missing from
your company's integrated brand. One of the most important tools for
keeping employees on track, the brand principle, is the one that's most
often missing from company brands.

Together, brand tools allow your employees to keep your brand
promise. And best yet, they already exist within your organization in
the form of actions you are currently taking – all you need to do is reveal
and reinforce them. In general, employees will use your company's
principle, personality, values and story in making most day-to-day
decisions and in customer interactions – but that assumes the tools are
supported by senior management, clear and well communicated.

FIGURE 3.1: WHAT CREATES A UNIQUE CUSTOMER EXPERIENCE?
Your brand promise drives your company activities, leading to a unique and compelling customer experience.

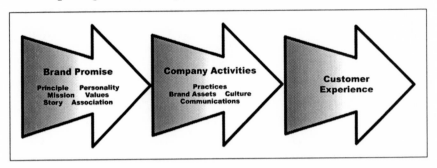

The result of using brand tools is unbreakable relationships with your core customers. Unbreakable relationships occur only when customers have a strong head and heart connection with your company. This means your employees act in a way that results in the customer emotions of loyalty and trust, and that customers have an intellectual belief that your brand is serving their needs in exactly the way they want to be served.

DEFINING YOUR BRAND TOOLS

One important distinction between living and not living your brand is whether *all* employee actions and company activities strengthen the brand. That's where your brand tools come in: they are guidelines for how to act on brand. Think of these tools as the DNA of the organization, the driving force for everything a company does, the propellant for all actions and decisions, and the belief system from which the organization lives, unconsciously or otherwise.

Your brand strategy then functions as a macro plan for using the tools to get to your company's destination. Both the tools and the brand strategy need to be consciously applied to the customer experience – from their first interaction with your company to the last. A distinct and compelling customer experience is the culmination of all brand tools and strategies. Creating easily used brand tools is the first step in achieving brand clarity and act as a guidepost for employee decisions (which is particularly helpful when leaders aren't present).

When authors Joe LePla and Lynn Parker developed the integrated branding concept in the late 1980s and early 1990s, they identified these six organization guides, the brand tools, that when acted on, will deliver your valuable brand experience. We discussed these to some extent in the previous chapter: your mission; values; story; principle; personality; and associations. Collectively, they build your integrated brand and help define your customer experience.

FIGURE 3.2: INTEGRATED BRANDING TOOL USAGE METAPHOR
This illustration explains how leaders use brand tools to live their integrated brand.

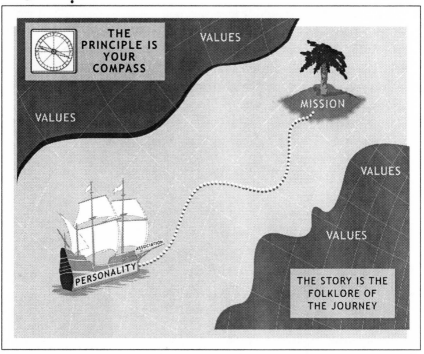

The illustration above shows the function of each brand tool, using another journey metaphor. Imagine, you're taking a boat trip to an island. The island is your destination, that is, your mission. How do you get there? First, you have to stay within the banks of your values: you probably won't arrive in one piece if you run aground – in fact, you may never arrive at all. But knowing the boundaries for action is not enough; you also need a compass to stay on course toward your mission. That's your brand principle, your compass for action. Of course, not every boat is the same. What your boat looks like and how the sailors talk and act will have an impact on who wants to travel with you. This is your personality. Your story is the tales you tell about where you've been and where you're going. Your associations are the things people remember most about your boat and crew. These could be everything from the flags you fly to the color of your boat to the distinctive sound of your horn. As a group, these tools permeate your journey, providing essential definition and guidance along they way. They allow you to get there faster, more safely and with a full cargo of happy customers and employees.

For brand tools to be effective, they must also move from being cleverly crafted words to being working concepts that are the basis for employee actions. No matter how nicely a compass is made, it won't get you to the right place unless you use it. Brand tools require senior management commitment and use to begin transforming a company. Otherwise they are just words.

Here's another way to think about each tool:

The mission…

> is *what* you do;
> answers the question of what business you are in;
> inspires people;
> forces choices.

The values…

> influence *how* you work;
> are cherished beliefs;
> provide input to corporate culture;
> identify standards of behavior;
> shape discussions.

The story…

> is what you say to others;
> describes brand behavior in context;
> is your organization's collective myth;
> is the basis for your elevator statement;
> provides context to your mission.

The principle…

> is your unique approach;
> acts as a filter for decisions and behaviors;
> is your key differentiator;
> provides a compass for on-brand action.

The personality…

> is your tone and manner;
> adds emotion to customer relationships;
> builds trust;

> drives your visual and verbal communications;
> provides guidelines for how to act.

The associations…

> are extra ways for customers to remember you;
> bring your brand to life through the five senses;
> provide shortcuts to the brand.

Let's look at each of these tools in more detail. After each definition, we'll show you real world examples, then at the end of the chapter, you can see how the tools work together in a case study.

MISSION

There's a lot written about what a mission is, or isn't, but for branding purposes, let's agree it describes what your organization is trying to achieve, your reason for being. It should answer the questions of what business you're in, why you exist and what you are trying to accomplish. The 'what business you are in' section of the mission is also called the strategic role. For more information on strategic roles see Chapter 5: Brand Strategy: Turn Customers into Committed Champions, 'Strategic planning to counter competitive, regulatory and industry threats.' To be useful, your mission must be clear and short. To get people rallying around it, it must be inspirational; it has to point in a direction that gets people excited. A good mission statement energizes employees to pursue common goals. It also forces choices, helping determine where to focus resources. The leader's role is to use the mission to rally and focus other employees by putting it in the context of their area of work.

Mission examples:

GROUP HEALTH COOPERATIVE

'We exist to transform healthcare, working together every day to improve the care and well-being of our consumers and communities.'

CAPITALSTREAM

'We streamline commercial finance.'

LOUDEYE

'Enabling a totally new experience of audio and video on every Web page.'

SOCIETY FOR TECHNICAL COMMUNICATION

'Designing the future of technical communication.'

VALUES

If mission defines *where* and *what* you do, values define *how* you work. What kinds of deep beliefs does your organization cherish above all else? What are you never willing to give

SOCIETY FOR TECHNICAL COMMUNICATION

up to achieve your mission? What is sacrosanct, to the point that your organization will forgo extra profits rather than ignore it? Values are the building blocks of employee and public trust. Values can include such profound issues as integrity and trustworthiness. On the other hand, they may encompass some of the lighter virtues, such as creativity, or having fun. Every company has its own set of shared values that can't be easily ignored or broken. If you have not determined values, you will still be living some, you just won't know what they are.

Leaders will make sure that their actions are always consistent with company values because this creates employee trust and cultural continuity. This, in turn, powerfully influences how people work and the kind of customer experience they deliver.

While well-defined values can be a key tool for affecting the employee brand experience they are often no more than words in an annual report. In an article by Megan Mulholland, in *The Post-Crescent*, she states:

'According to Bill Holland, executive vice president of the North Central Group of Chicago-based Right Management Consultants, the problem is that many organizations have "a limousine program." "That's where the CEO meets with the human resources person on the way from a meeting in a limousine and asks, 'Why don't we have one of those programs?'"[1] If senior management doesn't sponsor values and resulting employee programs, employees won't understand their relevance or limit that relevance to a shadow of what it could be. For instance, in speaking about the potential of a value of diversity to an organization, Holland says: "Diversity is more than race and gender; it's about organizational performance. Diversity is a process and end result by which people are valued for what they bring vs. being penalized for who they are."[2]

Value examples:

- Group Health Cooperative: Respect, integrity, scientific discipline, pioneering spirit, stewardship;
- CapitalStream: Customer needs, ambitious goals, integrity, teamwork, quality, personal responsibility, balance, learning, innovation, and fun;
- Loudeye: Leading edge, customer-driven, favorite place to work, excellence, empowerment;
- Society for Technical Communication: Open-minded, effective, member-focused, ethical.

STORY

Your story is, well, your story. Throughout history, human beings have communicated the tribe's goals, values and beliefs through storytelling. Myths, anecdotes and family stories are all staples of entertainment and teaching. Every company's story is different, but like the classic hero's journey, they'll all have some similar elements. Your company has a story, whether or not you've articulated it. While a story seems basic, almost trivial, it is a *highly* useful brand tool, particularly for training people in how to live the brand and consistently communicating to others who you are.

Stories give context to how the company acts. A simple story answers many questions the customers have including: *'Who are you?; What are you doing?; Where did you come from?; Where are you going?'* In many organizations, storytelling is left to the salespeople. Leaders need to strongly encourage employees to become company storytellers. Hundreds or thousands of employees all explaining why they are excited about what the company is doing is a powerful force for developing deep customer relationships.

A good brand story involves:

- the birth of an idea;
- unique formative events;
- how you overcame challenges;
- brand strengths;
- the creation of key messages;
- ultimate success.

Story Example

Loudeye's story is an example of what this brand tool can look like:

loudeye™

What do you get when you combine a biker movie with a lemonade stand and a group of talented friends? More than just a kick in the pants. Loudeye, originally encoding.com, evolved from those three elements. In 1997, Microsoft employee Martin Tobias produced a biker movie that he wanted to put on the Web. The complexity of the task showed him the need for products and services that would help people efficiently turn content into digital media. Throw in some talented friends to start it up and encoding. com went from just an idea to a full blown digital media company built with one goal in mind: to enable a totally new experience of audio and video on every Web page.

Experts began turning out the Web's richest digital media, from videotapes, CDs and photographs to movie footage. RealNetworks signed on as its first customer, and the first pillars of the streaming media infrastructure went up.

The pioneering encoding effort expanded and grew into the best data management, indexing, watermarking, digital rights management, archiving and distribution services for on-demand content available. Not long after, Loudeye further expanded its suite of services to provide complete audio and video broadcasting capabilities for enterprises seeking to deliver live content; such as product launches, sales meetings, remote training sessions, corporate communications and major events.

Low turnover and quality in the company's products and services reflect Loudeye's ability to grow and service customers faster, better and smarter.

PRINCIPLE

Your brand principle is your company's unique approach to its business category and mission. It is the most important brand tool because it acts as the compass for all employee decisions and actions – resulting in a unique and valuable customer experience. It is the explicit agreement among employees about how to build, focus and differentiate the brand.

A good principle reflects what is really valuable to customers. It is evident at customer touchpoints, is clear, is brief, and is something every employee can own and act upon. A principle is never stated word for word to customers; instead it is lived by employees and experienced by customers. Once you have unearthed your principle, it then becomes the driving force behind living your brand.

Note to Marketing Managers:

How does positioning fit into this model? The principle is a long-term internal guide for company and employee behavior. Positioning is how you are currently differentiated in the market – an external, shorter-term facet of your principle. Positioning is a way of conveying much of your brand, but in a competitive context. Your position should cover your business, your benefit, and your differentiation in a clear and concise way. Your principle, on the other hand, is your unique approach to your mission.

Here are some examples of brand principles. In each case, they describe the approach to the company's business that clearly delineates it from the competition. Employees in any department or work group can use this guide by asking themselves: *'In this action (or decision), how will I demonstrate our brand principle?'* The leader's role is to make decisions using the principle, let employees know how principle-based actions have created greater company success and exhort other employees to use the principle themselves.

- Group Health Cooperative: Assuring superior coordinated experiences;
- CapitalStream: Making change an ally;
- Loudeye: Pioneers of better;
- Society for Technical Communication: Creating opportunity.

PERSONALITY

A company's personality helps to create an emotional relationship with customers. It's conveyed via the company's tone and manner, its look and feel, and its visual and verbal identity. It drives the emotive part of the brand, as well as the way marketing materials are designed. Once your organization has agreed on the elements of personality, then you can reflect it, as appropriate, in all external communications and actions.

The difference between values and personality traits is that values are core beliefs that drive your actions, while personality traits are how someone else would describe your actions. Values are your internal guidelines, while your personality is your public face.

Leaders demonstrate the company personality while periodically checking to make sure that the company face is consistent to customers. In addition, they hire people who are most able to reflect that personality to customers.

Here are some personality examples:

- Group Health Cooperative: Welcoming, trustworthy, dedicated, progressive, collaborative, expert, and proud;
- CapitalStream: Confident, passionate, charismatic, gives a damn, self-aware, energetic;
- Loudeye: Hip, smart, committed, unconventional, passionate;
- Society for Technical Communication: Smart, class act, fun, friendly, visionary, engaged.

ASSOCIATIONS

Brand associations are those things that the company attaches to itself to create memorability, a kind of a mental shortcut to the brand meaning. They can be as diverse as Kodak's yellow, McDonald's golden arches, the Michelin man, or Intel Inside's four-toned musical signature. Associations often arise later in a brand's development, when a company is looking for more ways to build brand meaning with its customers. To build an association, a company typically comes up with a concept it wishes to reinforce with customers, then works with a creative firm to develop ways to express it. New associations can be added over time, building up a rich set of touchstones to the concepts behind the company's brand.

For example, the Seattle Children's Home decided to create an association around the concept of transformation, because it is a Seattle-based non-profit that transforms fragile children's lives. We arranged for the organization to work with Walsh & Associates, a graphic design firm known for its brand-based design approach. Walsh created a compelling visual of a butterfly in flight, which is now an integral part of the Home's printed and electronic communications.

Associations are foundational tools for integrated branding because they are a mental shortcut to the brand promise, and act as a quick reminder of the brand.

FIGURE 3.3.1:
MCDONALD'S GOLDEN ARCHES

FIGURE 3.3.2:
THE MICHELIN MAN

FIGURE 3.3.3:
SCH BUTTERFLY

Point of Interest

A Brand Tools Inventory

Take a moment to inventory your company's brand tools: mission; values; story; principle; personality; associations.

- *Which ones currently exist?*
- *Are they easy to base actions on as written?*
- *Are they used by most everyone in the company?*
- *If not, which departments or groups aren't using the tools? Why aren't they?*
- *How can you make your brand tools even more effective?*

Brand tools also cause prospects to go from strangers to best friends much more quickly. Some tools – such as the story – are used almost exclusively at the beginning of the customer relationship. Customers experience the effects of most tools at ever-deeper levels over time. The important role that brand tools play in building best customers means that management needs to spend the necessary time to get the brand tools right – both to think them through and to make sure they are lived throughout the organization. Integrated branding also requires being clear on whom your best customers are; because that is the group you are designing your brand tools for.

Brands are like people: We imbue them with personality and we interact with them as if they were people. Here are five steps that transform prospects into best friends using your brand tools:	
1. Experience them as a unique person	Personality
2. Share life stories	Story
3. Explore common values, stated or unstated	Values
4. Discover unique behaviors that you appreciate	Principle, Association
5. Share deepest goals	Mission

AFTER BRAND CLARITY

Brand tool clarity is the huge first step on every leader's journey to living the integrated brand. The benefits of an integrated brand increase as you go further in the journey. The next step in your journey is aligning practices, brand assets, culture and communications using the brand tools.

If you have brand development responsibility as part of your jobs, see LePla and Parker's earlier book, *Integrated Branding: Becoming Brand-driven Through Company-wide Action,* for more detailed information on developing brand tools.

Sakson & Taylor's Brand: A Case Study

O nce there was a company that had a serious employee relations problem. This company was in the

business of hiring technical writers who were then placed on site at clients' locations. The writers felt that they didn't belong, either at their on-site assignments or with their employer: They didn't really feel like employees of either company. There was talk of forming a union, and a lot of grumbling in chat rooms about how the company's practices were unfair.

Because the company paid well and offered industry-leading benefits, company management was upset, defensive and felt misunderstood. That tone came across in their emails, driving the two groups further apart.

This company was ripe for integrated branding. By understanding its mission, values and story, it could better impart to employees their purpose, what they were signing up for, and offer a company experience that displaced workers could feel a part of. By understanding its brand principle and personality, managers could give proactive direction and performance expectations instead of being reactive.

The company went through the process of creating its brand tools. It interviewed dozens of employees (disgruntled and not), customers, prospects and the entire senior management team.

Resulting tools. The brand team decided on a principle of excellence through caring. The personality was caring, resourceful, playful, professional and confident. Their values were win/win/win, responsible, community-focused, innovative, integrity, respect, excellence and clear communication. And their association was the perfect match.

After coming to consensus on these tools, the company found a number of ways that it could lead from the brand. For example, it gave the management team tools to define corporate norms of behavior. This made discussing what was or wasn't 'professional' more positive by creating norms for professionalism and ways to discuss.

behavior. It reduced the number of times an employee would make a promise to a client before getting buy-in from other team members. Changes in contract wording that took out onerous non-compete language made every employee a win/win/win partner. It reduced micro-management by team leaders because employees had broad guidelines for behavior they could follow. And it increased direct communication between employees when there was a conflict or a problem because of the explicit value now placed on clear communication.

While these cultural changes were great, brand clarity also had a positive effect on the company's bottom line. Because employees started to feel a part of the company, turnover decreased. Productivity went up. And marketing efforts were more successful, leading to increased business. All this occurred because employees understood the brand and were given the tools to act from it.

EXECUTIVE LEADER LOG

The tools seem to pair up, complementarily. Mission and principle seem to go hand in hand. So do values and personality; together, I wonder, don't they capture company culture? And story and association seem linked, as well. The principle, personality and association sound like 'customer experience' twists on the mission, values and story, respectively. What are the best brand tools to use in the various stages of creating alignment of our practices, brand assets, communications and culture? How can we use our story to successfully introduce the other brand tools, once we have them? Will the story help create context for the other tools?

HUMAN RESOURCES LEADER LOG

Which tools will be most useful for hiring? For managing employee performance? For fine-tuning a healthy culture? It sounds like the principle tool should be used all the time, sometimes in conjunction with another tool or two. Think about ways to train people how to decide which tools to use and how to use them, depending on the situation and the decision to be made.

SALES LEADER LOG

It would be great to see brand tools used across the board in this company, not just in sales. Constantly experiencing the brand in action will make us better salespeople. I think I should advocate for brand clarity from that point of view – it will light up the eyes of our CEO.

NOTES

[1] Mulholland, Megan, "'Diversity Specialist Speaks in Appleton, Wisconsin,' (30 September 2000), *Knight-Ridder Tribune Business News: The Post-Crescent*

[2] Ibid.

CHAPTER

ALIGN TO DELIVER A UNIQUE CUSTOMER EXPERIENCE

On a journey of 100 miles, 90 is but halfway.
    –Chinese proverb

When you have completed 95 percent of your journey you are halfway there.
    –Japanese proverb

We've shown you how individual employees can use brand tools to guide their actions and decisions. The next steps are to learn how to use the tools to guide your company's group actions and decisions and commit to the level of branding that's right for your company. This includes understanding the four types of company-wide brand activities (practices, brand assets, culture and communications) and how you, as a leader, can be effective in making these group activities more on-brand. These steps will make your organization road ready.

ALIGNING GROUP ACTIONS

Creating a compelling customer experience requires aligning all company activities, which are made up of practices, brand assets, culture and communications. Classifying company activities into definable areas allows you to more easily manage them. In some cases, this means aligning activities based on your brand tools. In others, it means investing in a particular activity that enhances your customer experience. Please note, a company's culture and its brand assets are often also part of a company's practices, or culture may be an asset itself – there is some overlap – but these classifications make it easier to discuss how to align them.

Practices are group activities that allow you to effectively conduct business. They include everything from how you make your sales, to product development and quality control processes. They also include actions that happen solely within one department or require coordinated actions from several departments.

Brand assets are a subset of group activities that customers would find beneficial. Brand assets are typically intangible and can include your compelling customer experience; unique industry approach, including strategic role and principle; associations; company reputation; industry leadership position; quality control systems; employee experience and training; company culture; customers; compensation and rewards; and delivery systems.

Prior to conducting branding discovery, companies usually can't identify their brand assets. But defining brand assets is critical because it allows an organization to successfully manage and build them. Because they are often invisible on the balance sheet, their use as a competitive advantage is often squandered.

To identify your brand assets, ask, *'What company activities do customers mention as valuable?' 'What other activities would they find valuable if they knew about them?' Which brand assets should we strengthen to most effectively build our customer experience?'* At vacation ownership company Trendwest, one brand asset is the flexible vacation possibilities they offer customers – from drive-to weekends to guided tours. Using its brand principle of accommodate and delight as a guide for what kind of flexible products and services to add, the company would find other ways of providing its customers with even more vacation options. This might mean creating an opt-in database of customers who would like to be notified of last-minute resort deals at drive-to resorts. While staff members responsible for marketing their drive-to resorts might have used their principle to arrive at this action anyway, focusing on flexible vacation possibilities as a defined brand asset allows Trendwest to more easily build it.

Culture is the learned behavioral patterns of the organization based on shared beliefs and values. These patterns become the norms for action – 'the way we do things around here' and often use 'code phrases' when they are invoked. For instance, a supervisor uses the phrase full participation as the shorthand, cultural-norm explanation for why she has asked everyone in the sales department to voice their opinion on a new service offering.

Cultural norms are powerful influencers of action. When you are aligning actions to a newly revealed brand, using senior management to model your revealed brand or combining multiple cultures due to an acquisition, understanding your cultural norms becomes particularly important. The following are some of the questions you may want to ask to discover your company's cultural norms:

- What would you miss most if you left the culture?
- How do you handle conflicts?
- How do you deliver, hear and act on feedback?
- How do you present alternative points of view?
- What company behaviors do you use to justify taking a particular course of action?
- What do we point out to others as inappropriate actions? What do we use as justification for pointing these behaviors out?
- What 'unspoken agreements' do we have that allow us to interact with each other more effectively?

Communications are positioning, message themes, associations, and the look and feel of all your external and internal communications, from your advertising, to your Web site, to all-employee meetings. While communications that aren't based on how your company acts create confusion and cynicism with customers and employees, communications based on brand are one of the most important tipping points for employee and customer brand acceptance.

Here's an example of why alignment of group actions is essential for 'walking the talk and talking the walk.' If you say that your brand principle is success at critical times and your service people aren't available to immediately solve customer problems, then your practices aren't aligned with your brand. If customers don't see concrete benefits of 'success at critical times,' then you lack supporting brand assets. If your team over-analyzes crisis situations – causing frustrating delays in response time – your culture is not supporting 'success at critical times.' If your advertising is about innovation but doesn't also speak to reliability, your communications aren't aligned with the brand experience this principle would create. Employees and customers experiencing any of these disconnected actions would be much less inclined to emotionally bond with your brand and would probably not develop an intellectual understanding of what you stand for – a critical hurdle to creating unbreakable relationships.

Alignment is where the rubber meets the road in keeping you ahead of the competition. It allows all company actions to enhance your customer experience. While the benefits are huge – long-term valuation of 25 to 30% greater than competitors, product and service premiums from 10 to 25% – even in mature markets, and unbreakable customer relationships – alignment requires continual management acknowledgement and sponsorship until living the brand becomes second nature to all employees.

BRAND COMMITMENT LEVELS

Before jumping into any brand discovery process, you need to determine at what level senior management is willing to sponsor it. For example, aligning all company activities to your brand takes a degree of commitment your management team might not be ready to support. Based on senior management's commitment, companies arrive at one of the following three levels of branding – communications, customer touchpoint or integrated branding.

FIGURE 4.1: BRANDING COMMITMENT LEVELS
Know which brand level you want to achieve before starting the journey.

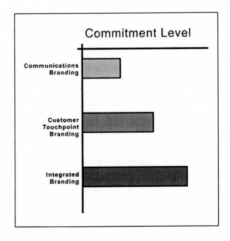

COMMUNICATIONS BRANDING

At this level, the marketing department understands the need for branding and has the support of upper management to develop the company's visual brand identity, messages and communications. Branding in this context might mean integrated external communications, with upper management supporting the resulting strategic focus, messages and visual brand conveyors. At the communications branding level, company practices, brand assets and culture alignment happen accidentally, if at all, while communications alignment is high. Even communications alignment can be a stretch if the main emphasis of the branding project was simply a corporate identity – a company logo, colors, typography and graphic templates.

The problem with communications branding is that the world's best look and the most appealing advertising won't be effective if the company's product, services and actions don't back up your communications. As an example, a regional telecommunications company has been advertising its responsiveness to customer needs, yet is notorious for not meeting promised installation dates and providing the wrong phone numbers for business customers in directory assistance. Customers dismiss the company's communications brand and may even be using word of mouth to tell non-customers why the company can't be trusted.

FIGURE 4.2: COMMUNICATIONS BRANDING
The company communicates its brand value through every communication - but departmental brand actions aren't always consistent.

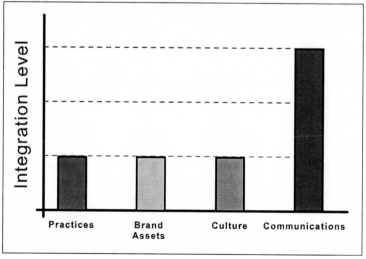

CUSTOMER-TOUCHPOINT BRANDING

At this next level, branding is coordinated – at least partially – to the customer experience of the company. Management ensures everyone who touches the customer, including marketing, sales and customer support, are using the brand tools to provide an integrated customer experience. Senior management is often a strong customer advocate in these companies – so the brand is also supported in the company culture.

What's lacking at this level is aligning employees, practices and brand assets in non-customer touchpoint departments. This results in products, services and department practices that may conflict with the customer experience you are trying to deliver. An example will demonstrate why this can be a serious problem: An Internet infrastructure company was known for acting as a pragmatic partner with customers, but its products were overly complex, making them very hard to learn. The complexity of the product, designed by a team of engineers far removed from customers, was resulting in customer confusion and dissatisfaction.

FIGURE 4.3: CUSTOMER TOUCHPOINT BRANDING
In addition to communications, the company consistently demonstrates its brand value in every department that interacts with customers - other departments' actions aren't always consistent.

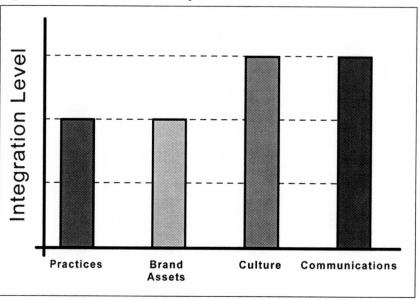

INTEGRATED BRANDING

At the integrated level of branding, senior management and other company leaders guide their actions based on the company's brand principle, while demonstrating its consistent personality and values. Everyone believes in and advocates for the mission and tells a company story with consistent messages. Finally, senior management holds everyone else in the company to the same yardstick of acting and communicating on brand. The benefit of brand integration is that every employee action, company practice and even the corporate culture help deliver a valued and differentiated customer experience. And because employees do this day in and day out, year in and year out, the result is cumulative brand value and a progressively larger lead over the competition. At the same time, these brands don't have the problem of practices, brand assets or culture conflicting with communications, which often happens at the first two brand commitment levels. In the race to capture the heads and hearts of customers – and, of course, long-term market leadership with the highest valuations – integrated branding stands head and shoulders above the other brand levels.

FIGURE 4.4: INTEGRATED BRANDING

All departments and employees consistently demonstrate and communicate brand value.

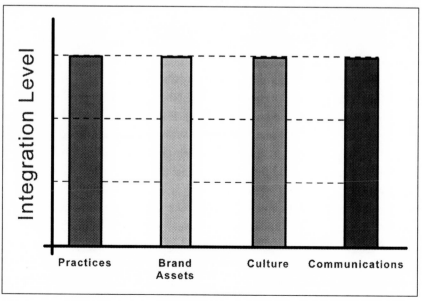

At the integrated branding level, part of a leader's job is to recognize and nurture brand assets, such as the quality of doctors at Group Health or the variety of natural health disciplines offered by Bastyr University, or the walkable neighborhoods planned by Newhall Land. And corporate culture and company practices either resonate with the brand or are fine-tuned until they do, so employees don't perceive any disconnect between the brand they are being asked to demonstrate for customers and the way the company does things internally.

A UNIQUE CUSTOMER EXPERIENCE

The result of creating an integrated brand is a shift in the company's focus from delivering products and services to delivering a unique and compelling customer experience based on your strategic role.

Companies that practice integrated branding become adept at looking at themselves and competitors through a customer-experience filter. For example, take an IT consultant that has identified the need for the enterprise architect strategic role. A company that has this strategic role is one that designs and builds the entire technological house – and makes sure all of the rooms and house systems work together in an optimum way. This is in contrast to competitors who see themselves as system integrators. The problem with 'system integrators' as a strategic role is that it is not unique and too low on the food chain. The firm that does the architecting would be working with higher levels of management and be very likely to control any system integration that is required as well. This company's focus will allow it to easily move to the next technology wave whatever it may be. Similarly, Polaroid would have done better by viewing its industry as instant images, not instant photographs. While the company now offers digital cameras, it lost what could have been a significant lead in the digital camera category because it viewed its category to be based on film. In mastering the telegram, Western Union got stuck on a specific way of delivering immediate, long-distance messaging. There have been multiple successors to telegrams, first fax machines, then email, and now a move to unified messaging, where one receives email, phone and fax messages all on the same device. If Western Union had defined its strategic role as immediate, long-distance messaging, it would have been much more likely to recognize and invest in innovative ways to deliver the experience.

Using a customer experience rather than product perspective is also very important in mature markets. Estée Lauder president and COO Fred Langhammer asks, 'How many more neckties or lipsticks does anyone need? We're saturated with consumer goods; it becomes very important to have brands that provide an exciting experience as well as excellent products.'[1]

Besides protecting your market share, a customer experience focus provides new, high growth business lines for a mature brand. IBM Global Services has allowed IBM to gain an entirely new revenue stream and positioned itself as a 'wise partner that could guide companies through their transformation into nimble Net-savvy players ...in a year in which most technology brands took a bath in terms of their valuation, IBM held steady, at U.S. $53 billion.'[2]

How can a leader determine whether his or her company is product or customer-experience based? One way is to look at the numbers of product variations that are on the market. Product-based strategies usually result in too many product choices and choices that don't represent real customer needs. In fact, consumer-products makers churned out more than 31,000 new products in the United States in the year 2000, up from a little more than 10,000 per year in 1986. 'The more-is-better approach can backfire,' warns Mark Lepper, the chairman of Stanford University's psychology department, who studies how variety affects the odds that people actually buy. Lepper set up a table with 30 jars of jam and gave shoppers who stopped for a sample a discount coupon for their next jam purchase. He also had a table with six jams. He counted the coupons to see which group was more likely to buy. Of the shoppers who faced 30 choices, only 3% actually bought jam; of the shoppers who had six choices, 30% purchased jam.'[3]

Jack Trout and Steve Rivkin, in their book *Differentiate or Die*, identify three key ways to combat the choice explosion: 'If you ignore your uniqueness and try to be everything for everybody, you quickly undermine what makes you different; if you ignore changes in the market, your difference becomes less important; and if you stay in the shadow of your larger competitors and never establish your "differentness," you will always be weak.'[4]

MAPPING OUT YOUR CUSTOMER EXPERIENCE

In addition to defining the strategic role they want to play, companies also need to map out their current customer experience. A customer experience model allows you to view all of the ways your organization impacts its customers. Since most companies have more than one audience, you will want to create a model for each one.

The model should include both company-initiated and customer-initiated interactions. For instance, a dealer may react to a company communication by ignoring it or your end-customer might react to inconsistent service by complaining. Once you've created this customer model, you will want to consider forming a standing customer-advisory group. You can use this group to track real-world reactions to proposed and implemented changes to the customer experience.

OBTAINING SPONSORSHIP TO ACHIEVE INTEGRATED BRANDING

Leaders need to do more than simply agree about the importance of having an integrated brand – they must demonstrate sponsorship for the resulting employee- and company-activity alignment it requires. A sponsor is someone who has the power to dedicate time, resources and people to make your project happen. Someone who sponsors integrated branding would also actively model living the brand, allocate budgets for alignment project management and benchmarking, and evangelize integrated branding benefits over time.

For example, if a company needs to align its sales practices with the brand, the sponsor may be the sales manager. He or she will support the efforts of a project team to evaluate what needs to be changed, approve the budget for the change (if necessary), and help evaluate how effective the project was, once completed. Sponsorship ideally should cascade throughout the company beginning with senior management. As departmental plans develop, sponsorship is required for implementation.

Create a Customer Experience Map

Point of Interest

1. Create three columns and label them customer experience and company activity. In the customer experience column, list all of the experiences your customer has with the brand and write down your goal for each experience. This includes direct communications, the Web, your product or service, third parties, your employees, the media or peers.

2. Next to each customer experience in the company activity column, list all of the company activities including practices, brand assets (if you know them), cultural norms and communication activities that directly impact that experience. Depending on the number of company activities that impact a particular customer experience, you may want to take an entire page for each experience.

3. In the third column, list whether and how each company activity furthers this desired customer experience based on your goal for the experience and your brand tools. If you haven't revealed your tools yet, use the model to ask *'What type of impression is the customer receiving from this experience?' 'What will it cause them to feel or think about our company?'*

4. Using the same list of experiences and activities, walk a hypothetical customer through a set of typical company experiences beginning with his or her very first exposure to you. *'Does the sequence of experiences or time between interactions impact his or her perception of you?' 'Have you taken actions that develop loyal and committed customers?' 'Have you given customers opportunities to form both personal relationships with you and join groups or clubs related to your brand?'*

You can use this customer experience model to analyze specific customer touchpoints as well as for getting a big-picture perspective on your entire customer experience. If you're ready to take it to the next level, you can also consider how the company's support activities – such as training, IT, HR, administration and others – indirectly impact each customer experience.

Daryl R. Connor in his book, *Managing at the Speed of Change*, identified the sponsor as critical to any organizational change.[5] Not getting sponsorship for branding – at any level – is a major reason why so many brand processes fail. The following checklist can help you define what committing to sponsorship will require in terms of actions, time and resources. Sponsors:

- directly and openly communicate their decisions;

- explain how their decisions fit into organization goals;

- provide the resources they expect the effort will take;

- understand how their decisions impact existing priorities, communicating the impact to employees, and helping others adjust, as needed;

- know how to measure success;

- share responsibility by holding others accountable for execution of their decisions;

- help redirect employees, teams and even other leaders if things get off track;

- recognize and reward efforts that align with their decisions.

GETTING SPONSORSHIP FOR INTEGRATED BRANDING

The first step to getting sponsorship is to ask for it. When people are afraid sponsors will say no, they tend not to be straightforward about a project's time, resources and energy needs. This sets up fuzzy expectations at the front end of a project that increase its chance of failing. In the case of integrated branding, outlining the entire scope of a project upfront will help management weigh the effort with the possible results. You may still end up with a 'no,' but you may also get a 'yes,' if not for the entire project, then perhaps for a logical first step, such as a brand environment report or a communications brand. The golden rule of sponsorship is that you'll want to make sure you've gotten the leader to commit to all the actions that demonstrate sponsorship, otherwise you'll still lack support when the time comes to do the project.

There are a number of ways to make it easier for leaders to commit to sponsoring an integrated branding project:

- Create clarity for them. Help them to understand the priorities, resources, skill needs, and costs at each step of the project. Don't expect sponsors to always do this analysis themselves.
- Set up simple measures of success. Sponsors will want to know how it is going and if they need to adjust its direction. Find short-term ways to measure success – such as anecdotes from employees or quick deliverables.
- Keep sponsors updated and solicit their feedback. Since the brand discovery process can take a few months, it's important to periodically restate goals and show how much progress the company has made towards accomplishing them. Sponsors are more likely to take a risk and sponsor initiatives if they are confident they will get pertinent information as the project progresses. Less information and less feedback equal less control for the leader and a much greater possibility of failure.

Testing for Sponsorship

Point of Interest

Ask the following questions to determine if integrated branding is currently sponsored in your organization:
- *Have leaders clearly and continuously communicated your brand promise and the value of your integrated brand to employees? Have they made the downside clear if employees don't execute on your brand promise?*
- *Have leaders identified and communicated measures of success for living the integrated brand? Will leaders know if the company is executing on its brand?*
- *Are employees who are successful rewarded and recognized?*
- *Have leaders demonstrated that executing on the integrated brand co-exists with other business priorities, and is not allowed to get lost?*
- *Have leaders allocated necessary resources or time to living the brand?*
- *Have any of the above demonstrations of sponsorship occurred on more than one occasion?*

Keep asking these questions. Keeping the sponsorship conversation alive is a critical skill for leaders who want to live their integrated brand.

Overcoming Barriers to Company Alignment

Once you've got sponsorship, you then need to determine which company activities need alignment to be road ready. There are six predictable barriers to overcome when aligning company activities with your brand. Understanding these challenges will help you reach the level of branding you're aiming for.

Maintaining a High-Trust Environment

Any initiative involving the actions of employees, whether it's living the integrated brand or designing a better mousetrap, will be more likely to succeed if employees trust leaders. If employees are asking, *'Why should we do what they want?'*; *'What's in it for us?'*; *'Are they serious, or will this idea pass with time?'*; you may have some serious trust issues.

Trust grows when leaders do what they say they will do, and base their actions on a set of well-defined values. Other integrated branding tools, including the mission and principle, also help management build and maintain trust by creating consistent, predictable actions and decisions – but only if company leaders live them. Identifying brand tools and then not acting on them will dramatically lower employee trust levels. For example, if management says it values quality, yet every discussion and decision is made based on profit, employees will question whether anything management is saying is true – resulting in a more cynical work environment and less enthusiasm for new initiatives. Step one for building company-wide trust is to walk the talk – ensure that your leadership actions match what you say is important.

Step two is to involve employees by asking for their input and sharing management thinking on problems that affect them. Studies suggest that organizations that share power and decision making with employees foster more trust and perform better than more hierarchical organizations.

Some of the most innovative brand work happening right now is in the area of employee branding. Companies such as global human resources consultant Watson Wyatt are measuring the return on the care and feeding of employees through its Human Capital Index (HCI) study. A multi-year study of 750 large, European and American publicly traded companies, HCI found that superior human capital practices such as clear communications of company values and goals are a leading indicator of financial performance. The study also shows a strong correlation between communications integrity (employees having easy access to communications; business plans and goals being shared with employees; employees having input into how work gets done; the sharing of financial information; and company action on employee feedback) and increasing shareholder value.[6]

Don't despair if you work in a more hierarchical organization. It's possible to create high-trust relationships between employer and employees in more rigid hierarchies. But it's even more important in these organizations for management to walk the talk, due to lack of a broader employee perspective on management workings.

Your company doesn't have to be perfect in order to create an environment of trust. The following trust builder test will help you to determine if your company's (or department's) environment is one that is ready for integrated branding.

Trust Builder Test

Point of Interest

Answer on a scale of 1 to 5 with 1 being low and 5 being high:

- *To what extent do leaders explain how goals and decisions fit into the overall mission?*
- *To what extent do leaders demonstrate their stated values through their actions?*
- *To what extent are leaders open about the state of the company and its financial position?*
- *To what extent is there a well-understood feedback mechanism to and from leaders?*
- *To what extent are leaders accurate and honest in their communications?*
- *To what extent do leaders recognize and reward actions that align to what they say is important?*

There is more to trust than six questions, but answering at a level of three or above on all of these questions indicates that your organization has a sufficiently high trust level and will therefore be more successful with company-wide initiatives, such as integrated branding. If most of the answers to the questions were at a two or below, leadership needs to revisit its communications and actions to grow trust.

GIVING EMPLOYEES INCENTIVES TO ALIGN COMPANY ACTIVITIES

The second challenge in alignment is motivating employees to make alignment happen. A company creates change not just by giving employees clear directions for how to live the brand through brand tools, but also through instilling employees with the power to take action. Companies can do this through rewarding appropriate employee behavior. Creating recognition and compensation plans using brand-based objectives *shows* them that management believes brand is a core business practice of the company.

This bottom line orientation also helps employees understand the importance of tying brand action to return on investment. A company's ability to turn its existing brand assets into greater product margins and stock valuation is a critical test of your integrated brand's strength. Leaders who are ready to sponsor company activity alignment in their own areas of responsibility will be very supportive of company-wide recognition and compensation plans. In Chapter 11: Convey Your Brand's Meaning and Chapter 12: Measure Your Brand's Effectiveness we review these plans in more detail.

COMPANY ACTIVITIES: ON-BRAND OR OFF-BRAND

Another challenge to getting road ready is aligning company practices, brand assets, culture and communications with your brand principle, personality and values. The first step is a brand alignment analysis to determine which activities are 'on' or 'off' brand. The analysis includes looking at:

- *What is or isn't in alignment?*
- *What departments would be affected by bringing activities into alignment?*
- *What is the cost and time needed for alignment?*
- *Who should be responsible for alignment priorities and on each alignment team?*
- *Which alignment projects get priority?*

If you were examining the alignment of a company's patient practices in a healthcare organization, you might look at how doctors make the experience valuable right now, such as offering first-level diagnosis and providing a sounding board for options. You might also examine what physician assistants do – perhaps being a patient advocate and empathizer – and what other specialists add, such as expert advice.

If your principle is highest practice quality, you would determine how to make all of these activities of the highest quality. This might cause you to consider adding more communications between the primary care doctor and specialists as well as offering additional patient-advocate training. You would then determine the cost and time needed for alignment to take place and whether aligning this practice would have a lesser or greater impact on the customer experience than other company activities.

One way to determine which activities to focus on is to have leaders and employees in each division answer the following questions:

- *What are the major practices, brand assets, cultural norms and communications that directly or indirectly impact the customer experience?*
- *To what degree do these demonstrate our brand principle, values and personality?*

PRIORITIZING FOR THE CUSTOMER EXPERIENCE

Since you'll never have the money or time to do everything at once and you want to maximize return on investment, you'll have to prioritize. One way to achieve the best financial return is to prioritize based on which activities will have the greatest impact on your customer experience.

The first step is to create the customer experience map discussed earlier in this chapter. Step two is to conduct a strength and weakness inventory of company activities listed within your customer experience map. The goal of the inventory is to put a value on all of the company practices, brand assets, cultural norms and communications that are currently adding or detracting from the customer experience. (You've already made a start on this through designating whether activities enhance the brand or not.)

Begin the strengths and weaknesses inventory with information from your customer experience map on page 65, the brand environment report (see Chapter 2: Bring your Brand Into Focus) and any other existing research – which has customer-experience-based information. Then add your own internal expertise by conducting a facilitated session with departments to identify other company activities. In the second half of the meeting, prioritize activities based on their relative impact on the customer experience, approximate costs to fix or improve, linkages/ involvement with other departments and time to change.

We recommend that you create a brand alignment team for high priority alignment projects. They can be a sub-committee of the standing brand team and work in conjunction with department heads to tackle the alignment projects and help oversee project management. Both the brand alignment team and the department heads should be held accountable for the successful completion of each project.

Strengths and Weaknesses Inventory

Assess the relative impact of a company activity on the customer experience by answering the following questions. Assign values based on a 1-10 scale where 1 is hardly at all and 10 is highest.

- *How much greater of a head or heart connection will eliminating this negative activity or improving this positive activity create between customer and company?*
- *How much more would a customer be willing to pay for a company product/service if this changed?*
- *How much more likely will the customer be to repeat his/ her purchase of the company product/service?*
- *How much more likely will the customer be to recommend the company product or service to others?*

The completion of this final step should result in having a prioritized alignment list.

ELIMINATING OFF-BRAND ACTIONS

After you've gone through the prioritization process, we recommend bringing together department heads to assess which company activities should become fix-it or enhancement projects. Depending on the political structure of the company, this might take place in two separate meetings – the first with a working group that explores linkages of various departments in a given project. The second meeting would be a presentation where the brand alignment team presents to the larger brand team or CEO for clarification or budgetary sign-off.

While not all changes will create costs, it's important for the brand alignment team to have some idea going into these meetings what budget is available. Often alignment actions will fall under budget expenditures that have already been authorized. For example, enhancing customer awareness around the quality of rooms offered by a hotel chain might be piggybacked on an already-budgeted advertising campaign. Budgets may also fall into multiple departments, further offsetting the cost for any one group. If the change has a significant impact on the customer experience and therefore the company's bottom line, additional budget may be justified as an investment rather than as a cost.

We recommend using a project manager from outside of the department or company for activity alignment, because this is not typically something the department head will have time to handle. This person will have the advantage of not losing sight of the goal in the day-to-day press of getting work done. Typically the department or functional heads maintain the sponsorship, while executing the alignment activities falls to the project manager and employees.

We also recommend creating ways to measure the project's impact once it's completed. You can do this either through direct customer research or using a standing customer-advisory group, or as part of a more general, annual, brand-benchmarking program (if your organization conducts one).

CORRECTING MISTAKES

No matter how carefully you go about improving the customer experience and securing sponsorship for activity alignment, you will still do things that are not on-brand. Mistakes happen. That means that building in the practice of correcting mistakes is essential for all brands. When competently handled, mistakes will strengthen your relationship with a customer.

Each company will handle mistakes differently, but we've found that the first line of action should always belong to the person closest to the transaction – whether that is a sales person, customer service representative or even an independent dealer. Your policy on mistakes should be comprehensive, clear, and in alignment with your brand, and completely empower that person on the frontline. The second part of your mistake process should be to always ensure that the mistake has been followed up to the best possible conclusion – that is usually a satisfied customer, but on some occasions may be a customer who believes you did your best. The third and final part of the process is to look at why the mistake occurred, and institute processes for eliminating such mistakes in the future.

A FINAL CHECK

Look at your company through the eyes of your customer. Go back to your customer experience model and simply ask whether you can answer 'no' to the question of *'Are there still major disconnects between what we are promising and what the customer will experience?'* You should also be able to answer 'yes' to the question of *'Are you delivering a consistent and valuable experience to customers each time they touch the company?'* While you'll never get everything right all of the time, our experience is that companies can make major changes in their customer experience in a short period of time when they have defined their brand tools, received executive sponsorship for a well-defined brand project and aligned both employees and company activities to them.

We believe that the relatively new discipline of aligning company processes with the brand will be one of the most important methods for increasing productivity, product margins and shareholder value in the coming years. While many companies have implemented specific components of integrated branding, far fewer have viewed integrated branding as a critical guide to how a company works. This is both an opportunity and a threat – the companies that live their brand will gain a significant advantage over the competition. Since that advantage builds on its own successes, those who are first out of the gate should be able to sustain their lead over the long term.

EXECUTIVE LEADER LOG

My company talks about brand development, but do they mean communications branding? Few companies commit to integrated branding. I'm much more interested in the payoff from aligning our organization behind our brand, versus the payoff of merely aligning our external communications. Talk to exec staff about what it would take to commit to integrated branding.

HUMAN RESOURCES LEADER LOG

Performance Reviews: In self-reviews (at all levels?) ask 'what are you already doing—every day, every week, every month, every quarter—to keep our promise?'

Management Training: Have our managers been trained to see the link between their departments' best practices and the customers' experience – even when their department is not directly touching the customer?

Recruiting and Hiring: Ask about what promises the candidate's made lately – promises they've kept and promises they've failed to keep (and what they learned as a result)?

SALES LEADER LOG

How can I mix up sales folks with other teams? Customers will nail our salespeople to the wall if the company breaks the promise sales makes – I want to get sales and non-sales efforts to move towards each other, cooperate more and get themselves aligned.

NOTES

[1] Hymowitz, Carol, (17 July 2001) 'In The Lead', The Wall Street Journal, B1

[2] 'The Best global Brands,' (6 August 2001) Business Week, p 54

[3] Nelson, Emily, (20 April 01), 'Too Many Choices', The Wall Street Journal, B1

[4] Trout, Jack, Rivkin, Steve, (September 2000), Differentiate or Die, Soundview Executive Book Summaries, p 2

[5] Connor, D. (1993) Managing at the Speed of Change, Villard Books, New York

[6] Watson Wyatt Worldwide (2001/2002 survey report) Human Capital Index

BRAND STRATEGY: TURN CUSTOMERS INTO COMMITTED CHAMPIONS

This was really the way my whole road experience began, and the things that were to come are too fantastic not to tell.

–Jack Kerouac, *On The Road*

While strategy is supposed to be a critical senior management practice, it often gets lost in the frenzy of daily business. Even in companies that have an annual strategic planning process, strategy is often the words on paper rather than approaches that lead a company to its goals. Brand strategy is the itinerary that you use to build your integrated brand. For a majority of companies – even those who have done some form of brand work – actions are almost always driven by short-term tactics. Why? Because it's very difficult for most people to act in the present to gain some nebulous, future reward. But it's a leader's job to see tomorrow's goals and work towards achieving them.

An effective brand strategy encompasses all of the ways you plan to improve your customer experience. It includes aligning actions by all departments to your integrated brand, not just marketing actions. It addresses everything from new product and service development to aligning and enhancing your practices, brand assets, culture and communications. (See Chapter 4: Align to Deliver a Unique Customer Experience for definitions of practices, brand assets, culture and communications). It focuses on what you need to change and the priorities and timetable for that change. Brand strategy answers the question of *'What is our brand focus this year?'*

A strategy also helps you coordinate company activities in response to current threats, trends and opportunities – something that brand tools alone can't do for you. For example, if you make cars and safety is your brand principle, you may invest in too many safety strategies while your competitors out-flank you by focusing exclusively on the current public concern of child safety.

Your brand strategy is a core component of your organization's annual plan. By making it the centerpiece, you'll always focus talent and resources on what makes your company's products or services compelling and unique. It will also focus your company on those actions that have the greatest impact on the bottom line.

Why concern yourself with brand strategy if you're not in senior management or the brand manager? Because every employee has a role in executing the brand strategy. Besides using your tools in day-to-day decision making, helping to execute the brand strategy will have the single greatest impact on creating brand, hence company, value. And if you are closer to the front lines, the information you gather and the ideas you generate can be invaluable for refining brand strategy.

The 'employee branding movement,' often led by human resources, is correct in its understanding that employees need to turn company objectives into action. Unfortunately many employee-branding efforts actually hinder company brand building by focusing employees on something that isn't directly related to the company's brand principle. If human resources gives employees a slogan such as quality in every action but the company's brand principle is delightful customer experiences, employees will miss opportunities for building the brand. While quality is always important, focusing employees on 'quality' when the company wants to own 'delightful customer experiences' will result in reduced brand effectiveness.

What's in a Brand Strategy?

How does a brand strategy differ from a typical corporate strategy? In several ways. The first and most important is that using a brand strategy changes company perspective. A brand strategy focuses action on activities that create a more compelling, unique and more consistent customer experience – while a typical corporate strategy looks only at enhancing specific products, services or financial results.

Here's an example of a brand strategy: A vacation ownership company, such as Trendwest. Trendwest, wants to enrich people's lives through a variety of great vacation experiences (mission). It does this by accommodating and delighting (principle) its customers who buy 'vacation points' that allow them to use 38 resorts and a variety of guided tours and cruises. Meanwhile, the competition has also started to use this points system that Trendwest pioneered. As a response to this, Trendwest's current brand strategy might be to enhance how customers feel accommodated over their lifetime of vacation experiences through Trendwest adding more customer choices to their offerings. In addition to creating more weekend 'drive to' destinations, it might also add staffing for 24-hour telephone reservations or event directors at special properties.

This shows the role that brand tools play with the brand strategy. Without the direction set by Trendwest's mission and principle, the company could just as easily assume its brand planning should focus on expanding the number of resorts and *reducing* the types of vacation experiences to choose from. On the other side, without the shorter-term focus of the brand strategy, Trendwest might use its brand tools in ways that don't answer competitive pressures and positionings.

Mapping out your brand strategy allows you to more effectively leverage all aspects of your brand. It provides an annual opportunity for all leaders to focus on their strategic role and customer experience and determine where the experience aligns with the brand and where it needs to be fixed. It also allows you to direct group and individual activities – your practices, brand assets, culture and communications – to enhance the customer experience.

When you first reveal your brand, it's important to prioritize which company activities need the most alignment and enhancement. A brand strategy allows you to most effectively prioritize, while looking at how company activities can work together to strengthen the brand. (See Chapter 4: Align to Deliver a Unique Customer Experience for more information on alignment.)

As part of brand strategy planning, you also need to understand the impact changing practices in one department will have on others. To go back to the vacation ownership example, if you decide to create drive-to resorts, you need to train vacation planners to show customers how to most effectively take advantage of these products. And you need to consider the ways facilities and on-site staff can accommodate the differing needs of weekenders during their drive-to experience. While strategic planning is a good idea in any company, if you want to sustain brand integration, it is a mandatory one.

Finally, understanding how your practices, brand assets, culture and communications work to serve your brand strategy can impact the success of product and service extensions, and mergers or acquisitions. In our experience, companies that try to extend their brand into new product areas without a sound customer-experience rationale will fail. And there are a lot of examples that might have made good economic sense, but made no sense to the customer. How else would you explain a maker of casual clothes offering fine men's suits, or a department store offering insurance? The questions typically unasked up front are, *'How will this product enhance our customers' brand experience? And, if it doesn't, are we willing to take on the expense of creating a wholly new brand?'*

Proposed mergers or acquisitions rarely look at the impact on customer experience. Companies tend to spend most of their time on financial due diligence or product and service fit. Rarely do they take the additional steps of analyzing whether the other company's brand and culture, practices and brand assets are a good fit with their own brand promise and customer experience. If you are looking to expand market share or offerings through a merger or acquisition, your brand strategy must address the brand-tool and company-activity-alignment issues that such a transaction will present. (See Chapter 17: Branding Issues for Mergers and Acquisitions to learn about an expanded due diligence model.)

TAKE THE FIRST STEP

A goal within a brand strategy is something you are willing to forsake maximum short-term profitability to achieve. While this doesn't sound difficult, many senior management teams are creatures of habit when it comes to the bottom line. They are afraid to make investments in brand communications, aligning company practices, and building company brand assets if they can't see immediate results in greater sales. But, there's no point in conducting a brand process or creating a brand strategy if you aren't going to support it with at least some investment.

Brand Strategy for a Hypothetical Community Planner

Our goal in the next twelve months will be to create positive public opinion of our company as reflected by research sample interviews where 60% of county residents respond with one or more positive statements when asked about our company. This will result in political support for our projects and a higher valuation on houses and commercial property in our community.

Our strategy will be to effectively communicate the beneficial value of current and past brand assets such as our community centers and boulevards to the general public through changing the way we live our culture and the way we communicate.

While our company practices are already aligned to create a positive public reaction, our culture and communications need to change to fulfill this brand strategy. Our cultural norm in this area has been *'our work will speak for itself.'* We will shift our cultural norm by having our president and management team model new behavior that lets the public know about the good works we do as we do them. We will let employees know that this shift is occurring and encourage everyone to ask *'Are we calling attention to it?'* as the way to get this cultural norm acted on throughout the company. We will shift our communications to a proactive 'calling attention' to our positive practices and brand assets including communicating the benefits of community planning and the complexity and depth of the work that we do in the community.

We will also add modeling the *'Are we calling attention to it?'* cultural norm as a component of all managers' job descriptions. Human resources will hold a training session on how managers can help employees to integrate this while also giving managers guidelines for assessing how well they are modeling it.

We will measure our progress toward this goal through annual resident research. Our goal for the first year will be a 30% positive mention rate (up from the current 12%), and our two-year goal will be a 60% positive mention rate. We will re-evaluate and fine-tune our brand strategy at the end of year one.

Brand Strategy Questions Every
Leader Should Ask

Point of Interest

Does your company have a brand strategy? If not, here are some of the questions you can answer to create or advocate for one:

- What areas of the brand promise (based on your brand tools) does the customer experience currently not deliver?
- What is the current competitive situation that the brand must address?
- What are the current threats that the brand must overcome?
- If you could wave a magic wand and create the perfect customer experience based on your brand, what would it look like? Make sure that your new-and-improved customer experience meets the criteria of unique and compelling.
- Given current company brand assets, practices and culture, how much of this experience could you realistically provide in one year? In two years?
- What would leaders need to sponsor to ensure the success of this strategy?
- What resources and capital would it take to make it happen?
- If you believe this is the right thing for the company to do, what are the logical next steps to make it happen?

A leader's first step is to advocate for sponsorship of a brand strategy and goals for their respective areas. The leader can also help to make goals as concrete as possible. This usually requires that you provide some estimate of return on investment. You'll find a wide variety of outcomes can measure brand investment return – including enhanced product and service price premiums, customer stickiness, margins, profits, revenues and company valuation. Most often, you'll want to set shorter-term milestones – such as the change in public opinion in the above community planner example – on your way to bottom line results.

Beyond these immediate returns, the pot of gold at the end of the integrated branding rainbow is a highly profitable business with sustainable margins and market share. A brand integrated around the customer experience can expect to be an industry leader year in and year out.

Perhaps your senior management team is willing to take only a small step with its first brand strategy. Don't despair; this can open the door to larger commitments later.

Part of any ROI framework is measuring and comparing brand-activity results quarter-to-quarter and year-to-year. For instance, tracking changes in price-premiums of specific products and services as well as the effect of the overall brand on all product and service pricing. You can also track everything from the effect of brand actions on buying behavior to company valuation. (For more detailed information on measurement, see Chapter 12: Measure Your Brand's Effectiveness).

A BRAND-PLANNING TEMPLATE

What is the goal of a brand strategy? It's to capture the hearts and minds of your customers and lead them to the loyalty and commitment levels of brand equity. (See Chapter 1: Figure 1.2, Brand Equity Pyramid) Your brand strategy will enhance your company's unique and compelling customer experience through all company activities.

The following outlines a typical brand strategy. While yours may include other components, the purpose is to show how to think about executing on a strategy that builds your integrated brand. An effective brand strategy needs to realistically address budgeting expenditures, activity alignment, the product or service competitive environment and future company direction. The strategy's time period should be based on how long it will take to reasonably achieve your goals. The plan should be revisited annually or more frequently, as market factors change.

There are three components to an effective brand strategy:
1. Internal: your company brand direction as played out in your customer experience; new or existing product and service development; company activities; budgets.
2. External: economic cycles; competitive threats; regulatory threats; industry threats such as a sea change in your customer-experience area (for instance, from black and

83

white to color television, or from mainframes to networked computers).

3. ROI and improvement: how you will handle implementation, benchmarking, contingencies, feedback and fine-tuning.

The brand team, senior management team, and division and department heads are responsible for making sure the company lives the brand through all its company-wide, product and service, and departmental activities. They also act as a touchpoint for all parties when it comes to creating a brand strategy.

WHAT TO CONSIDER WHEN DEVELOPING BRAND STRATEGY

The following is a detailed look at the components of a brand strategy. You can use this to get a clearer picture of where the company should make changes to improve its customer experience. You can then use this information to craft a brand strategy.

COMPANY ACTIVITIES

These activities are discussed in detail in Chapter 4: Align to Deliver a Unique Customer Experience. The brand strategy prioritizes company activity alignment, enhancement and new activity creation. Company activities include:

- Practices
  - *How can you leverage current practices to deliver a more on-brand customer experience?*
  - *What practices should you add or eliminate to better deliver your customer experience?*
  - *Are you correctly prioritizing your investments in practices?*
  - *Are your costs appropriate for your industry, customer demand and brand goals?*
- Brand assets
  - *Which brand assets do your customers most value?*
  - *Which brand assets would be valued by customers if they knew about them?*
  - *Are there additional brand assets you should be building or buying?*

> *— How much should you invest in each asset in the next 12 months? 24 months? What outcome are you expecting from that investment?*
> *— Are you communicating brand assets in a way that increases customer awareness and perception of their value?*

- Culture
  > *— How do you demonstrate your principle, personality and values through 'the way we do things around here?'*
  > *— Do you have any cultural norms that you need to change or enhance to align with your brand?*
  > *— What other cultural norms do you need or should you eliminate to live your integrated brand?*
  > *— What charitable causes should you be championing to demonstrate your brand?*
- Communications
  > *— What misperceptions and awareness gaps do customers and prospects have about your strategic role and your unique approach to that role?*
  > *— Are you effectively communicating why customers should be loyal and committed to your brand?*
  > *— Where aren't you communicating consistently?*
  > *— Are you effectively communicating your expected customer experience to employees?*
  > *— Do your communications help employees understand the benefits of brand and living the brand?*

WHICH CUSTOMERS TO FOCUS ON

One of the other areas to think about in your brand strategy is whether you offer different levels of service to different customer segments. While the traditional approach of considering your core customers to be the ones who spend the most money is useful for maximizing revenues from that group, it often results in brands not giving enough attention to other customers who have reached the commitment and loyalty levels of the brand pyramid. These customers are most likely to stay with the company, pay higher prices and actively recommend the brand to others – all valuable traits even if they aren't necessarily the ones who spend the most money in a given time period.

PRODUCT AND SERVICE INITIATIVES

Product and service strategies seek to enhance current product or service value, while addressing what new offerings you should develop. These strategies define what you will offer to customers and represent your primary revenue generators. Your goal is to broadly interpret your strategic role while keeping a lock on your desired customer experience (as defined by your brand tools):

- *What are your opportunities for expanding existing products or services based on your strategic role?* (Such as geographical, market share or new markets.) *How would these changes impact the customer experience?*
- *What are your product or service weaknesses and how do they impact the customer experience?*
- *What new products or services should you add to enhance the customer experience or address current trends?*
- *What are your product and service pricing targets?* These should be based on the strength of your brand and the market maturity level.
- *How would new distribution channels and market perception of these channels affect your customers' perceptions of your brand?*

DEPARTMENTAL INITIATIVES

All departments, whether they generate revenue or directly interact with the customer, are key to delivering the customer experience and therefore play a role in brand strategy.

SALES

Sales answers the question of how customers make buying decisions. How you combine direct sales, wholesale, co-selling and retail will depend on the type of customer experience and customer your brand focuses on.

- *Are you able to demonstrate how the company brand promise is reflected in products and services, using your current sales tools?*
- *Is the current sales process enhancing the customer's brand experience or is it perceived as a hurdle customers must get past to experience the brand?*

- *Does the sales story give customers the big-picture reasons why they should be loyal and committed to your brand?*
- *Does your positioning effectively differentiate you from the competition?*
- *As your positioning changes, does it continue to build customers' understanding of your brand principle?*

MARKETING

It's marketing's job to build the type of company awareness that reinforces the customer experience and creates high customer interaction. Prior to having direct experience with the company, marketing efforts also are the basis for the public's perception of the brand.

- *Are you building unaided and aided awareness with prospects around your brand name and your brand distinctiveness?*
- *Are you building loyalty and commitment with customers?*
- *Are you increasing the level of repeat business and product or service cross-selling?*
- *Are you reducing misperceptions by customers and the general public about company focus and intention?*
- *Are you letting customers know about all of your brand assets?*
- *Are you viewing your internal audience as a customer for brand communications?*

HUMAN RESOURCES

Human resources plays a pivotal role in integrated branding. Integrated branding is also sometimes known as employee branding, a relatively new movement in certain HR circles. HR personnel can help ensure employees begin to understand and live the brand, from the hiring process to new-employee orientation, and in day-to-day actions. HR's effectiveness in aligning employees with corporate brand goals and strategies can mean the difference between delivering a great customer experience and failure to live the integrated brand.

- *In what areas and departments are employees having a difficult time living the brand?*
- *Do new employee hiring and orientation practices inculcate the employee brand?*
- *Are your compensation and bonus plans in alignment with your brand values, principle and mission?*

- *Do you have effective criteria for creating brand leaders throughout the company?*
- *How does your performance review process recognize and reward on-brand practices?*

CUSTOMER SERVICE AND SUPPORT

Service and support staff are on the front lines of the customer experience. Other than sales employees, they have the most interactions with customers and may be the only people who consistently deal with customers who are using your products or services. Their ability to create, or sabotage, a branded customer experience is critical to growing a successful brand.

The role of customer service has become more complex as Web and email responses have become preferred means of customer communication. The challenge from an integrated branding point of view is communicating the brand in whatever form the customer wishes to talk in. In the *InformationWeek* article 'Customers Get the Message,' by James K. Watson, Jr., Frank Meister and Joe Fenner, the authors say: 'Most companies are creating dedicated teams to handle e-mail requests. But given that getting "bounced around" among different representatives is such a common customer complaint, it makes sense to focus on skills development for all customer service representatives.'[1]

Some questions to consider for branding this department include:

- *Are support personnel accurately presenting your brand personality?*
- *Are support personnel trained to enhance customer relationships?*
- *Are they making decisions based on your brand principle?*
- *Do support personnel know how to encourage customers to commit more resources or energy to the brand – a key indicator of 'loyalty' and 'commitment?'*
- *Does your mistake-fixing process bring every problem to a successful conclusion from the customer's point of view?*
- *Are support personnel educated about new company, product or service brand initiatives?*
- *Does the customer receive a personalized, branded experience regardless of the communication medium he or she chooses to use?*

BRAND STRATEGY AND BUSINESS THREATS

ECONOMIC CYCLES

Economic-cycle contingency planning is an important aspect of any brand strategy. Simply put, a company that wants to maintain a special relationship with its customers must empathize with all situations that customers will encounter. By planning for the impact that economic booms and busts will have on customers, you can solidify customer relationships in good times and bad. On the other hand, if you don't anticipate how economic cycles will affect your customers, you run a greater chance of doing harm to your customer relationships. While this may seem an obvious danger in economic downturns, it's also true in expansions when it's human nature to take customers for granted.

American Express has paid heed to how customer needs change during times of economic uncertainty. An article in *Business Times* titled 'Branding, Inc.' explains: 'One way of dealing with a recession is to launch and brand products in ways relevant to the times. During Singapore's '98 recession, the launch of Amex Blue as a card that offered low interest rates — or real value — to cash-strapped consumers met the original target for the launch twice over in five months.'[2]

Customers' expectations of your brand may change significantly, based on the economic climate. In an upturn, customers will look to you to keep up with their expanding personal or business needs. In a downturn, they will be looking to you for ways they can do more with less. Your job in both situations is to tailor customers' brand experiences to their changing needs.

In a strong economy, new business opportunities abound and companies often grow as fast as they can scale up to meet demand. If this scale up has only one metric, say 'increased sales,' the company will not closely examine the impact of its growth on the customer experience. This can result in a decline in customer-experience quality in sales, delivery and product use. That's because when demand is high, inexperienced sales people may promise more than they can deliver, delivery times may dramatically increase and customers may be thinly supported on the back end of the sale. And in service companies, where people are the product, quality typically will drop as new, untrained employees are thrown into the fray.

An off-brand customer experience begets weaker customer relationships or even revolving-door customers and more negative word-of-mouth on the street. When customer demand is high, companies can hide some of their declining brand equity through acquiring new customers. When the economy slows, customers are even more likely to switch to competitors, who may capture them for good through offering a compelling integrated brand experience.

During a downturn, companies may lose their ability to provide an on-brand experience. Layoffs, office closings and other negative news can cause loyal customers to question their relationship with your brand. While it may not be possible to prevent all layoffs, we believe that planning for downturns will cause the company to cut unnecessary expenditures, keep its belt tight and create a crisis plan that can reduce the frequency and severity of layoffs.

By adding brand strategy goals to the typical annual planning objectives of increasing size, revenue or profits, companies can build their customer relationships regardless of the competitive or economic environment. While an annual plan needs to address short-term opportunities and threats, an integrated brand strategy provides balance by addressing the sustainability of the customer experience in any actions taken.

STRATEGIC PLANNING TO COUNTER COMPETITIVE, REGULATORY AND INDUSTRY THREATS

The best defense is a great offense. Differentiating by living your integrated brand is a much more effective way to deal with threats than in reacting to competitive moves. But there are times when countering the competition is job one.

As part of building your integrated brand, we recommend creating a competitive war room where you summarize in words and visuals each of your competitors' offerings and positions. This will help you understand how your brand looks and feels and is positioned in the marketplace. While many companies use war rooms as one-time exercises, we suggest you leave this war room in a conspicuous place, where senior management and other leaders can see it – and update it monthly. The war room should also contain an area for new product developments or potential trends that could be alternative solutions to meet your customers' needs. For instance, if your sales depend on telemarketing, you would track consumer sentiment and changes in local laws pertaining to that practice.

The continuous war room allows you to address threats from obsolescence, due to changes in technology, customer tastes, delivery systems, and changes in the law or geopolitics. This is why it's also extremely important to have the brand mission and strategy defined and championed by senior management. When you understand that your strategic role is more than your current product category, you'll create a clearer and faster path to new products and reduce company resistance to retiring old ones. For instance, General Motors went after a much younger crowd with a new product, service and sales system in its Saturn sub-brand, while putting its Oldsmobile brand out to pasture.

Home Depot decided that its strategic role was to be a resource center for the do-it-yourselfer rather than the traditional hardware store role. According to W. Chan Kim and Renée Mauborgne writing in a *Harvard Business Review* article entitled 'Creating New Market Space,' Home Depot asked 'Why do people choose hardware stores over professional contractors? The most common answer would be to save money...They don't need the city locations, the neighborly service or the nice display shelves...Home Depot has eliminated those costly features...executives at Home Depot have made it their mission to bolster the competence and confidence of customers whose expertise in home repair is limited. By delivering the decisive advantages of both substitute industries – and eliminating or reducing everything else – Home Depot has transformed latent demand for home improvement into real demand.'[3]

Another company that understands the importance of strategic roles is Switzerland-based SMH. It created the Swatch brand that turned the watch into a fashion and lifestyle accessory. 'You wear a watch on your wrist, right against your skin,' explains chairman Nicholas Hayek. 'It can be an important part of your image...Before Swatch, people usually purchased only one watch. Swatch made repeat purchases the standard.' Swatch now offers more than 350 watches in multiple 'lifestyle' lines and features a tagline of 'Discover Swatch, discover you.'[4]

Based in Great Britain, Virgin's role is as a consumer champion – a strategic role that has led them into owning over 200 companies – everything from airlines to mobile phones. They look for industries where customers are badly served and where they can further build their brand of making a difference while providing value for money, quality, innovation, fun and a sense of competitive challenge.[5]

ACTION AND REACTION

Executing your brand strategy will take you only part of the way to your destination. You also will need to measure, and make course corrections. You need to know and report on whether what was done has had a significant impact, whether you've met your milestones and improved the company's brand equity. You'll then use this information to figure out what to do next. The result of good execution, measurement and course correction is an almost unassailable brand position that can be sustained far into the future. (For more information on benchmarking see Chapter 12: Measure Your Brand's Effectiveness).

EXECUTIVE LEADER LOG

We're a small company that has never written an annual business plan – it's been a seat-of-the-pants operation from day one. The thought of a long planning process never appealed to us – but I can see how an annual brand strategy plan could really help focus our efforts, especially as our departments grow and take on their own plans and priorities.

HUMAN RESOURCES LEADER LOG

HR's past involvement in the annual planning process has been limited to salary and benefits forecasting and budgeting. A plan that starts and finishes with a brand strategy would open up doors for a much stronger contribution by HR to senior management.

SALES LEADER LOG

We've got a sales force working on a 100-percent-commission basis – and they like it that way. But it also means monetary rewards are tied directly to sales, however they get the sales. We'll need to do some heavy-duty retraining if we're going to start selling on-brand; that plus possibly a new sales-compensation model will need to be put in place. Talk to HR about possibilities for next year, and build those things into the brand strategy plan.

I'm in sales, not marketing, which is where I think senior management would expect brand-development advocacy to come from. But I think this company needs a clear brand strategy, plus a sales-method overhaul. Think about collaborating with the VP of marketing to take this to the CEO.

NOTES

1 Watson, James K. Jr., Meister, Frank, Fenner, Joe, (9 April 2001), *Information Week*, 'Customers Get The Message,' , p 62

2 (22 March 2002) 'Branding, Inc.' *Business Times* (Singapore)

3 Kim, Chan and Mauborgne, Renée, 'Creating New Market Space,' (January-February 1999) *Harvard Business Review*, pp 85-86

4 Corporate Design Foundation Web site, www.cdf.org, @Issue, Vol. 2, No. 2, *Swatch Design Time*

5 Virgin Web site, www.virgin.com, 'Welcome to the home of Virgin online'

CHAPTER

GET EMPLOYEE BUY-IN ON YOUR BRAND

The main skill is to keep from getting lost.

–Robert M. Pirsig, Zen and the Art of Motorcycle Maintenance

Once you realize the potential of integrated branding, it's obvious that customers need to understand your brand's promise. After all, integrated branding is all about creating a relationship that customers value. But it is not as obvious that employees need just as much, if not more, brand education than customers. Many companies invest in their integrated brand, and then focus only on customer communications, leaving limited budget for employee education. According to a report by The Conference Board, 'Engaging Employees Through Your Brand,' 'Companies that rate their corporate brand efforts "highly successful" shared a number of traits. They were more likely

- to identify employees as a key audience;
- to involve their advertising people in strategy settings as well as execution;
- to identify "delivering the brand promise to customers" as a key goal.'[1]

Getting employees to buy into the value of using your integrated brand won't happen overnight or after one executive memo. It will require ongoing explanation on how to make brand tools relevant to and useful for each employee's work. We've found the most effective way to do this is to communicate the destination to employees at the very start.

The essential prerequisite to 'communicating the destination' is to clarify how employees can use their map and compass – the brand tools. But it's equally critical to show them what it looks like to have arrived. In John Kotter's book *Leading Change*, he asserts that communicating the desired future is essential to creating behavior change. 'In the change process, a good vision serves three important purposes. First, by clarifying the general direction for change... it simplifies hundreds or thousands of more detailed decisions. Second, it motivates people to take action in the right direction, even if the initial steps are personally painful. Third, it helps coordinate the actions of different people, even thousands and thousands of individuals, in a remarkably fast and efficient way.' [2]

This chapter will give you examples of how to use integrated brand tools as well as develop ways to show people what arriving looks like before they get there. Please consider the brand communication process carefully. One of the most common laments of brand executives is not starting earlier or communicating enough about the brand: Tony Marchak of IBM, says, 'We would have done it earlier. We would try to tap into every single communication means that we have, whether it is done through the intranet, whether it is done through hard copy publications, whether it is line or senior executive communication, line communication at large, or HR communication.'[3]

Employee Branding at Shurgard Self Storage

Shurgard is an international, 1,000-employee self-storage company that prides itself on being better than the competition in all areas, including value, security, cleanliness and customer service. Its stated promise to customers is that they can "Expect More" from Shurgard.

Problem:

How best to get Shurgard employees aligned with the company's customer brand promise? While Shurgard had successfully launched its brand externally, with proof points and marketing materials, employees did not think about the brand promise when making everyday decisions or interacting with each other. Basically, there were multiple company culture norms that got in the way of Shurgard employees delivering on the brand promise to customers – internal and external.

Approach:

Parker LePla conducted 78 interviews with employees at all levels, asking questions about what "Expect More" meant to each employee, how they demonstrated it internally and externally, and what company-culture behaviors got in the way of being able to deliver on "Expect More." There were several areas where either people were confused about what "Expect More" meant and how they were expected to demonstrate it, or where company-culture behavior norms prevented them from demonstrating it, particularly in the areas of conflict, communication and accountability. After analyzing the research results, Parker LePla presented them to the company at its annual meeting and made recommendations on next steps.

Results:

In response to Parker LePla's recommendations, Shurgard set up an internal brand team with the charter to define "Expect More' in greater detail and depth, examine the company's cultural norms and make changes to bring the internal culture into alignment with the external brand promise. The brand team will also introduce internal proof points so employees will understand specific areas where they will be expected to deliver on the brand promise internally with each other.

COMMUNICATE AND DEMONSTRATE BRAND TOOLS

Communicating the destination takes two forms – communicating through words and conveying through actions – we call the latter demonstrating. Of the two, demonstrating is more powerful, because it is the visible proof of your brand promise. The table below outlines which tools to demonstrate and communicate. The tools work together to effectively help communicate your destination with employees, customers and other audiences.

THE LEADER'S ROLE IN DEMONSTRATING AND COMMUNICATING

As a leader, how do you decide when to demonstrate or communicate? The easy answer is you should be demonstrating brand actions with every decision you make. This means making sure all actions reflect the company's brand principle and personality to others. You'll want to use your brand values as boundaries for any action you take. You'll also want to take every opportunity to tell the company's brand story and to get others to do so as well.

TABLE 6.1 DEMONSTRATING AND COMMUNICATING USING
BRAND TOOLS

What	Demonstrate	Communicate	Example
Brand principle	X	X	Volvo demonstrates safety by creating a concept car based on safety. Volvo communicates safety through its tagline 'For life.'
Brand personality	X	X	Ben & Jerry's demonstrates its quirky personality through holding a contest to find a new CEO. Ben & Jerry's communicates its personality through ice cream names such as 'Cherry Garcia.'
Brand mission	X	X	Archer Daniels Midland (ADM) (an agriculture research and technology company) communicates its mission of 'Unlocking the potential of nature to improve the quality of life' through radio program sponsorships and its Web site and demonstrates its mission through nature-based products such as Xanthan gum.

What	Demonstrate	Communicate	Example
Brand associations		X	National Geographic uses a golden rectangle as a communications element on the front of its magazine, Web site, channel programming and logo.
Brand story		X	McIlhenny (manufacturer of pepper sauces) uses the founder, Edmund McIlhenny, and Avery Island, Louisiana (where its sauces are made) as the backdrop for communicating its story of growing the perfect peppers and making its unique sauces.
Brand values	X	X	McDonalds demonstrates its value of social responsibility by leading farmers into better animal-care practices. It is communicating that value by issuing a Worldwide Social Responsibility Report.

For example, a business consulting firm with a principle of creating perspective will want to make sure they provide both clients and co-workers with an understanding of how any project fits into the bigger picture. Doing this will be as important as successfully meeting the project objectives. At the same time, the firm will want to demonstrate its personality trait of collaborative by making sure they solicit and use others' ideas. Finally, the firm will want to use its value of long-term relationships as a guide for whether to bill the client for an activity that was not clearly defined as part of the project.

While modeling your brand is powerful, you shouldn't expect everyone to make the connection between your actions and the brand. Therefore, it's also important for leaders to communicate what you are doing as you are doing it - say 'Why did I set up a mid-project update with the client? Because of our principle of creating perspective,' for instance. This lets people hear how you applied the brand, while giving the actions you already demonstrated more authority.

What other tools leaders focus on will depend entirely on their areas of responsibility. Senior managers will spend a lot more time designing strategy to apply the mission, while other employees will use the mission only for inspiration or when asked about the company's goal. Marketing communications personnel will create communications reflecting the personality and associations that are also built on the principle's meaning. Human resources will use the personality as a hiring tool, the values to help define and redefine cultural norms and the principle to help employees align their actions to build the integrated brand.

Both demonstrating and communicating brand tools are important. Demonstrating them creates a force of authenticity words alone can't achieve. Demonstrating the personality creates customer interactions with the company and its products or services that are predictable and enjoyable. But communicating tool meaning, so people have a context for what you are demonstrating, is also critical[4] – so that your words reinforce your actions.

As a leader, you want to ensure that your area of responsibility – whether it is product development, operations or something else – gives employees and customers insight about what your brand stands for. That means examining all company activities with a view to what they are demonstrating and communicating – even such details as the design of your facilities. Timex, for example, opened a new company headquarters in Middlebury, Connecticut. According to its architect,

Douglas Disbrow of Fletcher Thompson, in a *Fast Company* article, 'Certain knowledge gets contained if space is defined in a certain way.'[5] In talking about the challenge of branding the space, *Fast Company* says, 'One design feature may help: an oculus-a round 'eye' punched into the building's domed roof-that directs a band of sunlight onto a solar calendar laid out on the floor. The building itself is a watch.'[6] Imagine what a powerful brand statement this building makes about the Timex customer experience to both its employees and visitors.

CREATING A COMMON BRAND LANGUAGE

A common language that creates a shortcut to brand-based action encourages brand tool usage through articulating cultural norms. One of your roles as a leader is to cultivate a common language to help employees build the brand. Edgar H. Schein, Professor of Management at the Sloan School of Management, MIT, and author of numerous organization development books, states: 'To function as a group, the individuals who come together must establish a system of communication and a language that permits interpretation of what is going on. Categories of meaning that organize perceptions and thought, thereby filtering out what is unimportant while focusing on what is important, become not only a major means of reducing over-load and anxiety but also a necessary precondition for any coordinated action.'[7] Having a common language can help individuals and workgroups identify and value brand actions and results as they happen.

When it started up, Avanade (a joint venture formed in 2000 by Accenture and Microsoft) conducted a week long, new-employee orientation called Quick Start. During Quick Start, employees and executives discussed and shaped their desired values and continued defining their brand promise. The term passion for technology caught on as a cultural norm for permission to explore technology advances, new software and hardware, training, knowledge-sharing and many other activities. Employees were heard saying *'We can show our customer our 'passion for technology' here by doing "x"'* or, *'Sometimes our "passion for technology" costs us time up front, but we all believe it will be worth the investment down the road.'* The phrase 'passion for technology' is globally understood at Avanade and is used worldwide in the company. It is not its brand principle, which is two steps ahead, but it supports the brand principle and, by its common use, helps direct employees to demonstrate behaviors that are on-brand.

Test Employees' Understanding of Your Brand Promise

In response to the three questions below, consider which statement sounds most like your expected employee responses (or better yet, ask a few employees and learn firsthand).

If your employees' statements are closer to the 'a' responses, reconsider how you are communicating your brand to employees.

Do you have a brand?
  a) 'Yes, but I don't know what it is.'
  b) 'Yes, and I can recite it in a 30-second elevator conversation as needed.'
What is your brand?
  a) 'Our brand is our logo and tagline.'
  b) 'Our brand can be described using brand tools such as principle, personality and values.'
How does your brand influence your work?
  a) 'Brand is for marketing to worry about. If I'm not in marketing I don't care about our brand.'
  b) 'Our brand can help me make decisions about how to execute my work, ultimately leading to our desired customer experience.'

VISUALIZING THE DESTINATION

Besides demonstrating and communicating the steps to living the integrated brand, you also need to give employees a sense of what it's like to have arrived. In a way, every time an employee successfully takes an action that is on-brand, they have made it to the destination. But it's also helpful to give them a glimpse of what the destination looks like for their job. Providing a glimpse of the destination comes in many forms – including clearly communicating on-brand behavior and brand strategy, marketing campaigns and tying employee compensation to that future.

COMMUNICATIONS CLARITY

Communications clarity helps leaders at every level guide employees to a desired future. A story will help illustrate this. Two leaders take

20 campers on a hike, all of whom have varying levels of ability. The terrain makes it impossible for the leaders to see all the hikers at once or remain in their line of sight at all times. At the beginning of the hike, the leaders have the choice of being very vague by saying 'hike in that direction' or less vague by saying 'hike to the top of the ridge.' If the group follows the first direction, it requires the leaders' guidance almost immediately when they come to a fork in the trail.

Alternatively, the leaders can provide more clarity about the destination and how to get there. They could say 'head to the top of the west ridge, when you come to a fork, always take the one bearing west, and wait at the top for the rest of us to get there – it should take about three hours.' This clarity enables hikers out in front to provide leadership – even when the leaders are not present. They have the right tools to determine which trail to take and an idea of how much time it will take to reach the destination.

Richard Deuree, former president of Proctor & Gamble, reportedly disdained writing any memorandum of more than one page. He explained to an interviewer, 'Part of my job is to train people to break down an involved question into a series of simple matters. Then we can all act intelligently.'[8]

The leader's first job in showing the destination is to clearly outline how every employee can get there. This communication begins with very big picture brand tools and brand strategy and continues with the department's and employee's specific role in getting to the destination.

COMMUNICATING THE VISION

An external marketing campaign is one of the tipping points that get employees excited and bought into your brand direction. The best time to build morale and change behavior around brand is when you have just gone through a branding or re-branding exercise and are at the point of rolling it out to all audiences. We recommend that leaders identify one brand aspect that is most compelling to customers and build a one-to-two-year advertising and public relations campaign around it. This campaign will get employees emotionally charged about the destination experience while building employee pride in the company's brand direction. Think back to the initial campaigns for Intel Inside or the 1984 Apple Computer advertisements to see good examples. These campaigns took the public by storm but also served to focus employee excitement and energy around brand direction.

A second way to communicate the destination is by engaging employees in a long-term, internal communications campaign. Part of the content for such a campaign is answering the question of what complete departmental brand alignment would look like. These 'what-if' scenarios work well when conducted as employee brainstorming sessions. For instance, using the Avanade principle of two steps ahead, what might the destination look like for the Avanade sales department? What should happen on a typical Avanade sales call? What types of information should sales people provide to prospects? How can they keep existing customers two steps ahead? Answering these types of questions gives departmental employees a clearer vision of the brand destination.

THE DESTINATION AND EMPLOYEE COMPENSATION

Perhaps the most powerful way to communicate the destination is to help employees understand how reaching the destination will directly benefit them. You can break this picture into career and monetary rewards. On the career side, what new skills and experience will aligning your department bring to employees? How will that help them further their careers? From a compensation point of view, what should the relationship be between compensation and living the brand?

There are three kinds of employee rewards for living the brand. The first is tied to their desire to make a difference in overall company success – due to the ability of integrated branding to increase margins, profitability, market share and long-term company sustainability. Making a difference also results in larger bonuses, job security and career advancement.

The second reward is an enhanced sense of self worth resulting from being part of a successful brand. If you work for a company with a strong brand and strong corporate culture, you are much more likely to take pride in the company's strong brand and feel good about the part you play in it than if you work for a company with a weak brand and weak culture.

A third reward type results from tying brand-based company goals directly to employee compensation or bonuses. Continental Airlines, for instance, gives all employees a bonus when the company reaches a certain level of on-time flights. Washington Mutual bases a portion of tellers' compensation on customer satisfaction. Brand compensation can also be tied to individual performance.

Dell Computer has a series of metrics that everyone's bonus is measured against including some that are directly tied to how the company delivers its customers experience. Dell's Scott Helbing says, 'So every employee knows that if we are not delivering on the customer experience, which is the brand promise, we're not getting paid...We emphasize this more with the sales force than the employees in general, but a lot of different segments and groups talk to their people about it.'[9]

Other ways to communicate the destination include:
- brand-tool-development seminars. Tri-Med Ambulance, for example, a 50-person ambulance company in Kent, WA, set aside two mornings at a local hotel to give all the drivers, EMTs and paramedics time to come together and learn about the brand tools, practice using them in small groups, and brainstorm other ways the company could better live its brand;
- special brand promotions. Cotelligent, an IT consulting firm based in San Francisco, gave every employee a Cotelligent-branded Swiss Army knife to represent the company's flexible nature;
- company-wide meetings. At Sakson & Taylor, a beach-themed party (complete with drawings for island vacations) was the launch event for all 500 employees to celebrate and learn about the brand tools;
- new employee orientation. Trendwest, a vacation ownership company, seamlessly incorporates the company's brand tools within a larger employee orientation process;
- internal newsletters;
- intranets and online e-learning. The Seattle Chapter of the World Entrepreneurs' Organization uses an intranet to demonstrate ways the organization is living its key promise: 'live with intent';
- periodic emails from senior management;
- in-office visuals (posters, handouts, memos);
- press coverage about the company. When a 500-person connectivity software company in Seattle received coverage

in an article that showed clearly the company's personality trait of 'respect,' it posted reprints for all employees to see.

Most Used Methods For Communicating the Brand From 137 U.S. Companies according to a (2001) The Conference Board report.	
Outside print and broadcast media	80%
Internal printed materials	77%
Internet campaign	66%
In-house meetings	58%
Intranet campaign	51%
Role modeling by CEO	40%
Road shows	40%
Role modeling by heads of business	40%
Middle management training	33%
Recognition and rewards program	32%
Variable compensation	20%
Formal peer programs	14%
Informal peer programs	14%

Qpass approached the challenge of educating employees about its brand in a fun, engaging and extremely creative way. With the help of a design firm, it developed a set of 30 Qpass trading cards. Each card had a different (high-tech yet funky) image on one side and a component of the company's brand promise on the other. The text on the cards included everything from mission, values and story, to personality, positioning and even rules for logo placement.

To get a particular card, employees needed to answer brand questions posed by company executives or recite brand messages on demand. The grand prize for the first person to amass the entire set of cards was four, box-seat tickets to a Seattle Mariners' baseball game. The reward for Qpass was communicating its brand in a way that actively engaged and excited employees. According to the VP of marketing, the cards were 'a creative way for each employee to feel and touch the brand. Everything employees do is a reflection of the company.'

FIGURE 6.1: QPASS BRAND CARDS
Qpass developed these to educate customers about the brand. Courtesy of Qpass and Methodologie.

Sakson & Taylor used a company-wide party to demonstrate its brand principle of excellence through caring to employees who typically worked off site. The party gave everyone a chance to come together as a team and allowed management to launch its integrated brand in an emotionally compelling manner. It also gave employees opportunities for one-to-one discussions with senior managers, where the new brand was communicated and employees got a clearer understanding of the brand destination.

Harley-Davidson uses a variety of tactics to communicate its brand destination. These include a twice-monthly, employees-only newsletter, an internal television system, an intranet called RIDE (Rapid Information Deployment Express), town hall meetings and having employees work at specific customer events to immerse them in the Harley-Davidson experience.[11]

Seattle Children's Home has created a large mural showing its association of a butterfly (representing transformation) in its executive boardroom. It has also landscaped its campus to create a safe refuge from the world based on its principle of improving the futures of the kids it serves.

EXECUTIVE LEADER LOG

If I want employees to embrace making big behavior changes to be more on-brand, I should lead by example. The harder it is for me to change, the more leadership I will demonstrate when people see I am actually doing some things differently.

HUMAN RESOURCES LEADER LOG

Customer-facing departments such as sales can brainstorm how to demonstrate the brand to our company's external customers. While internal-facing departments, including ours, can brainstorm what we could be doing differently, from their point of view, to demonstrate the company's brand to them.

Rewarding changes in behavior to be more on-brand (the bigger the change, the bigger the reward) might be best, say, during the first year. That would put the need for (and benefits of) change front and center. Even our best, most on-brand performers can improve – especially if the CEO is the first to make behavior changes.

SALES LEADER LOG

Starting to better demonstrate our brand should begin with our best customers – the impact with them will be so strong, I suspect, it will create the excitement and motivation to work on-brand behavior into ALL our sales situations. Maybe we'll even end up converting some not-best customers to 'best' status.

NOTES

[1] Dell, David, and Ainspan, Nathan, and Bodenberg, Thomas, and Troy, Kathryn, and Hickey, Jack, 'Engaging Employees Through Your Brand,' (2001) *The Conference Board*, p 8

[2] Kotter, J *Leading Change*

[3] Dell, David, and Ainspan, Nathan, and Bodenberg, Thomas, and Troy, Kathryn, and Hickey, Jack, 'Engaging Employees Through Your Brand,' (2001) *The Conference Board*, p 28

[4] LePla, J and Parker, L *Integrated Branding* (2002), Kogan Page, London

[5] Lieber, R 'Timex Resets Its Watch,' *Fast Company,* November 2001

[6] Ibid.

[7] Schein, E *Organizational Culture and Leadership* 2nd edition

[8] Peters, T and Waterman, R *In Search of Excellence*

[9] Dell, David, and Ainspan, Nathan, and Bodenberg, Thomas, and Troy, Kathryn, and Hickey, Jack, 'Engaging Employees Through Your Brand,' (2001) *The Conference Board*, p 34

[10] Dell, David, and Ainspan, Nathan, and Bodenberg, Thomas, and Troy, Kathryn, and Hickey, Jack, 'Engaging Employees Through Your Brand,' (2001) *The Conference Board*, p 22

[11] Dell, David, and Ainspan, Nathan, and Bodenberg, Thomas, and Troy, Kathryn, and Hickey, Jack, 'Engaging Employees Through Your Brand,' (2001) *The Conference Board*, p 21

CHAPTER

ARE YOUR CULTURAL NORMS SUPPORTING YOUR BRAND?

Decide who you must be, then do what you must do.

–Epictatus

By answering *'Where are we going?' 'Why are we going there?'* and *'Are we ready to go?'* the previous mile markers helped you point everyone in your company in a common direction. But like drivers who have finished studying their maps, now it's time for you to start putting the foot to the pedal.

The next two chapters transition leaders' attention from how they demonstrate and communicate the brand to how to get everyone else moving.

Living an integrated brand comes from effective day-to-day execution by employees at all levels. *But what does effective look like?* At any given moment, an employee will have opportunities to act, make decisions, and communicate in a style that demonstrates the company's brand promise – or not. The leaders' challenge is to create an environment which influences employees' behavioral choices, even when their leaders are absent. Although this may sound like some management sleight of hand, it's not. It happens every day, through cultural norms that exist in every workplace. This chapter examines the power of cultural norms and how to align them to your brand.

The following story illustrates the power of cultural norms: A patient walked into his doctor's office for an appointment. Even though the doctor worked in a large clinic, and the patient hadn't been there in a while, due to good signage, he was able to easily find his way to the right place. When he checked in, the receptionist asked him three pertinent questions and noted his arrival time. He thanked him for being on time. The patient validated his parking using the self-serve parking validation stamp on the reception countertop. Before he had a chance to pick out a magazine and get comfortable in the lobby, the doctor's medical assistant took him to an examining room. She also asked pertinent questions and said the doctor would be just a few minutes. Before he could read more than a paragraph or two in his magazine, the doctor arrived. The doctor apologized for keeping him waiting. What's more, this was the third time the man had had this on-time experience. Another family member also had a similar on-time experience with this doctor.

What the patient observed repeatedly at this office wasn't an accident. Behind the scenes, the doctor had made an investment in, and was taking specific actions that led to the on-time experience. These included:

- installing several directional signs so patients didn't waste time getting lost;
- training the receptionist on the on-time value;
- self-serve parking validation to free the receptionist's time for on-time activities;
- training a medical assistant on the on-time value;
- designing the doctor's first comments and questions to reinforce the on-time experience.

If the patient had a normal wait, he would have still received good medical care but the quality of his experience – and therefore his loyalty and commitment to the doctor – would have suffered. The doctor and her staff would have missed the opportunity to create an unbreakable customer relationship – moving this customer from 'preference' to 'loyalty' or 'commitment' on the brand equity pyramid. (See Chapter 1: Why All Leaders Need to Be Brand Driven).

One of the reasons for the success of this patient's experience is because the leaders in the doctor's office had successfully created a clear, integrated brand that influenced employees' behavioral choices in the moment. These brand-based choices then became rules of the road over time. Another way to think of rules of the road is as 'the way we do things around here.' In this case, the principle of on-time experience resulted in timeliness becoming one of the office's rules of the road.

LOOK FOR RULES OF THE ROAD

Rules of the road are cultural norms that shape employee behavior within an organization. They are behavioral shortcuts that allow employees to successfully take actions and make decisions. *Merriam-Webster's*

Collegiate Dictionary defines a norm as 'a principle of right actions binding upon the members of a group and serving to guide, control, or regulate proper and acceptable behavior.'[1]

The problem with rules of the road is they can get in the way if they aren't aligned with your integrated brand. Once you identify which ones currently operate in your culture, you can determine which to keep or change.

Rules of the road derive from your brand tools – a shared sense of what you do (your mission), how you work (your values), what you say to others (your story), your approach (your principle), and your tone and manner (your personality – especially the personality of founders and early employees). Cultural norms are the levers behind most company actions. Taken as a group, they define your corporate culture.

FIGURE 7.1: CORPORATE CULTURE MODEL 1
Where do cultural norms come from?

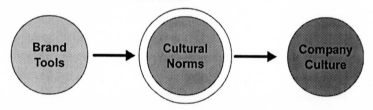

To further define the relationship between cultural norms and corporate culture, think of norms as drops of water in a bucket. Together, they make up the contents of the bucket, but individual norms may vary from bucket to bucket. Culture types fall into larger categories (see Chapter 8: Factor in Your Corporate Type) that can contain a wide variety of cultural norms. In organizations that live their integrated brand, it's every leader's role to understand the rules of the road that impact their work and ensure they are in line with the brand tools. Once they've identified the rules, leaders can take the following three steps:

1. Reinforce rules that demonstrate on-brand behavior.
2. Downplay existing rules that *do not* demonstrate the brand.
3. Create new rules that demonstrate brand behavior.

Here's an example of one set of rules of the road from a service firm:

- 'Full participation.' Each person participates in all discussions, weighing in with their own perspective, whether that includes agreement, disagreement; or additional input.
- 'We leave personal career issues at the door.' Each person participates from a whole-company perspective, not from a

personal-career perspective. Decisions and discussions about individual career development are handled at the supervisory level.

- 'Confrontation, disagreement and fights are okay.' Strong emotions are communicated and acknowledged, but they are not allowed to rule decisions. Disagreements are not left unsaid. The caveat for all of the above is that personal respect and courtesy are expected as well.
- 'We don't tolerate passive-aggressive behavior.' It happens rarely, but when it does, employees call each other on it – sometimes in a gentle manner, sometimes not so gently. The group will not let someone 'shut down' and stop participating and communicating. If someone's not feeling heard they are responsible for getting heard. 'I'm talking now – listen to me!' is a valid request and gets instant attention. 'Being heard' does not mean being agreed with.
- 'Everyone supports the group's decision.' Each member of the group is held accountable for acting on decisions they helped to make (being present means you participated, see above). Once a decision is made, everyone is expected to act based on it until such time as the decision becomes irrelevant or someone presents a good case for changing it and persuades the group (as a whole) to make the change. Each employee is empowered to quickly call each other on it if someone is not living by the agreement.
- 'We acknowledge and appreciate individual strengths.' Differences are okay. They make the organization stronger. Weaknesses are okay as well. If an employee has a personal need (for example, the need to think about something overnight; or the need to not discuss something via email), they ask for it.
- 'High trust environment.' Employees expect the best of each other – even when they see things that could suggest otherwise. Leaders try to model consistent behavior based on the organization's brand tools.

SOME PLACES WHERE KNOWING RULES IS IMPORTANT

If you're just beginning the integrated branding discovery process (back at Chapter 2: Bring Your Brand Into Focus and Chapter 3: Tools to Live Your Brand) you'll need to discover your current rules of the road. If you've already done a lot of branding work, you'll be able to figure them out pretty easily. As part of the brand research process, understanding your current rules will help in defining what's unique and compelling about the brand experience you deliver. It will also tell you which of your rules need to be changed to align with your revealed brand.

For example, Group Health revealed a brand principle of assuring superior, coordinated experiences. An existing rule of the road was to 'share information' among the primary-care physicians, specialists, pharmacists and other personnel that needed it. If the company had had an opposite rule of 'building departmental knowledge,' it would have had to downplay this rule to encourage employees to coordinate patient experiences.

WHERE TO LOOK FOR RULES OF THE ROAD

Don't look for your rules to be written down somewhere. You can discover them only by looking at how employees do their work. Look for the following to discover your company's rules.[2]

ACTIONS THAT GET RECOGNIZED OR REWARDED

When people act in ways that demonstrate rules of the road, they have an easier time getting things done. Look for types of actions others acknowledge and publicly reward through recognition programs, awards, bonuses and promotions. For instance, does your company give out an award for the most creative brainstorming ideas? If so, 'creative brainstorming' could be one of your rules of the road.

Another way to determine what behaviors might be rules is to see what types of repetitive actions senior management makes and what actions they acknowledge as important.

ACTIONS THAT SHAPE WORKING RELATIONSHIPS

Language use, the type of information employees communicate and even the questions they ask will illustrate rules of the road. For example, if you notice employees questioning peers but not senior management, your organization may have a rule of the road influencing who you can question and still maintain a positive relationship with.

ACTIONS THAT GUIDE PRIORITIES AND DECISIONS

You will identify some of the most important rules whenever employees are making decisions or prioritizing actions. When it's time to make a tough call, both brand values and rules will be hauled out to guide and justify employee actions. For a company that has a brand value of customer satisfaction, you might hear a rule of 'When in doubt, do what serves the customer'. If the company instead had a value of enhancing the bottom line, you might hear a rule of 'When in doubt, make the decision that results in increased revenue generation.' Or, this company will lead with cost questions versus customer satisfaction questions. Both are important questions in any business decision. It is the consistent emphasis on one type of question or the other that will give you a clue.

Cultural norms may show up in many little ways, such as people always coming to meetings on time, employees always asking questions about cost, the expectation that staff will always support statements with data, and people always copying others on email.

Some rules change based on the audience. An example of this is if employees are always on time to customer meetings, but almost never on time to internal meetings. If there is an audience that seems to have its own set of norms, it's based on a rule that relates specifically to that audience.

ACTIONS THAT USE A COMMON LANGUAGE OR REPRESENT A RITUAL

Often, rules of the road get propagated and cemented in corporate cultures through common language and rituals. For example, at Microsoft there has been a strong value placed on being individually excellent. Common language heard at every level in Microsoft is 'no brainer,' meaning some course of action is so obvious that employees don't have to debate its merits. At Qpass, recruiters hit a large, loud gong that can be heard throughout their halls, offices, and lobby each time the company hires a new employee. This ritual is one of many ways they publicly demonstrate their value of 'good people are essential.'

To simply illustrate how values show up in rules of the road, let's examine a military organization. Everyone agrees that the military values respecting the chain of command. This value is even written down and taught to new officers and enlistees as something they must do. Those who follow this requirement are eligible for promotion and those who do not are subject to military discipline. This value then shows itself in several rules that have developed over the centuries, such as the display of rank on sailors' sleeves, shoulders and collars for all to see, and deference to those of higher rank and seniority.[3]

Let's look at how some of the rules play out in more detail.

Repetitive actions: Military personnel greet each other with both a handshake and a salute.[4] Civilian courtesies are not given up in the military; but the addition of the salute emphasizes the importance of chain of command.

Actions that influence priorities and decisions: The captain is always responsible for what happens – even the mistakes.

Looking for Rules of the Road

Point of Interest

Step 1: For two weeks, observe employee actions. Keep the following five questions with you. Note all rules of the road you see. What actions are:

- *recognized and rewarded*;
- *shaping relationships*;
- *influencing priorities and decisions*;
- *always the same, or always the same with a given audience*;
- *reflected in a common language or ritual?*

Step 2: Look for underlying themes in the rules of the road you identify. What values do they illustrate? List a few values you think employees believe in.

Step 3: Ask others to do the same, then compare your findings.

Actions that remain the same with a given audience: Rank determines actions as simple as riding in a car or walking down the street. The place of honor is always on the right, so the senior person in the party will sit or walk on the right. If three people are traveling, the most junior person rides or walks in the middle (or least comfortable location).[5]

Common language and rituals: All officers are called 'sir' or 'ma'am' and often referred to by their title (i.e. 'General Jones'). 'Mister' is reserved for junior officers (officers who are not field grade), and enlisted personnel are referred to by their last name. Non-commissioned officers are referred to by their title as a matter of respect, including respect downward. For example, an admiral would call a senior chief petty officer 'senior chief.'

ALIGNING RULES OF THE ROAD TO YOUR BRAND PROMISE

Once you have identified your company's rules of the road, prioritize them from most to least important. The most important rules of the road will be the ones that most accurately distinguish your culture and may be considered best practices. Then ask yourself, *'Do these practices align with our brand?' 'Do they help us deliver our customer experience?'* The strongest rules, the ones you see most often in a variety of circumstances, represent a powerful opportunity to demonstrate your brand. For example, if your company's brand principle is precision at every turn, and rules include how each employee handles such details as 'arriving to meetings on time;' 'prepared, complete and specific email messages;' and 'highly polished group presentations;' then your rules align well with your brand promise. If your rules included 'free-form meetings with no agenda;' 'emails with no supporting data'; and 'very casual group presentations'; then your rules would not align well to 'precision at every turn.' The company still may produce products that have high precision – just not the highest precision. You'll have lost opportunities for employees to demonstrate and reinforce 'precision at every turn' to customers, partners and co-workers.

Below are more examples of rules-of-the-road alignment. Your challenge as a leader is to identify rules not in alignment with the brand, and then change or eliminate those rules.

TABLE 7.1: ALIGNING RULES OF THE ROAD TO BRAND PROMISE

Brand Promise	Aligned Rules	Mis-Aligned Rules
Caring, personalized service	'Provide a 24-hour toll-free telephone number'	'Answer the phone when convenient'
	'Meet at customer's location'	'Visit the customer site only if there is a problem'
	'Listen well'	'We answer complaints in writing only'
Two steps ahead	'Leading edge'	'Completely proven'
	'Teach innovation'	'Teach what customers have to know'
Innovation for patient benefit	'Reward patient-friendly innovation'	'Reward leading edge technology'
	'Does the patient benefit?'	'Is it cool?'

Aligning your existing rules of the road helps increase return on brand investment by eliminating actions that are counter to your brand direction.

REINFORCING RULES

You can enhance rules that align with the brand by making sure that leaders reinforce them. The more often one is used, the stronger it becomes. Leaders can reinforce rules through:

- role modeling;
- talking openly about them;
- recognizing and rewarding individuals and teams for rules-based actions;
- involving employees in discussions about maintaining certain behavior;
- redirecting undesirable behaviors.

Unfortunately, many leaders call attention only to undesirable behavior. As Kenneth Blanchard, author of the *One Minute Manager* and other popular management books, said, 'catch them doing something right.'[6] Recognition and rewards do not have to be formal or costly to the company. A mere 'thank you' goes a long way to reinforce existing rules of the road.

TABLE 7.2: REINFORCING RULES OF THE ROAD
This table gives some examples of how to reinforce rules of the road that align well to the brand promise.

Brand Promise	Aligned Rules of the Road	Reinforcing Actions (examples)
Caring, personalized service	'Provide a 24-hour toll-free telephone number'	Allocate budget for toll-free numbers and customer visits.
	'Listen well'	Ask those who are doing a good job of actively listening to be part of corporate-sponsored communications training.

Brand Promise	Aligned Rules of the Road	Reinforcing Actions (examples)
Two steps ahead	'Leading edge'	Recognize and reward employees for using new products.
	'Teach innovation'	Evaluate engineers based on how well customers tested the product on their systems.
Innovation for patient benefit	'Reward patient-friendly innovation'	Make resources available to measure patient use.
	'How does the patient benefit?'	Redirect any group that does not explore ways to involve patients in feature decisions.

Reinforcing Rules of the Road

- Choose a few rules that strongly demonstrate your brand.
- Generate a list of leadership activities that can reinforce those behaviors.
- Ask others for ideas.
- Pick one or two ideas from the list that you will begin doing ASAP.

DOWNPLAYING RULES OF THE ROAD

It's impossible to suddenly drop an established rule because it is a learned behavior. You need to create a plan for gradually downplaying those rules that conflict with your brand. The first step is to get senior management and department leaders to flag that a particular rule is changing, and then model the new behavior. Here are some other ways to eliminate undesirable rules:

- Eliminate recognition or rewards that reinforce off-brand behavior.

- Educate leaders who may be role-modeling undesired behavior unconsciously.
- Let others in your work group or peer group know what behaviors to eliminate and why.
- Create recognition and rewards for replacement behaviors.
- Provide necessary resources to support replacement behaviors.
- Remove leaders, end partnerships, or demote individuals who, with time and feedback, cannot downplay the undesirable behavior.

TABLE 7.3: DOWNPLAYING RULES OF THE ROAD
This table gives some examples of how to downplay rules of the road that do not align well to the brand promise.

Brand Promise	Mis-Aligned Rules of the Road	Downplaying Actions (examples)
Caring, personalized service	'Answer the phone when convenient'	Provide pagers for employees
	'Visit the customer site only if there is a problem'	Add a line item in the travel budget for personalized-service travel.
	'We answer complaints in writing only'	Work with employees to create alternatives for capturing customer complaints, in addition to written forms.
Two steps ahead	'Completely proven'	Reward employees for using products that are leading edge.
	'Teach what customers have to know'	Reward engineers for anticipating specific customer bugs and outlining specific bug fixes.

Brand Promise	Mis-Aligned Rules of the Road	Downplaying Actions (examples)
Innovation for patient benefit	'Reward leading edge technology'	Ensure all technology investments benefit can be tracked to a patient benefit.
	'Is it cool?'	Publicly recognize those groups that involve patients in decision-making.

Downplaying Rules of the Road

- Choose a few rules of the road that strongly conflict with your brand.
- Generate a list of leadership activities that will downplay those behaviors.
- Ask others for ideas.
- Pick one or two ideas from the list that you will begin doing as soon as possible.

CREATING NEW RULES OF THE ROAD

After a review of your existing rules of the road, you may identify some new behaviors that can powerfully support your customer experience. Establishing cultural norms is a very effective way of getting employees to correctly use your brand tools. For example, a family restaurant in a popular shopping center wanted to distinguish itself by providing 'fun for the entire family.' The restaurant invested in fun colors, menus, balloons and food presentations. But it discovered this was not enough. It needed to get the servers to deliver a fun experience. The leaders worked with the servers to discuss ideas about how to demonstrate more fun without stepping outside of their personal comfort zones. One idea was to wear a lot of bright, fun, silly buttons and decals on their uniforms. The idea caught on and employees explain when they are doing actions aligned with this norm as 'show horsing'. It has become a rule of the road for all employees, not just the servers.

Creating new rules of the road should not be undertaken lightly – and it will take time. For a new rule to be adopted companywide, it must align with your brand tools. Effective rules help you create a more compelling and unique customer experience. This is the distinction between 'nice-to-do's' and rules of the road. Many companies pursue 'nice-to-do's' that are behavioral traits no one specifically disagrees with, such as 'teamwork,' 'open feedback' and 'information sharing.' People will typically try in the best of circumstances (when the boss is in the room or when they have time) to do the 'nice-to-do's', but these behaviors do not become rules. Rules of the road are cultural norms that occur even during tough times. Ways leaders can propagate new rules include:[7]

- deliberate teaching and coaching;
- role modeling, particularly in times of crisis;
- immediate recognition of desired behaviors;
- immediate re-direction of non-desired behaviors;
- use of a new desired behavior as a criterion for advancement;
- ensuring necessary resources to demonstrate the new desired behavior.

TABLE 7.4: CREATING RULES OF THE ROAD

This table gives some examples of actions leaders can take working toward the creation of new rules of the road.

Brand Promise	New Rule of the Road to Create	Leader's Actions (examples)
Caring, personalized service	'Customer-based work hours'	Formally announce a new work-hours policy to the organization. CEO measures how often senior management role-models flexible hours. Measure overtime if the customer is experiencing more flexible communications due to flexible work hours.
Two steps ahead	'Customer futures'	Secure sponsorship for promotion criteria based on how well employee moves customer into the future and understands their business plans. Train managers on new criteria. When promotions are announced, publicly recap criteria for promotion.

Creating Rules of the Road

Point of Interest

- Choose only one rule you'd like to see your organization (or at least your area of influence) adopt.
- Test it to ensure it is sufficiently compelling and not merely a 'nice-to-do'.
  - *Will this significantly help us achieve our mission?*
  - *Is this in line with our values?*
  - *Will this directly demonstrate our brand promise?*
  - *Will this make our customer experience more compelling or unique?*
- Generate a list of leadership activities that announce and promote this behavior.
- Ask others for ideas.
- Work with senior management to secure demonstrated sponsorship (see Chapter 4: Align to Deliver a Unique Customer Experience for more on sponsorship).

EXECUTIVE LEADER LOG

Alignment of employee actions and our brand begins with awareness. What are our current rules of the road? At the next management retreat, get the managers thinking about our rules of the road and which ones we need to keep, drop or create to live our brand. Give them the assignment to get back to me with their keep, drop and create lists within three weeks. Consider whether we need to conduct research to fully understand our current cultural norms.

HUMAN RESOURCES LEADER LOG

I can use our rules of the road that align to our brand as part of new-employee orientations. Perhaps even for new-manager orientations. I wonder what rewarding these behaviors would look like? Talk to HR team about this. Employees who work directly with customers should be rewarded for brand-commitment-based, risk-taking behaviors, too. Even when the risk doesn't pay off. How can we instill a culture that cultivates on-brand risk taking?

SALES LEADER LOG

Does our sales staff have different rules of the road for customers versus internal employee interactions? If so, do both sets of rules support our brand? Are there any new rules of the road that would really scream our brand to customers? At the next sales summit, talk about rules of the road and ask the group to identify any we have been using when working directly with customers.

NOTES

[1] Merriam-Webster Web site: www.merriam-webster.com

[2] Adapted from: Schein, E (1992) *Organizational Culture and Leadership 2nd edition*, Jossey Bass Publishers, San Francisco

[3] Courtesy of: Commander Stanley C. Stumbo, U.S. Navy (Retired)

[4] About.com Web site: www.usmilitary.about.com

[5] Ibid.

[6] Blanchard, K, Ph.D (1999) Key note speech at Linkage Leader Development Conference, San Francisco

[7] Adapted from: Schein, E (1992) *Organizational Culture and Leadership 2nd edition*, Jossey Bass Publishers, San Francisco

CHAPTER

8
Factor in Your
Corporate Type

FACTOR IN YOUR CORPORATE TYPE

*A journey is like marriage. The certain way
to be wrong is to think you control it.*

–John Steinbeck

Like it or not, you're destined to live your integrated brand within the context of your corporate culture. It's all around you. You can't escape it, so the better you understand it, the better you'll be able to use it to navigate the way ahead. In this chapter, we'll help you identify your cultural type, which will give you a greater ability to align your cultural behaviors with your brand.

Corporate culture is often referred to as the personality of the organization. But it is more than that. It includes your personality, your values and cultural norms (a.k.a. rules of the road).

FIGURE 8.1: COMPANY CULTURE
Where does company culture come from?

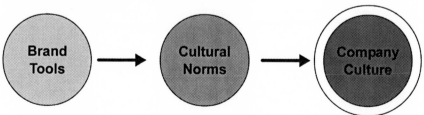

Corporate culture impacts your company in many ways including:
- what actions get resources and rewards;
- how crises are handled;
- how decisions are made;

- rituals;
- hiring criteria;
- language usage.

If it sounds simple, it isn't. According to Edgar Schein, noted author on corporate cultures, 'Culture is the product of social learning. Ways of thinking and behavior that are *shared and that work* become elements of the culture. You cannot create a new culture. You can however demand or stimulate new ways of working and thinking; you can monitor them to make sure they get done; but members of the organization do not internalize new behaviors and make them part of the new culture unless, over time, they actually work better.'[1]

In Chapter 7: Are Your Cultural Norms Supporting Your Brand?, we examined strategies for reinforcing, creating or eliminating cultural norms, with the goal of supporting on-brand actions. In this chapter we'll talk about the larger categories that cultures fit into – this clarity will give you a greater ability to manage your brand using your culture by showing you the most effective ways to manage change in your environment.

SIX CULTURE TYPES

We've identified six corporate culture types. Through identifying your company's predominant type, you'll get a big-picture view of your culture as a starting point for cultural change. Don't place a value judgment on a particular culture type – any type can be successful.

The following is not a one-size-fits-all model. These culture types are approximations used to help you self-assess – not a list of every possible culture. But most cultures will resemble one model more closely than the others.

The Six Culture Types

'Follow the leader'

'Follow the process'

'Customer is always right'

'What else is possible?'

'Competitive'

'Harmonious'

The first step to identifying your company's culture type is to review each type's characteristics and challenges. *Which most sounds like the culture you are working in?* Once you've determined your type, check out its change-management survival skills.

FIGURE 8.2: FOLLOW THE LEADER
'Follow the leader' culture type illustration

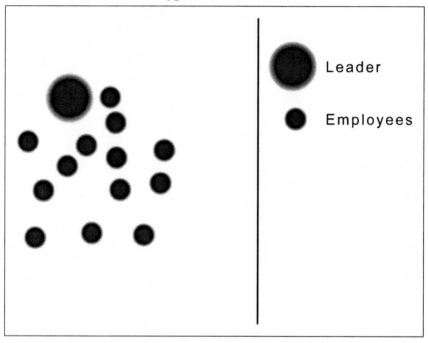

'FOLLOW THE LEADER'

'Follow the leader' cultural characteristics include: adherence to a chain of command; clear roles and job functions (i.e. what you do and do not do); clear processes, standards, operating procedures; directions; plans; and tradition. Any organization can have a 'follow the leader' culture. A few typical examples include some (but not all) hospitals and public safety services such as fire and police departments.

Leaders in this culture spend time making decisions rather than reviewing decisions made by others. Leaders are often on an electronic lifeline to the company, typically a cell phone or pager, that they use continuously throughout the day to direct the activities of others. They are busy communicating plans they have made and measuring progress against those plans.

Leaders keep a tight rein on resources, like to hold people accountable and they give rewards for productivity that follows their plan. They expect directions to be followed and have little tolerance when subordinates question their decisions. In a crisis, employees will wait for the leader to decide how to respond.

They often have a 'president's award' and other visible ways of manifesting authority, such as larger offices or offices physically removed from employees' offices or workspaces for senior management. Authority is also reinforced by nicknames such as 'Chief' or 'Boss,' or the more pejorative 'Head Honcho' or 'The Man.'

CHALLENGES FOR 'FOLLOW THE LEADER' CULTURES

Leaders in these cultures can expect two challenges on the journey to living the integrated brand. We call these: 1) 'You are only as good as the leader,' and 2) 'It's not my job!'

CHALLENGE 1: 'YOU ARE ONLY AS GOOD AS THE LEADER'

Since this culture follows the leader, a committed CEO and senior management team must effectively demonstrate sponsorship for living the integrated brand. (See Chapter 4: Align to Deliver a Unique Customer Experience) 'Follow the leader' employees will not pay attention to the brand unless top-level leaders not only think it is important for the success of the company, but they personally demonstrate the brand in their everyday decisions and actions. Efforts to act on-brand will be difficult in this culture.

To survive this challenge, secure and maintain demonstrated sponsorship from senior management for living the integrated brand. Securing sponsorship will take time and dedication. The quick test for whether brand is sponsored includes:

- *Have leaders clearly and continuously communicated your brand promise and the value of your integrated brand to employees? Have they made the downside clear if employees don't execute on your brand promise?*
- *Have leaders identified measures of success for living the integrated brand? Will leaders know if the company is executing on its brand?*
- *Are employees who are successful rewarded and recognized?*
- *Have leaders demonstrated that executing on the integrated brand co-exists with other business priorities, and is not allowed to get lost?*

- *Have leaders allocated necessary resources or time to living the brand?*
- *Have any of the above demonstrations of sponsorship occurred on more than one occasion?*

It's unusual for any organization to score perfectly on the above test for sponsorship. However, just asking the questions and keeping integrated branding top of mind will help you get sponsorship.

CHALLENGE 2: 'IT'S NOT MY JOB!'

In a 'follow the leader' culture, there is a lot of emphasis on the right people doing the right things. Leaders focus on role clarity. But opportunities to demonstrate your brand promise to customers aren't always predictable. The person responsible may not be available at the opportune time, or the task required may not fall neatly into anyone's job function. 'It's not my job!' can get in the way of delivering your brand experience.

Another way to make sure you're delivering the brand promise is to establish an escalation path for 'it's not my job issues.' If your employees have a superior who can quickly and easily give them permission to act outside of their job scope, you may be able to overcome the 'it's not my job' syndrome. For example, if a customer asks a security officer to perform an additional service, such as checking the lower-floor bathrooms more frequently, the officer could get permission based on a pre-established process.

In a suburban fire department in Oregon, management encourages customer service and recognizes fire fighters who find creative ways to demonstrate that value. Without being specifically told to, the fire fighters have often finished hanging Christmas lights, painting houses and even splitting wood after they rescued individuals who were injured doing those activities. The station's 'customers' often experience service they didn't expect, and the fire station wants it that way. The fire department believes that its customers will remember this above-and-beyond service when it comes time to vote for bond measures that keep them well staffed and funded.

In another example, the pilot of a major airline heard about a passenger's dismay at being continually bumped from cross-country flights over a period of several hours. The pilot – wanting to execute upon the airline's promise of treating customers with dignity and respect – personally walked the passenger to a reservation desk and helped the customer and the reservation clerk find the quickest possible flight home. This was not the pilot's job, but it often takes stepping out of the normal confines of a role to deliver the right customer experience.

How to grow an integrated brand in a 'follow the leader' culture:

Encourage employees to do what it takes to provide your brand experience. There are a number of ways to get employees to go above and beyond their normal cultural restraints. Here are a few:

- Offer public recognition in the moment (or shortly after).
- Create small but meaningful spot bonuses or brand-keeper awards.
- Create a place on the standard performance review to acknowledge on-brand behavior (both inside and outside of the normal scope of the job).
- Give employees feedback in the moment if it appears as if they have missed a unique opportunity to demonstrate the brand, even if it was not their job.
- Lead by example.

Lastly, show leaders how the customer experiences your product or service. Leaders with first-hand knowledge will better understand what it takes to execute on your brand.

Amazon.com sends its corporate headquarters staff to packaging plants every holiday season (this is the highest-volume-sales season). They help with the extra workload, but also see and experience the assembly line processes and people that ensure customers get their books and other merchandise on time. Some Microsoft leaders annually have skip-level meetings, where leaders spend time one-on-one or in small groups with employees at all levels to gain insights about their on-the-job experiences and challenges.

'FOLLOW THE PROCESS'

Characteristics include:

- extensive training on work processes;
- decisions made using detailed data;
- an emphasis on work flow and efficiency;
- well-defined roles;
- clear beginnings and ends to projects;
- inflexible work hours;
- a strict chain of command;
- rewards for seniority.

FIGURE 8.3: FOLLOW THE PROCESS
'Follow the process' culture type illustration.

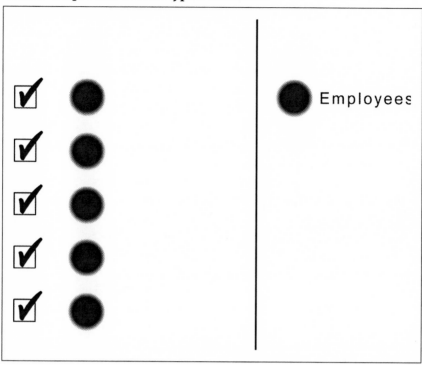

'Follow the process' leaders are primarily project and people managers. They are there to control a well-defined (but often complex) set of processes. They use sophisticated metrics to measure progress. Anything causing a change to a process is met with skepticism, and often implemented only on a trial basis. Any organization can adopt a 'follow the process' culture. You might find typical examples in government agencies or at banks.

Change happens very slowly in this type of culture. Leaders hire candidates based on previous job performance and a strong attendance record. A 'follow the process' culture may not sound appealing to everyone – especially to those who work in a much more open and autonomous culture. However, this culture lends itself to certain types of businesses. For example, a forensic DNA lab may thrive with a 'follow the process' culture where the work needs to be exact and predictable.

Challenges for a 'follow the process' culture:

1) 'Process is king,' and 2) 'If it ain't broke, don't fix it!'

CHALLENGE 1: 'PROCESS IS KING'

In 'follow the process' companies, maintaining the process can easily become more important than the customer experience. As customers, we've all been the victims of company-focused processes. In the worst case, 'follow the process' customers can feel downright abused.

Here's an example. In July 1998, the United States Internal Revenue Service (IRS) Reform Act was signed into law, creating the most sweeping reform of that agency in decades. President Bill Clinton remarked that the law ushered in what he called 'a new era of customer service and enacting taxpayer-friendly rules intended to curb the excesses of overzealous tax collectors.' [2] Phil Brand, a veteran of the IRS remarked, 'This is really about an attempt to influence the culture of the IRS in the broadest sense. The IRS has always viewed itself as a law-enforcement agency. Now they're being asked to view themselves as a financial-services agency with a tilt to customer service.'[3]

However, in April 2000, investigators from the congressional General Accounting Office (GAO) failed to find the widespread evidence of problems in the IRS alleged in 1998. 'Our investigation established that the allegations themselves had been based on an incomplete awareness of the total circumstances,' the GAO report said. 'We found that each manager had acted within his or her discretion... their decisions were approved by appropriate individuals and were documented in the files.'[4] The point being, the IRS apparently followed its process perfectly, and in doing so seriously alienated customers to the point that reform was initiated and eventually passed into law.

The way to survive the process-is-king challenge is by communicating the value of living an integrated brand. One good way to do this is to establish perspective through competitive comparisons. You might ask, *'Why should police agencies and citizens choose one forensic DNA lab over another?'* Or, you could speak of the positive bottom line impact of using the brand principle, personality and values. In the 'follow the process' culture, it's important to give successful examples of people living the brand principle while still getting quality work done.

You can also shift this culture by exposing employees to customers. When employees feel customer satisfaction or pain, they gain perspective on whether their internal processes actually serve the customer. If employees can't visit customers, ensure customer satisfaction is measured and communicated back to employees in a way that makes the customer experience real to them, and that employees are rewarded based on that measurement.

Howard Schultz, founder and Chief Global Strategist of Starbucks and owner of the Seattle Supersonics basketball team, does this well. Schultz is bringing the same tenacious approach to managing the Seattle Sonics that he honed while building the Starbucks brand. 'Schultz is part of a new breed of owners in the NBA who understands that professional sports teams are brands that need to be built and maintained,' explains Kurt Hunzeker, editor of *Team Marketing Report*, a Chicago-based monthly sports-marketing newsletter. 'At the end of the day, despite this being professional sports business and an NBA team, it's a brand,' Schultz said. 'The equity of that brand is built on trust and confidence. I think that trust has been eroded in the past.'

Shultz delivered this message to 500 arena ushers to convince them that their 'contact with fans can make a difference in the fans' experience at games.' [5]

CHALLENGE 2. 'IF IT AIN'T BROKE DON'T FIX IT'

In a process-driven culture, people expect predictability. As a result, it's difficult to change behavior. Employees may see change as a burden, or simply not part of their job.

To make a brand thrive in a 'follow the process' culture, keep it simple. Focus on simple, well-defined first steps. Keep communications short and sweet, but consistent. Consider pilot projects or trials for new ideas. If successful, communicate the positive results with zeal and extend the trial. Once employees see that the change is possible and that the change has had a positive outcome, they are more likely to support it.

Reward ideas that demonstrate brand and process improvements. Ask employees to nominate each other for rewards.

THE 'CUSTOMER IS ALWAYS RIGHT' CULTURE

Cultural characteristics include:
- responding to the whims of the customer take priority;
- spending lots of time, energy and resources on understanding the customers' needs;
- customizing products and services to meet customer needs;
- rewarding the building of relationships with customers and partners;

- tracking many different customer-satisfaction measures;
- conferring higher status on jobs and projects that are closest to the customer.

FIGURE 8.4: CUSTOMER IS ALWAYS RIGHT
'Customer is always right' culture illustration

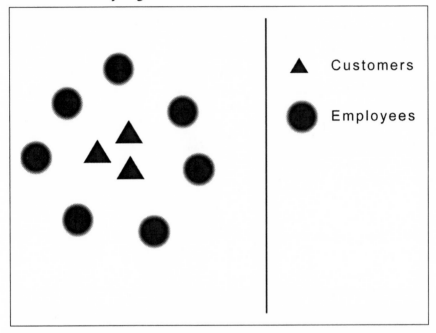

In a 'customer is always right' culture, leaders create and nurture relationships with customers and key partners. They spend time determining and meeting customer needs – even to the point of letting customers have significant influence on new products and features. In a crisis, easing the customer's pain is the first agenda item, fixing the problem is second. Again any organization can have a 'customer is always right' culture. A few typical examples include some (but not all) hotels or consulting firms.

For an example of a 'customer is always right' culture's priorities, consider the 6.8 magnitude earthquake that shook Seattle in February 2001 and hit a major retail business's headquarters hard. Nervous employees ran out of the building to ensure their safety. When addressing these employees on the street in front of their wrecked building, the first thing the CEO said was 'I have great news... the systems that serve our customers are still up and running.' The CEO's focus was on serving the customers – a value that he held to be at least as important as employee safety. Although an unpopular comment, this was a defining moment for the company's core brand value of serving the customer. Employees heard loud and clear that the customer comes first.

CHALLENGES FOR THE 'CUSTOMER IS ALWAYS RIGHT' CULTURE

We've phrased this challenge *'Who are we, anyway?'* In a 'customer is always right' culture, employees get yanked in many directions at the whim of customers. Sometimes they are even set to work on competing products or services – an expensive and confusing philosophy. The result is often a loss of identity and purpose, and dissipation of precious resources.

Worse still, customers won't get a consistent brand experience. In fact, if asked, any two employees might not be able to agree on what the customer experience should look like – since they are doing a myriad of things all aimed at customers.

Leaders in 'customer is always right' cultures can overcome this challenge by encouraging senior management to clearly determine their organization's brand principle, personality and values. (See Chapter 2: Bring Your Brand Into Focus) Clarifying your brand tools doesn't mean ignoring the customer. It does mean being clear on the value you bring to customers, no matter what the specific product or service you deliver. For instance, WestStock (owned by ImageState), a stock-photography company, which can be classified as a 'customer is always right' culture, has a brand principle of image guide, which helps focus the customer-centric company's employees as to how to deliver that customer service.

Not every leader will be in a position to determine the brand, but it is every leader's responsibility to advocate for brand clarity. An essential way to spread the brand principle, personality and values in a 'customer is always right' culture is to tell stories about when customers *didn't* get what they wanted because it didn't fit in with the brand promise.

What gets attention in a 'customer is always right' culture? Not serving the customer. The bias in this culture is to focus on customer relationships and less on the internal operations, processes and infrastructure necessary for great customer service. These functions customers don't see are still necessary to deliver satisfaction – and they include such items as database servers, automated billing systems, inventory and shipping systems, manufacturing and quality-assurance processes. During budgeting (see Chapter 11: Convey Your Brand's Meaning), leaders need to ensure they are working backwards from the customer experience and allocating resources to support this effort.

Lastly, a 'customer is always right' culture needs to ensure that employees know what stays *sacred* about their brand. A major food broker had a key customer – so key it represented the broker's entire revenue stream. It was imperative for all employees to demonstrate their unique value to this customer, in every interaction. At a leadership retreat, the chairman asked, *'How can we make it so this customer can't live without us? What unique values are we offering that will survive changes in their business?'* The group worked for two days discussing measurable actions and deliverables (such as regional buying expertise). They created a means to measure brand equity, not just short-term customer satisfaction. (For more on brand measurement see Chapter 12: Measure Your Brand's Effectiveness).

'WHAT ELSE IS POSSIBLE?'

Typical characteristics of a 'what else is possible?' culture include:
- constantly exploring market possibilities and deals;
- industry networking;
- emphasizing market analysis;
- constantly improving processes;
- having a vague or all-inclusive mission;
- following multiple strategies;
- stopping and starting;
- company divisions following different agendas.

In this culture, leaders spend a lot of their time building partnerships and new sources of revenue. Work focuses on creating or leveraging opportunities, not necessarily on doing what customers want or expect. Leaders are rewarded for bringing new ideas back to the organization leading to employees becoming confused about what matters. You may find this type of culture in a creative design firm or a technology company, however it can develop in any type of organization.

FIGURE 8.5: WHAT ELSE IS POSSIBLE?
'What else is possible?' culture illustration.

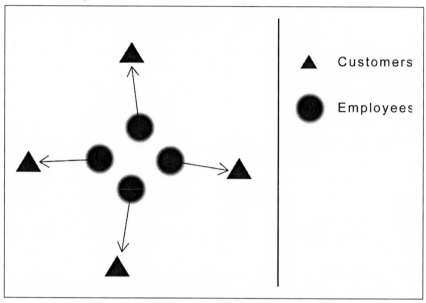

A telecommunications company directed its 200 employees to constantly explore ways to use its technology to make money. Groups were busy working on many initiatives. This made it impossible to prioritize the variety of projects and bring work to closure.

'What else is possible?' cultures are often in transition. Therefore it's hard to reward anything other than working long hours, as the goals that determine success get lost. Employees can easily become de-motivated because of this constant change in focus..

This culture's challenges are 1) 'Are we lost? It sure feels like it,' and 2) 'We don't believe anything is real.'

CHALLENGE 1: 'ARE WE LOST? IT SURE FEELS LIKE IT'
It is nearly impossible for leaders to inspire others to live the integrated brand when the brand isn't working. If the target keeps moving, eventually you stop shooting.

'What else is possible?' cultures brand safe things such as logos, names, short-lived ad campaigns and collateral materials that require less internal alignment and commitment. But these efforts further confuse employees. First, the concept of branding becomes associated with visuals and marketing instead of a unified strategy that aligns the organization behind a promise to the customer. Second, if employees cannot easily see how their current projects and services fit into what the jazzy ads are trying to convey, they wonder if they should be doing something different or, worse, if the company is lying to customers.

Encourage leaders to determine and communicate brand tools. As with the 'customer is always right' culture, this culture needs brand clarity. If employees have benchmarks for success, they can develop best practices that consistently demonstrate the brand, even when the scope of work changes.

A new accounting firm was pursuing many lines of business and asking its consultants to quickly become competent in all of them. Employees were scrambling to come up to speed. However, the firm had always lived a principle of quality at any cost with its employees and customers. Employees used the need to demonstrate quality at any cost as the rationale for asking for more time to learn these new procedures.

CHALLENGE 2: 'I DON'T BELIEVE ANYTHING IS REAL'

Employees in the 'what else is possible?' culture expect change and don't believe the company has consistent goals or strategies. Therefore they will hold off on committing to the success of any plan or initiative. Asking them to work in ways that execute on the brand is especially challenging. They are likely to fear that the brand promise will change soon like everything else they work on.

One tactic to survive this challenge is through being redundant, really. Brand sponsors need to communicate how actions are linked to the brand tools, and then model and reward on-brand behavior. These cultures also need to consistently integrate brand messages into corporate communications. If employees keep seeing the same brand tools, they will eventually begin to believe they are real.

Culture leaders can ask these questions to ensure their actions are consistent with the brand promise:

- *Of the alternative directions we're considering, which will deliver the most on-brand customer experience?*
- *Are there new directions we're considering that are clearly off-brand?*
- *How do my team's current projects fit with our brand tools? If they don't, how should we modify them?*
- *Am I rewarding exploration that enhances the customer experience, or am I exploring for exploring's sake?*

THE 'COMPETITIVE' CULTURE

A 'competitive' culture employs an 'us vs. them' mentality as a basis for its actions. 'We know what is right for you' is a popular (although typically unspoken) theme in employees' behaviors. Look for 'competitive' cultures in organizations that are based on competence such as academic organizations or expert services groups. Again, there is no perfect correlation between the type of organization and the type of culture. Characteristics of this culture include:

- strong group or company identification;
- an emphasis on group survival (sometimes at the expense of cost efficiencies, corporate strategies or customer satisfaction);
- group or company approval and credibility is valued more than customer approval and credibility;
- fewer resources are allocated to customer-satisfaction metrics than in other cultures;
- groups within the company do not necessarily know what others are working on;
- cross-group coordination is difficult.

FIGURE 8.6: COMPETITIVE
'Competitive' culture illustration.

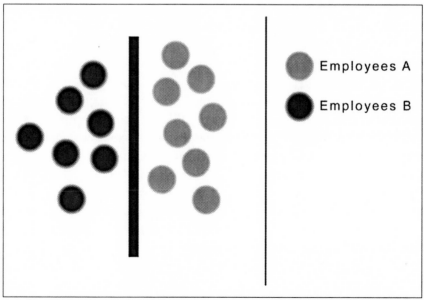

Leaders do what it takes for their group to win. They gather support, persuade others and improve processes to do it their way. Their ultimate reward is winning additional resources and internal influence as opposed to being recognized for customer satisfaction or bottom-line contributions. Groups are generally good at reacting to change and can shift focus quickly if their survival is threatened.

Other characteristics include:

- people outside a group are treated with suspicion;
- decisions are based almost exclusively on inter-group input;
- crises are handled by circling the wagons;
- hires are made on how well candidates fit into the group and support its agenda;
- short-hand and jargon (understood only by those in the group) are used to describe products, services and processes;
- groups tend to work in close proximity to each other to maintain team spirit.

Challenges for a 'competitive' culture include:

1) 'My brand, not yours,' and 2) 'Lack of cross-group coordination.'

CHALLENGE 1: 'MY BRAND, NOT YOURS'

Groups within the company will continually try to define their own brand (or tweak the existing one) to fit their way of doing things. This often results in conflicting customer experiences.

How to survive this challenge:

Involve leaders from all groups to determine the company's brand principle, personality and values. Leaders within the company are more likely to support a company-wide brand principle, personality and values that they helped create. During this participative process, they will also hear the importance of maintaining a consistent brand and resolve how their group's goals can co-exist within an umbrella brand identity. This process is best done with a trained facilitator as there may be competing leaders or groups present that can derail the process.

Don't let on-brand corporate communications become an afterthought. Keeping the brand promise fresh in everyone's mind is critical. Departments will inevitably feel the urge to re-write the brand principle, personality and values as well as slant communications to their approach. For example, a restaurant company with a brand principle of regional classics, had one franchise location that decided to serve what was popular to meet revenue goals. While pursuing this off-brand strategy, the franchise lost sight of the company's customer experience. Customers who dined at other franchise locations were disappointed and confused when faced with this one's inconsistent experience.

Test sponsorship. Clear executive sponsorship for using brand tools is the glue that can bind these groups. (See 'Test for Sponsorship' in 'follow the leader' type description above.)

CHALLENGE 2: 'LACK OF CROSS-GROUP COORDINATION'
In this culture, every group wants to be the dominant group, setting direction for everyone else. It's difficult to consistently deliver one brand and get groups to work together.

Communicating a company brand is a catalyst for cohesion in the 'competitive' culture. Groups need to allocate resources and rewards based on taking on-brand actions. Measuring brand recognition with customers and feeding the results back to groups helps create even more cohesion.

'HARMONIOUS' CULTURES
This culture has a strong preference for group consensus. Characteristics include:
- consensus-driven decision making;
- broadly defined roles that appeal to everyone;
- competing agendas in attempts to please everyone;
- decisions that take a long time;
- employee-satisfaction-driven vs. customer-satisfaction-driven;
- high importance on positive relationships among employees;
- a tendency for the best clients to become personal friends;
- easily allocated resources for social gatherings.

In a 'harmonious' culture, leaders spend a lot of time polling employees and determining courses of action that appeal to everyone. They measure employee satisfaction regularly and control decision-making processes to ensure everyone is involved. Even in a crisis, employees are brought together to determine the best course of action. Rewards go to those who execute their job functions, but do so in ways that maintain relationships with others. The organization brings employees together on a regular basis and likes to give public recognition for a job well done. These companies hire candidates based on their ability to work well with others as much as having the right experience for the job. The work environment is often open with few office doors. We've seen many non-profit organizations adopt this style.

FIGURE 8.7: HARMONIOUS
'Harmonious' culture type illustration

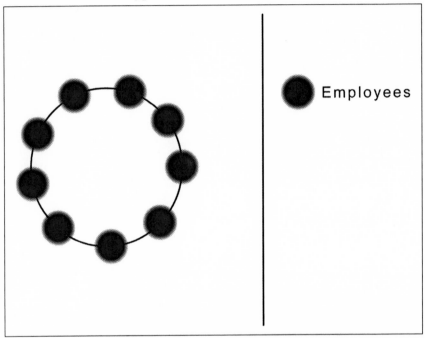

Challenges for a 'harmonious' culture: 1) 'The brand can change as people change,' and 2) 'Decisions are based on the least-common denominator.'

CHALLENGE 1: 'THE BRAND CAN CHANGE AS PEOPLE CHANGE'

The brand is often an extension of personal values as well as organizational values. Leaders take employees' opinions and personal values into consideration when creating brand tools and ways of demonstrating that brand. As a result, the brand often is more of a reflection of influential people inside the organization than company value. An additional risk for these cultures is when new influential people enter into leadership positions, because they often lobby to alter the brand to better fit their personal values.

On the other hand, if an influential person leaves the organization, a defining force behind the brand may vanish. The existing brand will lose a strong advocate and may easily morph into something that is a better personal fit for those who remain.

To survive this challenge, clarify and promote the bottom-line value of a *consistent* brand promise. You need to convince employees that the brand isn't there to please them, but to ensure long-term success.

CHALLENGE 2: 'ACTING ON THE LEAST-COMMON DENOMINATOR'

In a 'harmonious' culture, great strategies sometimes get passed over because they do not gain enough consensus. The strategies the organization decides on run the risk of being overly conservative and traditional to meet the approval of the largest group. Therefore companies can miss defining opportunities in the effort to please everyone. AFLAC, the supplemental insurance company, might never have created a duck as an association if the company required wide, group consensus. No doubt, it would have struck certain people as simply too risky.

Leaders need to set an example by defending on-the-fringe ideas. One way to demonstrate this is to not shut down constructive conflict to maintain group harmony or to quickly reach consensus. It's also important to make time for brainstorms and meandering conversations, without immediately reaching consensus. Try floating a few crazy ideas and see what happens.

What is Your Corporate Culture Type?

Cultural typing helps leaders align their cultures to their brands. Now that you understand the six types, answer the following questions to identify which type fits your company:

- Review the characteristics of each culture type. Which type description best illustrates cultural norms you often experience?
- Review the challenges associated with your type. What can you personally do to address these challenges on an ongoing basis?

Once you know what culture type you have, and you decide how to navigate its predictable challenges, it's time to focus on getting people hired and organized into ways that will deliver on your brand promise. This is the subject of the next chapter.

EXECUTIVE LEADER LOG

It's interesting to think back to our founding days. What did we do consciously or unconsciously to shape the culture we have today? I think we have a 'competitive' culture – would others agree? I do reward groups for doing their own thing. Perhaps I should look to see if they are demonstrating our corporate brand as they forge ahead. I think we've too often let our culture type be the driver behind decisions, rather than using our brand as the key driver. I'll make a point in weekly staff and management meetings to use the brand filter before the 'culture filter', rather than the other way around.

HUMAN RESOURCES LEADER LOG

How does our corporate culture relate to our brand? I think it would be valuable if at least HR did an assessment based on this question. It would be an interesting conversation for HR to have with the execs about how our culture can help us get the most return from our brand investment. We could add a lot of value by recognizing any areas where our culture may be making it difficult for our employees to live our brand. In the past we just labeled these as 'management problems.' Also, helping our people managers understand the differences and overlaps between our brand and our culture should help improve our performance reviews. Understanding the strengths and pitfalls of our particular culture – and how surviving the challenges inherent in our culture may show up as disruptive employee behaviors – may help us be a more nimble organization. And awareness of these issues will probably reduce some internal conflicts.

SALES LEADER LOG

I'd like our culture to be more like 'customer is always right' and less like 'competitive.' I realize the transition could take a while and would need a high level of sponsorship. Discuss with other execs and determine the risks for our organization. Corporate culture seems more inwardly directed and the brand principle seems more outwardly directed – but this isn't the way it's supposed to be. Our brand personality may be the outward manifestation of our culture. A sales retreat where we brainstorm how to combine the use of our principle and personality to increase sales would be useful.

NOTES

[1] Schein, E (1999) *The Corporate Culture Survival Guide*, Jossey-Bass Inc., San Francisco

[2] Baker, P (1998) 'Clinton signs IRS reform bill', *The Washington Post*

[3] The Seattle Times News Service (10 July 1998) 'Here's what they said about IRS reform bill', *The Seattle Times*

[4] Anderson, C (25 April 2000) 'IRS abuses? GAO probe couldn't find any', *The Seattle Times*

[5] Ernst, S (23 November 2001), 'Fans applaud Sonics outreach efforts', *Puget Sound Business Journal*

CHAPTER

HIRE, TRAIN AND ORGANIZE TO LIVE THE BRAND

Good company in a journey makes the way to seem the shorter.

–Izaak Walton (1593–1683)

Bringing the right people on board and organizing them to live the brand is the next mile marker for every leader. Whatever your position, if you're a leader, you have some influence over who gets hired, for what jobs, and how they are organized to do the work. A research study of 137 leading U.S. companies by the Conference Board, entitled 'Engaging Employees Through Your Brand,' found that HR executives felt that their corporate brand was a highly important tool in recruiting, retaining and organizing employees. The following percentages reflect a highly important rating from HR executives:

61%	helping employees internalize the company's values
45%	achieving reputation as an employer of choice
38%	recruiting employees
38%	retaining employees
29%	achieving organizational integration
27%	sustaining organizational integration
24%	facilitating integration following merger or acquisition[1]

Avanade, founded in April 2000 as a joint venture between Microsoft and Accenture, creates web-service solutions for Global 2000 companies.[2] As a new marketplace player, Avanade knew it needed to hire and train more than a thousand employees in less than two years for the company to realize its market potential. In this chapter we'll show how Avanade was able to quickly get up to speed.

There are four areas where leaders can help equip a company at this stage of its journey:

- Job clarity: Decide what jobs are necessary to deliver your branded customer experience.
- Recruitment process: Recruit and hire candidates that are more likely to be able to live the brand and deliver the best customer experience.
- Orientation: Create the right first impressions for new hires.
- Organization structure: Design the division of work, teams and hierarchy to most effectively create brand value.

Having a clear understanding of brand tools and brand conveyors (See Chapter 2: Bring Your Brand Into Focus and Chapter 6: Get Employee Buy-in on Your Brand) is a pre-requisite for understanding this chapter. You need to clarify what your brand promise and resulting customer experience is upfront, before organizing employees to live the brand.

JOB CLARITY: A PLATFORM FOR BRAND ACTION

Defining jobs and roles is a key integrated branding lever. A defined job creates the right environment for focusing employees' attention, applying skill, achieving accountability, effectively allocating resources, and rapidly developing expertise to live your brand.

Just defining the scope of a person's job creates focus. For example, if an organization creates research positions, it is reasonable to expect people in those jobs to: Focus on research; have research expertise; be accountable to do research; receive necessary resources to conduct research; and develop their research skills as necessary.

Compare this to a company who designates engineers as responsible for development *and* research. Part of their job is research, but they are primarily responsible for product development. Since product development is deadline driven, the research function will have a lower priority – running the risk of creating lower quality or lesser quantity research.

How do you determine what the appropriate scope of work should be? In this case, the leader needs to weigh the importance of research to living the brand. If the company's brand principle is either stretching possibilities or technology explorers, separating it from product development would ensure that the company conducts the research necessary to deliver on the promised customer experience. On the other hand, if the organization's brand principle is delivering proven technology, a combined R&D position may work.

A simple way to assess whether a separate job function should exist is by answering the questions in the following Point of Interest. We recommend asking these questions quarterly, or whenever you are doing a brand or organization review. You'll want to bring employees into these discussions because they're closest to the action and will have the most knowledge of what's on-brand.

Besides determining job clarity, the branded customer experience also determines what jobs should be outsourced. The rule is that jobs that are critical to delivering your brand experience must be in the company's direct control. In his book *Jack: Straight from the Gut*, Jack Welch, former CEO of General Electric, writes how General Electric used a similar management concept. He refers to this concept as 'your back room is somebody else's front room' – which means focus on those things your company does best and let others focus on the things they do best.[3] The integrated branding process focuses on understanding where your real added value is and then putting your best people and resources behind that understanding.

Defining Job Using Your Brand

Point of Interest

1. *'What does it look like to the customer when we demonstrate our brand?'*
   Good answers to this question are behavioral, and product- or service-specific. If this question generates many answers, rank them in order of their effectiveness in building your brand. This means that you are once again using your brand tools – including your principle, personality, values, mission and brand assets as your guide. (See Chapter 4: Align to Deliver a Unique Customer Experience. Point of Interest: Create your own customer experience map).
   The more specific your answers are the better tool you'll have for defining job scope. Here are behaviorally specific answers:
   - *'The customer can install the product without having to read the instruction manual.'*

- *'The customer can always choose from a number of product options.'*
- *'The customer will go out of their way to find us, knowing they are consistently getting the best selection.'*
- *'The customers will never hear "I don't know" on the technical support hotline.'*

Non-behaviorally specific or vague answers might include:

- *'The customers will be satisfied.'*
- *'The customers will feel good about our product.'*
- *'The customers will "get it."'*
- *'The customers will think we offer quality products.'*

2. *'What must employees do in your department (actions and deliverables) to deliver on your customer experience based on Question One's answer?'*

   Answers to this will depend on the business of the organization. Make a list of must-do actions that will support your branded customer experience. Clarify between must-do and should-do actions and prioritize must-dos in order of effectiveness for building your brand. Making the tough decisions about a few things employees must do will help you focus on actions critical to the brand experience. Too many must-do actions will water down their importance.

3. *'Do we currently have jobs specifically tasked with executing our must-do actions?'*

   If yes:

   Review the job to ensure the focus, expertise, accountability, resources and training opportunities necessary to deliver the must-do list are appropriate, and identify any necessary changes. Possible actions can include time and resource re-allocation, knowledge-sharing forums, and increased autonomy or training.

   If no:

   Discuss the outcomes and costs of defining a new job function to create the must-do actions.

   If a separate job function isn't necessary, discuss how to add the must-do actions to an existing job function.

Here is an example of how Avanade answered these evaluation questions:

1. *'What does it look like to the customer when we demonstrate our brand principle of "two steps ahead" and our mission of "being the world's premier technology integrator for Microsoft solutions in the enterprise?"'*

Avanade's response:

- Customers will benefit from Avanade's on-going investments to build and maintain deep technical expertise on the Microsoft platform, enabling them to utilize leading-edge technology to meet their needs.
- Customers will see simpler processes when adopting and deploying leading-edge solutions.
- Customers will use Avanade's experience to deploy Microsoft solutions and integrate those solutions with heterogeneous enterprise solutions.

2. *'What must employees do (actions and deliverables) to deliver on this customer experience as outlined in Question One's answer?'*

- Continue to track the latest technology trends – and how those trends are turning into practices in each region of the world.
- Continue to invest in development of reusable assets and solutions which simplify enterprise adoption of leading-edge technology.
- Conduct real-time sharing of expertise and on-the-job knowledge with peers, so deep technical skills and a knowledge base will develop across the company.

3. *'Do we currently have jobs that execute on these must-do actions?'*

Avanade's must-do actions have been difficult to achieve in a marketplace where technology changes daily. And its consultants are not centrally located, which has made traditional training difficult. So Avanade created the Knowledge Resource Group (KRG) and invested in maintaining a leading-edge training organization. The KRG function is responsible for orchestrating knowledge sharing across Avanade.

Recruitment: Finding the Right Candidates to Build Your Integrated Brand

Candidates are drawn to companies that have strong brands for the same reasons as customers: Something about your brand promise intrigues them. Your brand sparks their interest and gives them head and heart reasons for liking your company. One technique that will assure a head and heart response is to treat every candidate as a customer. Delivering your customer experience to potential employees will have a significant impact on whether they see your company as a good fit. Even the most elementary or entry-level jobs are more glamorous in a company with an attractive brand. And positive recruiting experiences can build your brand image – whether the candidates are hired or not.

On the other hand, an off-brand experience may confuse candidates and limit your ability to hire the right people.

There are two recruiting activities where delivering your brand experience can create positive results: attracting candidates and conducting interviews. These activities allow you to set candidates' expectations for the role of brand in your company by both demonstrating your brand and telling candidates that living the brand is a core competency.

Attracting Candidates

Attracting candidates is similar to selling to prospective customers. The organization wants loyalty from job candidates (who become employees) and customers (who provide revenue). Candidates want more value for their time and productivity, compared to other employment opportunities. Customers want value for each dollar spent, compared to buying from a competitor. Keeping both groups happy leads to long-term company success.

Just as with customers, first experiences with job candidates are critical. This first experience occurs in recruitment ads, unsolicited head-hunting calls, and informational interviews.

Questions to consider when working with job candidates include:
- *Do your recruitment ads demonstrate your integrated brand?*
- *Do your recruitment ads integrate well with other company ads?*
- *Does the initial call to the candidate align with your brand personality?*

- *Is the company contact able to explain the uniqueness of your company, using its brand tools (mission, values, principle, personality, story, and associations), its strategic role and its career opportunities?*

Here are some examples of how recruiting activities can support or conflict with a company's brand principle:

Brand promise = approachable experts

Supportive recruiting behavior:
- Make time for calls from candidates.
- Portray a friendly, non-combative manner with candidates.
- Understand company offerings.
- Ask deep, relevant questions.

Conflicting recruiting behavior:
- Rush conversations.
- Degrade or judge candidate.
- Demonstrate a lack of product knowledge.
- Ask vague questions.

If you consider the number of contacts even a medium-sized organization's recruiters make each year – the number of chances to gain brand champions or turn people off is significant.

The Bellagio Hotel

Here's an example of how to live the integrated brand during the recruiting process:[4]

The Bellagio Hotel, a lavish Las Vegas establishment, needed to hire 9,600 employees in 24 weeks for its grand opening. It created a system for screening 84,000 applicants in 12 weeks, interviewing 27,000 finalists in 10 weeks, and processing 9,600 hires in 11 days.

To do this, the company created electronic job applications, processing documents and personnel files. But it didn't merely meet its aggressive hiring deadlines; the company created Bellagio brand champions by treating every applicant like a Bellagio customer.

The company wanted to give candidates the personalized-service experience Bellagio provides its guests. Typically, personalized service implies added time and attention, but the Bellagio didn't have any extra time when hiring these 9,600 employees. Still, the company did a number of things in its recruiting process to demonstrate its brand principle of personalized service:

- Applicants scheduled a time to apply and interview online, instead of waiting for hours in a line, which was the norm for large Las Vegas hotels.
- When applicants drove into the parking lot, a staff person welcomed them and confirmed their name. Then, the staff notified the greeter at the door (via microphone and radio) about who was coming.
- The greeter at the door greeted them by name and assigned them a computer terminal.
- Computers were available 12 hours a day, six days a week.
- Once applicants completed the application, they were thanked on-screen and directed to a staff person who personally completed the application process.
- If the applicant was invited back for a formal interview, they interviewed with a trained hiring manager who used an unobtrusively placed computer to rate the interview.
- Bellagio made job offers in face-to-face interviews, not over the phone.

CONDUCTING THE INTERVIEW

The first prerequisite for using the interview as a path to living the brand is to define what skills, experience and demeanor potential employees must have to fill job requirements. This includes requirements for living the brand within a specific job function. To determine all this, you'll want to ask yourself:

1. *'What does it look like to the customer when we demonstrate our brand?'*
2. *'What must employees do within the job we are interviewing for (actions to deliver on the list generated in question one)?'*
3. *'What skills, experience and demeanor must the candidate have to be a good fit for this job and our brand?'*

It's important to keep in mind which skills, experience and demeanor are must-haves when entering into an interview. It's easy to get distracted by strengths that are interesting and nice-to-haves. Also, candidates will often have differing strengths and weaknesses, which can all be accommodated by making trade-offs with others on the team.

It is also helpful to identify any brand-breaking behaviors you want to avoid at all costs in new hires, such as a demeanor that contradicts your brand. Since companies can't change employees' personalities, it's best to not hire individuals who may have the right skills, but the wrong personalities.

For example: If a company's brand principle is approachable, a brand-breaking personality would be someone who does not make eye contact with anyone, does not smile, and is visibly uncomfortable when meeting others for the first time. This would be particularly bad if the candidate were interviewing for a position that works directly with customers.

Audi recruits staff whose personalities reflect its brand. 'We aren't looking for good technicians or good salespeople, we are looking for good Audi technicians and salespeople - employees who empathize with the company's identity and, therefore, empathize with the customer,' explains Len Hunt, vice president of Audi of America. 'These tend to be people who enjoy relating to others and appreciate the unique traits and interests of each customer. We've found that brand-sympathetic staff, whether they are selling new cars, used cars or car parts, have boosted net profits an average of 8% at their dealerships,'[5] adds Hunt.

Companies that want to hire people who have the potential to live the brand must also look for a willingness to learn, openness to feedback and the ability to balance job flexibility with clarity no matter what their job function.

Hiring managers can use the following template to train others how to interview on-brand.

Interview template

Company: _____

Brand promise (principle, personality and values): _____

Open job: _____

Job description (must-do actions list included): _____

Skills and experience required (must-haves list included): _____

Interview questions: _____

Demeanor observations: _____

ORIENTATION: BORN INTO THE BRAND

Orientation is your first formal opportunity to educate new employees about the brand. It allows you to reinforce the expectation that using company brand tools for guiding decisions and actions will be a core competency for any position. As candidates, these new employees have already had one or more positive experiences with your brand. But they haven't been educated on the role they will play in delivering your branded customer experience. Below are a few ideas to include in your orientation:

- Demonstrate senior-management sponsorship for living the brand in every job function.
- Design integrated branding educational materials for orientation.
- Outline the company's brand investments to-date.
- Explain the bottom-line value of the brand to the company (repeat purchases, price premiums, etc.)
- Review competing brands and how the company compares.
- Include customer testimonials or introduce new employees to actual customers.
- Allow time to discuss the new employees' ideas for living the brand in their new positions.

- Explain how the corporate culture and the company's brand assets support the brand.
- Tell employees where they can go for questions about living the brand.
- Partner each new employee with a mentor who understands what living the brand looks like in practice.

In an article by Robert Rodriguez in the *Chicago Tribune*, titled 'Company Culture Can Help Determine Compatibility,' he describes the importance of brand orientation: 'Chicago's R.R. Donnelley & Sons' financial business unit has a two-week orientation for all new employees called 'Nuts and Bolts.' During this time, new employees hear about the company history, meet with numerous senior leaders, are allowed to meet with other new employees, and are set up with a mentor. Employees that participate in "Nuts and Bolts" are clearly aware that R.R. Donnelley's culture is one that values employees.'[6]

AVANADE NEW EMPLOYEE ORIENTATION

Avanade uses its employee orientation to kick-start living the brand. It did this by creating Quick Start, which is a mandatory three-day orientation. Typical new-employee questions are covered, such as, *'How do I get paid and what are the benefits?'* but the majority of the orientation is spent on educating new Avanade employees about the company, its desired customer experience, its uniqueness, and how each employee will play a role in growing the company. Below are some examples of things Avanade did in the program:

One or more executives personally attended each Quick Start to explain and clarify the company's vision, mission and uniqueness.

Employees learned and practiced an 'elevator conversation' that they could use for prospective customers and candidates that explained what they do and why Avanade is unique, in less than 30 seconds.

Employees played a game at the end of the orientation that tested their understanding of the business and its uniqueness. Prizes were given to those who correctly answered the questions.

Employees were given time to work in teams to specifically identify things each could do, as well as things their teams and Avanade could do to live its brand.

ORGANIZATION STRUCTURE: AVENUES AND BOUNDARIES

Another brand leadership opportunity is organizing positions so they work together to deliver the customer experience. There is no right organization structure that magically aligns employees to accomplish company goals. The key to living the integrated brand in any organization structure is to understand the strengths and weaknesses of each type and how they will complement your unique brand approach. The best advice is to first identify the core skills and practices you need to enhance your customer experience and then design an organization structure that will be the most supportive to this goal.

Don't confuse organizational structure with culture type discussed in Chapter 8. Organizational structures deal with role and function design, cultural type deals with your company's style of working. For instance, I might be working in a divisional structure where all job functions and information are organized to make the division successful, while our company's culture type promotes group consensus as the style for making all decisions in the division. You'll want to consider both structure and culture type in addition to your brand tools when making decisions on how to deliver your customer experience most effectively.

To be effective, every organization structure must encompass:
- flow of information;
- flexibility to respond to information;
- clear roles and decision authority;
- cross-functional planning and problem solving.

The following summary allows you to explore basic organization-design options, diagnose your situation and design the right organization to reach your goals.

There are four basic organization structures to consider: Functional, divisional, hybrid/matrix and empowerment.

FUNCTIONAL STRUCTURE

Functionally designed organizations coordinate employees based on the main activities the organization needs – such as engineering, sales and finance. This structure encourages collaboration, efficiency and quality *within* functional departments, but makes coordination and integration with other departments more difficult. One example is an international resort hotel chain where all of its hotels around the world are organized using functional departments from janitorial to spa services to sales.

Pros	*Cons*
Focus on functional goals	Low coordination between functions
Coordination and quality within functions	Few cross-function solutions
Function efficiency	Low organization/ goal visibility
Function skill development	Low cross-function knowledge sharing

FIGURE 9.1: FUNCTIONAL FORM
Functionally designed organizations divide and organize employees based on activities.

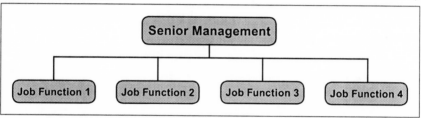

DIVISIONAL STRUCTURE

The divisional structure groups functions into divisions. Divisions focus on products, market-segments, regions, or clients, and can run like independent businesses. Division goals drive work coordination and job skills. You can see divisions structures at work in most hospitals. Hospitals have many departments ranging from pediatrics to oncology that can act independently of each other and deliver a complete customer experience – from setting appointments through to billing.

Pros	*Cons*
Focus on division goals	Low coordination between divisions
Cross-functional solutions within division	Little function-based skill development
Response to change within division	Poor economies of scale Duplication of functional groups company-wide

FIGURE 9.2: DIVISIONAL FORM

Divisional organization structure places necessary functions in divisions.

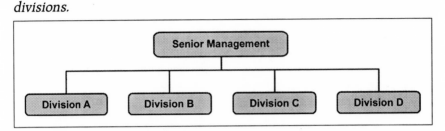

HYBRID/MATRIX STRUCTURE

Most organizations have a hybrid structure. While some functions are centralized, such as research, sales or manufacturing, others are handled at the division level. Hybrids can take advantage of the other structures' pros and avoid some of their cons. Their shortcomings are that central functions are not tailored sufficiently for each division's needs as well as the potential for divisions to have conflicting goals. When living their integrated brand, hybrid organizations need to focus on overcoming these weaknesses.

A type of hybrid structure is matrix, where both divisional and functional reporting relationships occur. At Avanade, consultants can report both to the on-site project manager and to the home-office technology executive. This is to ensure their work is focused on the project deliverables and also on developing their depth of technical knowledge – a company asset.

Pros	*Cons*
Dual reporting to function and division	Conflicting priorities
Flexible resource allocation	Authority confusion and long decision cycles
Information and knowledge sharing	Lack of job focus
Function-based skill development	Duplication of function groups company-wide

FIGURE 9.3: MATRIX FORM
In a matrix, both divisional and functional structures occur simultaneously.

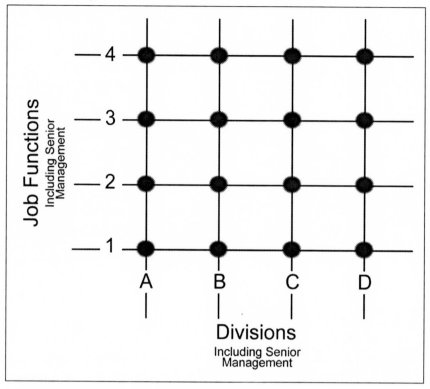

EMPOWERMENT STRUCTURE

Empowerment structure aims to turn traditional structures on their heads, blur organization boundaries, and give the power to those closest to the work. These structures are known by many names, such as 'bottom-up structures' or 'self-directed work teams.' They are highly adaptable and work best where there is a good mix of skills and experience, and the desired outcomes are predictable. Both Volvo and General Foods pet food plant have experimented with empowerment structures.[7]

Their disadvantage is they muddy accountability and strategic intent. They also lengthen the time it takes to make decisions and resolve conflicts since there is no formal hierarchy to fall back on for quick resolution.

Organizing your company's structure, job positions and hiring and orientation practices to deliver your unique customer experience will build an amazingly deep level of brand differentiation into everything your company does. Imagine the head start you'll have – even over relatively sophisticated competitors that may have identified their brand but haven't built it into the DNA of company design.

FIGURE 9.4: EMPOWERMENT FORM

Gives power to those closest to the work and blurs organizational boundaries. More autonomy and influence reside with employees versus management.

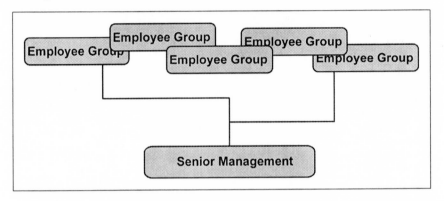

EXECUTIVE LEADER LOG

We've talked in the past about evaluating the jobs of those who directly face our customers to ensure they are demonstrating our brand. But, perhaps we should also be looking deeper into the organization, to our engineers, researchers and IT people. Do their jobs need to change to help deliver our entire product line in an on-brand manner?

HUMAN RESOURCES LEADER LOG

Talk to the brand manager tomorrow to see when we can sign up our recruiter for brand education!

SALES LEADER LOG

Are our sales engineers missing some cross-product training opportunities because we are organized by division instead of by function? Would our customers be more satisfied if our sales engineers were more knowledgeable about all our products, not just the ones produced out of their division?

NOTES

[1] Dell, David, and Ainspan, Nathan, and Bodenberg, Thomas, and Troy, Kathryn, and Hickey, Jack, 'Engaging Employees Through Your Brand,' (2001) *The Conference Board*, p 13

[2] Ibid.

[3] Welch, J (2001) *Jack: Straight from the Gut*, Warner Books, New York

[4] Breen, B 'Full House', *Fast Company*

[5] Garrett, Jill, (Summer 2001), *The Human Side of Brand,* GMJ, p 4

[6] Rodriguez, Robert, (14 January 2001), 'Company Culture Can Help Determine Compatibility', *Chicago Tribune*, C1

[7] French, Wendell L., and Bell, Cecil H., (1990) *Organization Development 4th edition*, Prentice Hall, Inc., New Jersey

CHAPTER

BRAND LEADERSHIP IN ACTION

If life is a journey, pay attention to how you walk.

—Angus Wong, author

ONE LEADER'S JOURNEY TO LIVING THE INTEGRATED BRAND: A CASE STUDY

Amir is the director of quality assurance (QA) at a three-year-old, 80-employee, embedded-software company. The company wants the customer to experience expanding possibilities in every interaction and has invested time and money to promote this brand principle and customer experience inside and outside the company. Amir directs 15 QA engineers, seven of whom were hired in the last year. Today, Amir's focus is to make final decisions regarding the QA strategic plan and the testing requirements for the next year. In the plan, which requires upper management approval, Amir must outline the quality goals and necessary resources, technologies, employees and testing processes that will work together to keep his employees moving forward, on-brand.

But there's one catch. Amir's boss, Lauren, the VP of engineering, is not available to help, since she is busy with an acquisition deal (the third such deal for this company in a year). While Amir has developed strategic plans before, he has never been the primary decision maker. He has several concerns with this new task. First, he realizes he doesn't know it all. There are no industry best practices to refer to for the emerging technology his company is delivering.

He is also concerned about staffing and implementation. Amir has three open positions for senior QA engineers, and most of his current staff members are in the biggest jobs of their career. His staff will be learning on the job, which will impact Amir's productivity projections.

And Amir knows talented QA engineers can easily go work elsewhere if they don't like their work or think they are underpaid.

Finally, Amir is concerned about his own success. He knows that a great QA strategic plan will put him in a position to be VP of engineering, should Lauren leave. But he's far too busy to put as much time into the plan as he would like. At this moment, he has to interview a job candidate who has a competing offer. Because Amir desperately needs to make this hire, his immediate concern is the candidate's resume and how he will sell him on the job.

Sound familiar? Amir's challenges are not unique. Every leader has to balance big-picture concerns with day-to-day demands. How can you keep people moving on the journey to living the brand while getting your job done?

While other chapters outline how to prepare for living the integrated brand and get people moving, this chapter will focus on how consistent leadership can keep people moving on-brand. Without effective leadership, living the brand remains just a nice theory. Every mile marker you need to reach assumes that you have the ability to lead others.

While leadership books espouse everything from complex competency models to modeling successful companies, the practice of leadership can still feel like guess work. This chapter will simplify what leadership behavior looks like so that you can use it every day.

A FRAMEWORK FOR EFFECTIVE LEADERSHIP

Effective leaders are those who simultaneously demonstrate their convictions while maintaining their connection with others. Effective leadership is walking the fine line between setting a stake in the ground to show others where to go, and listening to others' concerns and issues. And because living the brand is a new way for employees to think and act, it requires both the connection and the conviction part of the equation.

THE IMPORTANCE OF DEMONSTRATING CONVICTIONS

Convictions are a leader's strongly held and communicated opinions and beliefs in a given situation. In practice, these convictions help shape priorities, directions and deliverables, while motivating people to go in a direction with you. An effective leader not only has convictions on the big issues, but also clarifies his or her opinions on the little, unforeseen ones.

Having convictions *doesn't* mean you have all the answers. It *does* mean you set a direction that moves everyone forward. In Figure 10.1, you can see that actions that demonstrate conviction fall along a spectrum from low to high. It's important that the leader holds a few clear convictions on any given issue. In today's fast-paced world, employees admire clarity, not perfection.

Good employees typically say, 'Just show me what success looks like, then get out of the way!' Brand tools give employees a broad view on which path is right in a given situation. But clear convictions give employees 'handles' to more precisely align their actions, give feedback and measure their success. In an environment that lacks leadership, it's much more difficult for high achievers to be successful because they don't have as many signposts on the path. Leaders who have conviction increase employee morale and productivity.

FIGURE 10.1: DEMONSTRATING LEADERSHIP
Leadership is most effective when the leader both demonstrates conviction and maintains connection.

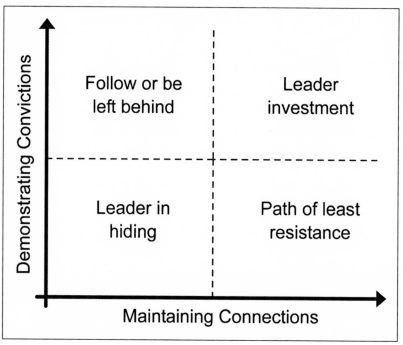

DEMONSTRATE CONVICTIONS THROUGH ACTIONS

Having conviction is only the first part of being an effective leader. As a matter of fact, in successful companies where analytical thinking and smarts are generally in high supply, people with convictions are pretty common. What isn't common is the demonstration of these convictions through consistent actions.

How do leaders demonstrate their convictions? Through what they focus on, measure, reinforce, reward and reprimand. Effective leaders minimize inconsistent actions. Acting with conviction requires both knowing what your convictions are and behaving in ways that demonstrate those convictions. This is easier said than done. It's easy to get sucked into the firefight of the day and unknowingly act inconsistently. But talk is cheap and employees know it. Employees perceive individuals to be leaders only when their convictions match their actions.

Cisco CEO, John Chambers, has conviction about ensuring customer satisfaction. Cisco keeps a 'critical customer' list of customers experiencing difficulties with Cisco or its products. Chambers demonstrates his conviction by nightly reviewing this status list, and giving customers his phone number so that they can contact him directly if they have a problem. According to Ed Paulson in *Inside Cisco,* Chambers spends as much as 50 percent of his time helping customers with problems.[1]

Amir's conviction is about the critical importance of hiring and motivating a strong staff that will execute the QA strategic plan in order to support the company's brand principle of expanding possibilities. He feels strongly that having the right staff in place is the most important part of allowing the company's electronics customers to use the company's software to expand their customers' possibilities. He can demonstrate his convictions by:

- selling executives on his plan to hire and motivate a strong staff;
- prioritizing hiring activities along with other QA team priorities, and adding hiring success to his quality measurements;
- making himself available for candidate interviews;
- clearly defining hiring criteria and suggesting key interview questions aligned with his beliefs regarding strong QA professionals.

If Amir demonstrates his convictions in these ways, others will support him through their actions.

On the other hand, Amir can sabotage his leadership through:

- presenting the QA plan with no mention of the importance of a strong and motivated staff necessary for execution;
- reviewing hiring status only when his human resources staff gives him a report, separating this activity from other departmental measurements;
- constantly rescheduling interviews due to other priorities, or not quickly responding to interview requests;
- totally delegating interviews to his staff-providing little clarity on his hiring or interviewing criteria.

Find Your Brand Convictions

Point of Interest

Step 1: Identify a goal – aimed at living your integrated brand – that will require you to demonstrate leadership for its successful completion.

Step 2: Determine what your convictions are. Write them down. Some questions to consider:

- What matters most if you are to deliver on your brand promise?
- What are the priorities?
- What does success look like to you? To others (customers, peers and employees)?
- How will success be measured?
- What are the key opportunities and threats?

Step 3: Identify how you will demonstrate your conviction in words, actions and measurement. Also identify any leadership killers (things you could do or get distracted by) you want to avoid.

Step 4: Compare your actions in the exercise to how you have handled similar challenges in the past. What would demonstrating conviction cause you to do differently?

None of these actions are unreasonable, but they won't provide the kinds of leadership that others will follow or create the results that Amir wants.

Once your convictions are clearly understood by employees, they can use you as a guide for whether specific actions will be on brand.

Ed Spencer, Honeywell's CEO from 1979 to 1987, defined a leadership building block called 'pretend I'm in the room.' He would tell his reports, 'Just assume I'm in the room with you. If a deal doesn't feel right – if you wouldn't do it with me sitting next to you – walk away.'[2]

MAINTAINING CONNECTIONS: THE GLUE OF LEADERSHIP

The best leaders don't stop at conviction. In fact, demonstrating convictions won't be effective if you don't maintain connection with the people you are trying to lead.

Connection is defined by the ability to maintain work-related communications, two-way information flow and mutual understanding. The simple truth is that staying engaged with others empowers you to lead them. This doesn't imply that leaders are friends with every employee or that leaders avoid conflict – as can often happen in consensus-driven cultures. Instead, connection creates empathy and self-awareness – you understand the impact you have on others and that they have on you. Without it, you won't know if your impact is uninformed, misinterpreted or disliked, and you will lessen the likelihood of employees carrying out your vision.

Connection is an ongoing effort, not a one-time announcement or pow-wow with employees. Too often, communication from leaders is one-way, which causes the leader to miss out on additional information and creates misunderstandings that slow productive action.

Connection is the process of transferring your convictions to others. Connection doesn't mean every employee needs to like every one of your ideas. But they will understand where you are coming from. It's the decisions that employees don't understand or that they haven't had a say in that are more likely to stop effective leadership in its tracks. If everyone is heard, and you respect each other, and everyone understands why you are moving ahead, they will follow your lead.

In practice, connection means consistently finding ways to involve employees in planning and problem solving – even when time is tight. It is making sure everyone understands why you are taking an action. Practicing connection means asking for and giving feedback, actively listening, speaking with respect, avoiding hostility and making yourself available for informal discussions – where employees form many of their work-related opinions.

FIGURE 10.2: COMMUNICATION FEEDBACK CYCLE

Maintaining connection requires open communications and feedback between leaders and other employees.

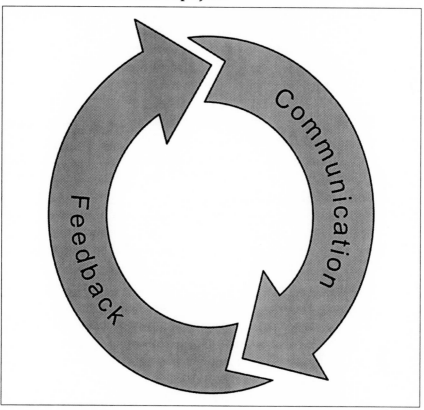

HOW CONTINENTAL AIRLINES EXERCISES BRAND LEADERSHIP

Let's look at an example of brand leadership in action. Continental Airlines does a great job setting priorities and making sure everyone knows and understands what they stand for. As a company, it demonstrates connection in a myriad of ways that attempt to align with the company's brand and its values of dignity and respect.[3]

- There are 600 bulletin boards in break rooms, offices, hallways and other locations throughout the Continental global system. They're updated daily, with on-time stats, percentage of flights completed the day before, perfect-attendance records, new destinations, the stock price, load factor and all other Continental measurements of success. The bulletin board is always in the same place in each office and organized the same way. The same information also goes out on company voicemail and e-mail lists.

- CEO Gordon Bethune tapes a voice message every Friday, with the 'view from the top' and the 'update of the week.' Employees use an 800 number to listen and leave comments or questions.
- Continental has a program called Officer Local Involvement (OLI) that builds trust with employees. Each officer of the company has a city they're responsible for. They visit quarterly and hold town meetings, where they review everything that's going on with the company and all its success measurements. In between the quarterly meetings, employees can call their OLI if they have questions. 'And they do call,' says Bonnie Reitz, Continental's senior VP of sales and distribution.
- Other communications vehicles include LED-display news boards in the offices and crew rooms at airports that feature the stock price, airport weather and any other news affecting the company. *Continental Quarterly* and *Continental Times* are two in-house organs that Continental publishes for employees.
- Continental gives managers a laminated 'brand' card. On one side are the beliefs the company wants customers to have, such as *'Continental employees deliver on their promises,'* and the other side what the company wants employees to think, including *'Management delivers on its promises. I can ask any question and get a straight answer.'*
- The company set up an 800 number, staffed by a response team seven days a week, for employees to report problems or make suggestions. The response team consists of employees from throughout the organization – pilots, flight attendants, gate agents and mechanics. They are required to research each problem or suggestion and get back to employees within 48 hours with one of three possible responses: 1) we fixed it; 2) we are not going to fix it, and here's why; or 3) we need to study it more and will get back to you by this date.
- Bethune has called employees at home to respond to complaints.

It is a natural tendency for leaders to avoid consistently acting in ways that maintain connection due to the speed of their business day or fear of conflict. Effective leaders know that they must invest the time in actions that maintain connection with others. The best-thought-out plans mean nothing if there aren't talented and motivated people willing to carry them out. McKinsey & Company's landmark study entitled, 'The War for Talent,' cites that retaining and using employee talent will be tomorrow's prime source of competitive advantage. From their research, including surveys of 13,000 executives at more than 120 companies and case studies of 27 leading companies, the authors discovered compelling evidence that better management leads to better performance. On average, companies that did a better job of attracting, developing and retaining highly talented people earned a 22% higher return to shareholders – a result mirrored in international human resource consulting firm Watson Wyatt's Human Capital Index. [4]

Back to Amir: He has only days to determine and present the QA strategic plan. Although time is tight, there are a number of actions Amir can invest in to maintain connection with others, such as:

- Call a meeting with key staffers to ask for their input into the plan – he needs to explain time is tight and prep them for the meeting by posing four or five critical questions in advance. He can also consider involving individuals who are not his direct reports, but who have crucial knowledge and influence.
- Refer to information and insights he received from others who were central to his planning process in presentations.
- Co-present the plan with others.
- Block out time on his schedule immediately following his presentation to get feedback and answer questions – making it easy for others to engage with him, instead of making it difficult to track him down.

The above actions would strengthen Amir's connections. Amir would also be setting an example for others by developing a departmental culture that is engaging rather than autocratic – a culture where trust has a good chance of developing.

Amir could damage connections by doing things such as:

- developing the plan alone or with input only from his boss;
- responding to questions about the plan defensively, versus listening carefully, fully understanding the questions or concerns, and then responding calmly and confidently;
- leaving on a business trip immediately following the presentation, making it hard for others to engage with him regarding the plan.

Maintain Connection

Step 1: Identify a goal – aimed at living your integrated brand – that will require you to demonstrate leadership for its successful completion.

Step 2: Determine who you need to be in connection with to be successful in the above challenge. Who is important for success – specific employees, customers, peers, or other groups?

Step 3: Identify how you will create and maintain connection via your words, actions, and processes. Also, identify the 'connection killers' you want to avoid.

Step 4: Compare your actions in the exercise to how you have handled similar challenges in the past. What could maintaining connection cause you to do differently?

PUT IT ALL TOGETHER

The proof of whether you are being an effective leader is if others follow you. But demonstrating your convictions while maintaining your connections is not an easy task. And understanding the relationship between conviction, connection and leading people is often an uncomfortable but necessary first step. This is why in figure 10.1 we call demonstrating conviction while maintaining connection a 'leader's investment.'

Edwin Friedman author of *Reinventing Leadership* and books on effective systems of people, called this type of behavior self-differentiated. 'The connected, non-reactive self is not a matter of personality types, and it applies, across the board, to all leadership styles.'[5] Self-differentiation in a leader is about the capacity to see things differently, to persist boldly in the face of resistance, to be willing to be vulnerable and open to feedback, to learn to endure (if not come to love) solitude, and to muster up the discipline that is necessary when a leader's initiative inevitably triggers sabotage. If this sounds like a thankless job, you're probably right. On the other hand, being a leader taking a group of people into new directions, is something that has its own rewards.

Demonstrating conviction and connection won't turn every person into an advocate. Even the greatest leaders of our time did not get every person to agree with them. Sometimes gracefully letting individuals go who are not willing to follow (or moving them to a different project) is an effective way to demonstrate leadership to those remaining.

BARRIERS TO EFFECTIVE LEADERSHIP

TRUST: THE PREREQUISITE FOR BECOMING A LEADER

Leadership cannot exist without trust. In Chapter 3, Tools to Live Your Brand, we talk about a high-trust environment being a pre-requisite for integrating your brand. But trust is also a necessity for all effective leadership. When trust is low, followers are less likely to take risks, tolerate mistakes, engage with passion or go above and beyond the call of duty.

In his book *7 Habits of Highly Successful People*, Stephen Covey describes trust using an emotional-bank-account metaphor.[6] Trust is not something you attain one time and then forget about. A leader's actions can be viewed as either withdrawals from or deposits into the trust account.

Withdrawals to the trust account include behaviors that are perceived to:

- Sand bag: Saving up concerns – putting a pinch of sand secretly in a bag, then unloading many concerns upon individuals at one time – it's like hitting them over the head with a sand bag.
- Breaking promises: People listen to what leaders have to say. Then they look for behaviors that are consistent with those verbal promises. For example, if leaders have openly made a brand promise to customers to help them 'expand possibilities', and then don't invest in research and development, they may be perceived as breaking that promise.
- Disengaging communications: These behaviors include interrupting while others are speaking, not listening actively, using harsh or culturally offensive language, over-using cynicism, and using closed non-verbal communication such as avoiding eye contact.

- Blaming: This includes using feedback only to find fault and ignoring efforts to solve problems productively or see broader perspectives.
- Indirect actions: This is attempting to get what you want by using indirect methods; that is, not being direct with your requests, conflicts or feedback. It also includes gossiping to a third party and going around people to get information or resources.

Deposits into the trust account include:
- Clarifying: Just as in job descriptions, clarity in behavior and communications is a motivator. People want to know what to expect and what success will look like. Communications or actions that distill important information, give context or punctuate meaning can build trust.
- Renegotiating expectations: Employee deliverables and roles change often. This is okay, if the leader renegotiates expectations and doesn't gloss over change, or expect individuals to always adjust on their own.
- Keeping promises: Simply doing what is promised and holding others accountable for what they promise builds enormous trust. According to Watson Wyatts' Human Capital Index research, accountability can also lead to increased market value. [7]
- Engaging communications: Any action you take that gives others proper respect will build trust, including allowing others to speak, listening actively, using culturally appropriate language, giving constructive feedback, and making frequent eye contact (in many Western countries).
- Following-up and checking in: Building trust also includes 'leadership by walking around.' Showing interest in others' endeavors by following up on how their work is going or simply checking in on how they are doing are both important. The key here is to be consistent with follow-up and check in. If it happens only when the leader suspects something is going wrong, this behavior won't build trust.
- Apologize: You aren't perfect and it isn't reasonable for you or others to expect you to be so. A sincere personal or sometimes public apology will go a long way towards building trust.

OTHER BARRIERS TO EFFECTIVE LEADERSHIP

There are things that can derail you on the road to conviction and connection, including:

History: Historically, companies have not rewarded effective leadership. Instead, it's taken a back seat to other skills, such as product planning, deal making, sales, engineering quality and financial analysis. As a result, most companies lack leadership know-how – limiting their ability to live their brands.

Undisciplined reactions: When faced with pressure, leaders can lose self-awareness or control. It's easy to fall into behavior patterns that are familiar, have been rewarded in the past or that decrease anxiety – such as going into a rage, taking passive-aggressive action or withdrawing. Leadership requires overcoming these anxieties and reactions.

Stamina: Leadership can call on reserves of courage, passion and perseverance. Push-back, conflict, questions and feedback from employees can wear down and overwhelm a leader. However, these employee actions are crucial for a group to work together most effectively. A leader must have the stamina to stay connected to others and further clarify their own convictions.

THREE LESS-THAN-EFFECTIVE LEADERSHIP STYLES

To understand what does work, it's helpful to see what doesn't.

The 'follow or be left behind' (see figure 10.1 upper left quad) style demonstrates conviction-only leadership at the expense of maintaining connection. In this style, directions lack employee involvement, open communication, shared understanding, give-and-take feedback, active listening or speaking with respect for others. Examples of this type of behavior include:

- announcing decisions via email without initiating any input, or follow up for questions or feedback;
- inviting employees to a planning meeting, but instead of encouraging open discussion, selling a pre-determined plan;
- being openly hostile when others question your ideas.

The 'path of least resistance' (see figure 10.1 lower right quad).

These are situations where leaders' only goal is to maintain connection – at the expense of demonstrating their convictions. This style lacks clarity, definitions of success, priorities, directions and deliverables. Examples of this type of behavior include:

- to avoid hard feelings, choosing a mediocre solution that gets 100% consensus, instead of asking others to work toward a better solution;
- not implementing well-thought-through plans involving several employees because of one vocal person's displeasure with the plan;
- placing more importance on the process and not offending anyone than on making a decision, which gridlocks or prolongs the decision process.

'Leader in hiding' (see Figure 10.1 lower left quad)

In this style, leaders' actions don't demonstrate conviction or connection. Leaders in hiding can be very vocal, but their behaviors don't demonstrate what matters to them (convictions), and they communicate in ways that don't engage others (connection). Examples of this type of behavior include:

- never available – being too busy (out of town, email back-log) to engage in issues that require personal opinions or discussions with others;
- analysis paralysis – using an over-reliance on quantitative data to stall having to express a conviction or speak candidly to others;
- blaming – clearly pointing out why someone else is at fault, but not suggesting a solution or being open to understanding the other side.

GROWING EFFECTIVE LEADERS

Once you become aware of how leadership shows up via conviction and connection, direct feedback can help you fine-tune your skills. The most effective feedback focuses on your behavior. Many people say they turned the corner in their quest to become effective leaders after getting specific feedback from people they respected.

Some organizations design feedback programs for their leaders. Others rely on leaders to solicit feedback. However it is done, the point is to do it.

There are three steps to growing effective leaders. We've already talked about the first two – using a conviction/connection framework that allows leaders to measure their progress and getting accurate feedback from employees and other leaders. The third is a focus on leadership accountability by senior management. All the resources and training groups in the world won't work without senior executive sponsorship for leader development. (See Chapter 3: Tools to Live Your Brand for more on sponsorship.)

Sponsoring leader development includes more than allocating a training budget. Executive staff must invest their own time developing and promoting leadership at all levels just as they would with any other core competency.

Effective leadership – both at the senior management and departmental levels – is the key to keeping people moving on their integrated-branding journey. It allows companies to execute their brand strategy in the most effective way by creating an environment that encourages intelligent participation and better group decisions resulting in the best direction for growth.

FIGURE 10.3: AMIR DEMONSTRATING LEADERSHIP
Using Amir as an example, the quadrants show how specific actions relate to effective leadership.

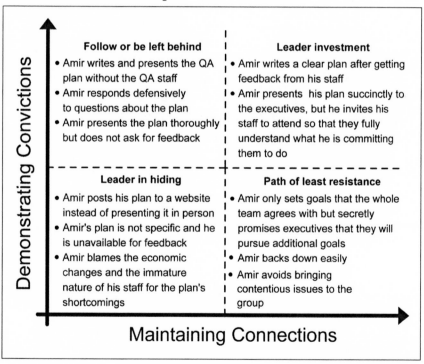

Demonstrating Convictions

Follow or be left behind
- Amir writes and presents the QA plan without the QA staff
- Amir responds defensively to questions about the plan
- Amir presents the plan thoroughly but does not ask for feedback

Leader investment
- Amir writes a clear plan after getting feedback from his staff
- Amir presents his plan succinctly to the executives, but he invites his staff to attend so that they fully understand what he is committing them to do

Leader in hiding
- Amir posts his plan to a website instead of presenting it in person
- Amir's plan is not specific and he is unavailable for feedback
- Amir blames the economic changes and the immature nature of his staff for the plan's shortcomings

Path of least resistance
- Amir only sets goals that the whole team agrees with but secretly promises executives that they will pursue additional goals
- Amir backs down easily
- Amir avoids bringing contentious issues to the group

Maintaining Connections

EXECUTIVE LEADER LOG

After all the work we have done to reveal and communicate our brand promise, I realize much of the ability for our organization to 'live it' will depend on the skill of our leaders. They are the ones on the front lines, guiding people day to day. Are we getting a good enough read on our leadership skills?

HUMAN RESOURCES LEADER LOG

Do we know if the frameworks we are using to develop our leaders are working? Are the core ideas of demonstrating conviction and maintaining connection meaningful to our leadership? Perhaps it's time to poll our leaders to ensure they are getting the development tools and opportunities they need.

SALES LEADER LOG

I think I'm a 'follow or be left behind' type leader with my staff and invest in connection only when I'm with customers. Am I missing some good ideas or feedback because of this? How can I maintain more connection with my staff, but keep my time investment to a minimum?

NOTES

[1] Paulson, Ed, (2001), *Inside Cisco. The Real Story of Sustained M&A Growth*, John Wiley & Sons, New York

[2] Jackson, Mannie, (May 2001), 'Bringing a Dying Brand Back to Life,' *Harvard Business Review*, p 60

[3] Bethune, G (1998) *From Worst to First*, John Wiley & Sons, New York

[4] Michaels, E, Handfield-Jones, H and Axelrod, B (2001) *The War for Talent*, Harvard Business School Press, Boston

[5] Friedman, E (1996) *Reinventing Leadership*, The Guilford Press, New York

[6] Covey, S (1989) *The 7 Habits of Highly Effective People*, Simon & Schuster, New York, p. 188

[7] Watson Wyatt Worldwide (2001) *Watson Wyatt Human Capital Index™*, 2001 Research, Watson Wyatt Worldwide

CHAPTER

CONVEY YOUR BRAND'S MEANING

*Landscapes have a language of their own, expressing
the soul of the things, lofty or humble.*

–Alexandra David-Neel, author and early explorer of Tibet

Employees and customers need multiple ways of identifying and remembering your brand's meaning. Landmarks make your brand more tangible. Just as physical landmarks vary in size and type, ranging from the Statue of Liberty to 'turn left at the service station,' brand landmarks help employees and customers figure out where they are now and where they're going next. These landmarks can be as obvious as your tagline, or as subtle as how you respond to crises. Landmarks are brand conveyors, or brand tools in action. After senior-management evangelism and leader modeling, brand landmarks are the most effective brand-reinforcement tactic for getting all employees to live the brand.

Because landmarks are brand conveyors, they are useful for both internal and external audiences. Internally, leaders can use stories, rewards, language, unique communications and facility design as landmarks. Customer landmarks might include names, product design, responses to crises, taglines and other distinctive communications.

Once you know what landmarks look like, you'll be able to identify your brand landmarks, suggest new ones, and discover places where landmarks would help employees live the brand more fully. If you decide a landmark is a good idea, you must also put in place resources to pay for it and measure it.

INTERNAL LANDMARKS

BRAND STORIES

Brand stories are a very powerful brand landmark. Stories demonstrate your company and its culture in a context people can easily relate to. When you have an individual or departmental success story, you can turn it into a brand story by putting the actions that created the success in the context of your brand tools.

Wells Fargo Bank chooses to demonstrate its commitment to its brand values of customer satisfaction and leadership and personal accountability by highlighting stories in its annual report of employees who went above and beyond and took personal ownership for a customer's problem and wouldn't let go until it was solved. Another company may tell the story of how the company tradition of giving select clients quirky holiday gifts began, indicative of the company's brand personality trait of creative. Another might address why the company created six different invoice templates to demonstrate a flexible personality.

One consulting firm starts every annual retreat off with the founders telling anecdotes about the company's history. This action reinforces key messages, sets a tone for behavior, and is the fastest and most enjoyable way of transmitting key brand tools.

'At 3M, every employee knows the story about how an employee came up with the idea for the Post-It products,' explains Robert Rodriguez in a *Chicago Tribune*, titled 'Company Culture Can Help Determine Compatibility.' 'The story is one of innovation and helps to promote the company culture of employee initiative and creativity.'[1]

A small-appliance manufacturer collects stories of employees who have lived its brand well, and compiles them into books for company-wide distribution.

Fruit-juice company Odwalla has launched a distinctive new bottle for its Samantha line of all-natural juices that 'features a four-sided wrap label with engaging graphics designed by Abby Carter, a children's book illustrator and one of the founders of the Samantha brand. The labels feature company stories and wacky fictional characters dreamed up by Carter ...that relay the playful irreverence that is typical of the Samantha brand.'[2]

In a large software company, salespeople report back on successful sales calls, identifying what parts of the brand the prospect responded to best. Here's a retelling of such a story:

'*The prospect (a large forest-products concern) already had many seats of our competitor's software product installed, and were not eager to support two different software packages. In addition, they wanted to know why our product was 20% more expensive. Because we brought a sales engineer along, we were able to demonstrate our corporate brand principle of consultative, by explaining how they could change their configuration, outfit fewer seats, and save a lot of money. In addition, we communicated our association of rock solid and convinced them there would be a lot less down time with the use of our product. The result is when it was time to upgrade, not only did they install our product, but they replaced the competitor's one as well. This sale was worth more than U.S. $1 million to our company, and was clearly a result of us living our brand in our product-design and sales processes.*'

When these types of success-with-context stories circulate through a company, they increase morale and employee commitment to living the integrated brand. You can also post these stories online for employee and customer audiences, as well as have the company president or CEO laud the team and the role that brand played in the accomplishment.

PAY AND BENEFITS

It also makes sense to compensate employees for brand-based actions, because there's a direct correlation between the strength of your brand and increased profitability. (See Chapter 1: Why All Leaders Need to Be Brand Driven). Such rewards can go beyond compensation to bonuses, stock-option grants, visible awards and prizes. Peter Drucker, known to many as the father of management, says 'you get what you measure.' Tying pay and benefits to specific performance is a very visible brand landmark that spurs on others. Here are three questions to help you build a pay and benefits brand landmark:

1. Is employee compensation based on the type of customer experience you are trying to achieve?
2. Are employees recognized for work and behaviors that specifically demonstrate the brand?
3. Are leaders recognized for brand-related activities?

There are several major companies that effectively use this landmark. Cisco Systems' Web site describes the company as the worldwide leader in networking for the Internet. The company got there by pursuing its mission to be the supplier-of-choice through leading all competitors in customer satisfaction, product leadership, market share and profitability. At Cisco, all managers have a compensation program that is in large part tied directly to customer satisfaction. The satisfaction level is ranked from 1 to 5, with the goal for the year set at 4.23. Employee bonuses are paid based on an annual customer survey that monitors 70 satisfaction items. Typical items measured include product quality, quality of the sales representative, ease with which customers can obtain Cisco-related information, and the level of fit between Cisco's products and the customer's networking needs, among others.' [3]

Washington Mutual ties compensation of many of its employees directly to customer satisfaction as well. Each working unit within the company has identified its customer group. Each does surveys (internally and externally) twice a year and evaluates service levels and customer satisfaction, including questions measuring timeliness of responses and problem solving. Compensation will vary depending on the work unit and the amount of time an employee interfaces with customers.

In another example, Continental Airlines raffles off eight fully loaded Ford Explorer sport utility vehicles, along with other cash and prizes, every six months, for perfect employee attendance, a metric for the company living its promise. Each lucky winner and a guest are treated to a trip to Continental's corporate headquarters in Houston to be thanked personally by chairman and CEO, Gordon Bethune, and other executives. The wining and dining concludes with a trip to the car dealership where they receive the keys to their new vehicles. According to Ryan Price, human resources director for the Field Services Division, the program has been instrumental in helping move Continental from the verge of its third bankruptcy in 1994 to Fortune's list of 100 Best Companies To Work For In The U.S., being proclaimed the 'Best Airline In the Industry' by Fortune, and multi-year winner of the JD Power Award for Customer Service. Awarding employees for perfect attendance is a win-win proposition for Continental, according to Price: 'The program may be seen as a costly perk to some, but it pays for itself year after year. When our employees are on time and want to come to work the ripple effect is tremendously valuable to Continental. We can avoid all sorts of replacement and re-training costs, but the net effect is that we are better able to keep our promise to customers. This program is one way we treat our employees with the same dignity and respect that we treat our customers. We need both customers and employees to be on time, and in turn we will treat them with dignity and respect. Even those who don't win the prizes, still get the message.'

Continental continued to demonstrate its commitment to its brand promise after the U.S. terrorist attack of September 11, 2001. The air-travel industry went into a serious slump due to customers' fear of travel, increased security measures and the resulting economic downturn. Continental had to lay off thousands of workers. Despite its cost, the Perfect Attendance Program and on-time bonuses remained.

FIGURE 11.1: CONTINENTAL AIRLINES ANNUAL REPORT
Continental Airlines' annual report cover page

Another highly effective internal brand landmark is an additional-benefits program. These benefits are above and beyond standard medical coverage and can include additional medical care, funds to purchase job-enhancing tools, family discounts at local venues, employee discounts, time off for volunteer work, stock options and many others. The specific additional benefits you may choose will depend on the brand promise you want to promote.

FedEx uses the annual Southern Heritage Classic football game, now called the Southern Heritage Classic Presented by FedEx, with an annual draw of 50,000 people, and the associated weekend of events for brand recognition, employee rewards and recognition and as a recruiting tool.[4]

When Avanade was in its first year, and building its employee base quickly, the company offered a 'gadget fund' to employees. In their first year, employees could spend up to U.S. $5,000 on technology gadgets of their choice for job-related use. The gadget purchases did not require management approval and were additional to any equipment (such as software, hubs, routers and computers) required to complete an assignment. By getting employees throughout the company (receptionists to engineers) to play with new technology, the company aligned employees' knowledge with the company's brand principle of two steps ahead. Eric Friedman, director of human resources planning and strategy, said 'the program was instrumental in the first year to demonstrate Avanade was serious about its desire to provide deep technical skills to customers, and to hire employees with a passion for technology. The program was not marketed outside the company, but just to new hires, who saw that Avanade was serious when we were willing to put a generous gadget fund into the additional-benefits program.'

Wells Fargo's brand promise centers around doing it right for the customer and superior customer service. To ensure employees think like owners, in 2000 the company awarded stock option grants of 100-400 shares to virtually every employee to thank them for the company's merger integration success and to encourage outstanding service. [5]

Australian-based Fosters Brewing Group leverages core employee competencies in brand building and brand management on a global platform, with the goal of becoming a world leader in premium alcoholic beverages. A key element of the group's business strategy is the employee rewards system. Short and long term incentive plans (including stock ownership, in which 67% of employees participate) reinforce the key value drivers for the group and serve to better align the interests of employees with those of shareholders. [6]

WEB SITES AND E-LEARNING

Electronic communication, via email, Web casts, e-learning or other methods, is often the least expensive and most effective way to create brand landmarks. When technical-writing consultancy Sakson & Taylor changed its logo in response to a brand development process, the concern management had was, *'How can we explain the logo change in a meaningful way to our 500 employees?'* Because many of the company's employees worked off-site at clients' locations, the company decided to use a Web site to explain how the new logo reflected the company's brand tools. The resulting Web site, available to all 500 employees, explained the brand tools and the logo. Using animation, each part of the new logo was deconstructed, explained and presented in the context of Sakson & Taylor's brand. The result was a clear understanding by employees of the brand tools, and how the logo reflected them. This gave employees a sense of pride and the ability to better live the brand.

MetaStories has taken the need for great brand stories and turned it into a successful company. Using rich media, MetaStories has provided organizations such as Discovery.com, The Bill and Melinda Gates Foundation and The Seattle Seahawks with an electronic storytelling channel. Said Brian Monnin, president and CEO of MetaStories, 'Our fundamental belief is that all learning and effective communication is rooted in stories that help people remember, explain, and comprehend. Then we add the use of interactivity, animation, photography, audio and video as building blocks for those stories.' According to MetaStories, rich-media stories stir attention, passions and reactions that don't necessarily occur with simple memos, emails or static Web pages.

Great Britain-based Virgin publishes 'the Virgin story' on its Web site to explain to employees and customers its company history and its brand approach to doing business. Among other things, the Web site explains the company's unique culture: 'Our companies are part of a family rather than a hierarchy. They are empowered to run their own affairs, yet other companies help one another, and solutions to problems come from all kinds of sources. In a sense we are a community, with shared ideas, values, interests and goals. The proof of our success is real and tangible.' [7]

FACILITY DESIGN AND LOCATION

While functionality is the first criterion for facility design, your buildings, offices and factories can do double duty as distinctive brand landmarks. You can create landmarks by asking the following questions:

- What kind of building and building details will help demonstrate your brand?
- What type of workspace allows employees to most effectively demonstrate their brand promise?
- Where do employees need to be located to best demonstrate the brand to customers?

One graphic design firm uses its high-concept lobby - all-black floors, dim lighting, Japanese waterfalls and shoji screens, nowhere to sit, stuffed ravens watching you as you wait - to demonstrate both its creativity and concept-heavy approach to design. REI, the outdoor equipment retailer, uses large stone fireplaces, recycled materials and a stream that is created from rain collected from its facilities' roofs to demonstrate its brand of getting outside yourself. REI also emphasizes its try-it-out approach to outdoor recreation by incorporating walking and biking paths and climbing walls into some stores so people can try out products on the spot.

Longaberger Baskets' headquarters in Newark, Ohio looks like a gigantic basket, letting customers and vendors know that this is no ordinary basket company.

FIGURE 11.2: LONGABERGER BASKET COMPANY HEADQUARTERS
Longaberger Basket company headquarters is shaped like one of its baskets

Susan Ivancie, senior director of corporate human resources at Medtronic, a medical technology company, explains the importance of physical landmarks in her company: 'Medtronic's brand is all around employees as they enter the building. Our vision is etched onto the building and our logo is very prominent in different locations. It's something they pick up on with a number of different senses, starting with the eyes. Our products are displayed all over the company...Our employees are continually aware of what Medtronic is about, the significance of the products we make, and how that is impacting people's lives.'[8]

For some companies (particularly retail businesses such as Nordstrom and Neiman Marcus, or shops on Beverly Hills' Rodeo Drive in California) location is linked to perceived brand value. For others, employees' proximity to each other or to partners is the only location issue. In any case, the workspace needs to deliver the right customer experience. Take, for example, the movie-rental store, Blockbuster, that promises always-available titles. Part of delivering on this brand promise is ensuring there is enough display space and storage space to stock enough movies that are always available. Delivering on its promise will help the store prioritize where to locate. For example, one location might offer more customer traffic, but not meet the display space requirements for Blockbuster.

FIGURE 11.3: FEDEX TRUCKS

To better reflect its brand promise of 'quick reliable delivery,' FedEx redesigned everything from its customer centers to its drop boxes to its trucks. It went so far as to redesign the electronic scanners carried by FedEx drivers, making them ergonomically easier to use. One graphic-design firm known for its warmth in personal dealings has a fireplace and couch in the lobby.

On a more subtle level, you can articulate key brand values in how you design your offices. In companies with less hierarchy, absence of executive offices may be a landmark. In companies that stress personal initiative, each employee may be given a budget to creatively decorate their personal space. If frugality is an organization value, then a lack of pretension or opulence in the office design and décor may be a good brand marker. IKEA's basic and minimalistic store architecture helps it to highlight the great values and high quality of the furnishings it sells.

LANGUAGE USE

At Starbucks, there are no employees, only partners. At Avanade, there are development centers, not regional offices. At Loudeye Technologies, there is a 'Maestra of the Message' in public relations. At Newhall Land, people aren't in 'land development,' they do 'responsible community planning.' Trendwest isn't in the 'timeshare' industry, but in the 'vacation ownership' one. Each of these uses of language helps clarify the companies' brand for both customers and employees.

At Starbucks, one of the core brand values is respect for the employee. In a practice practically unheard of in retail, the company gives every employee the opportunity to own company stock – which then becomes a powerful brand landmark as exemplified in the word 'partner.' Says Howard Shultz, chairman and Chief Global Strategist of Starbucks, in his book, *Pour Your Heart Into It* (1997), [9] 'If we linked everyone in Starbucks to the performance of the company as a whole... every employee would bring the same attitude to work as the CEO...From that day on, we stopped using the word "employee." We now call all our people "partners," because everyone is eligible for stock options as soon as he or she has been with Starbucks for six months.'

Discover Language that Symbolizes Your Brand

- Do you talk differently about things than do other organizations?
- What does that use of language say about your company's brand?

You may also want to look for language that's off-brand and talk to people about not using it.

EXTERNAL LANDMARKS

For audiences outside the organization, including customers, prospects, investors, the media and government, a different take on landmarks is necessary – they have to be more implicit. With employees, you have the luxury of pointing out what actions and communications reflect which brand tools, which is inappropriate with outside audiences. You'd never want to say, 'our brand principle is "x,"' because an effective brand tool is demonstrated – not told.

Each landmark must evoke the correct response, or you have lost an opportunity to connect with a customer, employee or other audience. Here are a few examples of external audience landmarks.

ASSOCIATIONS

AFLAC (provider of voluntary supplemental insurance in the United States and the largest foreign insurer in Japan). Did you hear the duck quack? Kodak. Did you see the yellow packaging? Intel Inside. Did you hear the four-tone jingle? Energizer. Did you picture the pink bunny? Avis. Did you think of 'we try harder?' Virgin. Did you picture Richard Branson?

These are all successful brand associations: Shortcuts to brand meaning and the most memorable landmarks for showing the world your brand. In reality, anything that reminds you of a brand is an association.

FIGURE 11.4:
ENERGIZER BUNNY

As landmarks, associations are a great way to ensure memorability. The harder trick with an association is to consistently apply it long enough so the market feeds it back to you. Companies typically get tired of their associations long before the marketplace does. For example, NBC made a mistake by dropping its peacock, which is now back and used in several different forms as a conveyor for a number of NBC values around entertainment. Fast-food purveyor Jack in the Box also dropped its clown imagery for a while, then brought it back to great effect.

To generate a strong brand association, you first must determine which of your brand assets you want to reinforce through it. Then, you need to pass that concept on to a designer or creative firm to render visually (Absolut's vodka bottle) or aurally (GE's 'We bring good things to life' or NBC's chimes). Through the use of multiple senses, you can help ensure your association's place in your customer's brain and link to your brand's meaning.

We all know these examples, but smaller companies without large budgets can also successfully use associations. Tri-Med Ambulance in Seattle drops off candy jars at nursing homes to reinforce the personality

Health New England: Using Health Related Books As An External Landmark

Point of Interest

Health New England's brand promise is based on providing personal and accountable service to its employers and members. As part of this promise, the organization has been addressing core health needs of its youngest member through a series of books addressing chronic health issues. The second in the Whiz Kidz series addresses childhood obesity.

Childhood obesity has become a nationwide epidemic. Experts blame too many sodas, too much fast food and not enough exercise—but simply reducing these factors won't be enough to help kids make better choices.

HNE's Seymour's Weight Loss Challenge is a story that gets parents and kids talking about the struggle with weight. The book is gentle, honest and practical and approaches the subject from a kid's perspective. It's also supplemented with a workbook, coloring book and CD/ROM virtual grocery store tour.

trait of sweet. George Brazil plumbers use a picture of George Brazil on each plumbing truck. Seattle Children's Home leverages its butterfly association in fund raisers, newsletters, donor gifts and in its landscaping.

Early on in a company's life cycle, one association is often enough. Later, you can add layers of brand meaning through additional associations. McDonald's is the master of associations, building on Ronald McDonald, golden arches, play spaces, Happy Meals, and many more.

TAGLINES

Taglines have many purposes; they can explain what you do to people who don't know, or they can accentuate a key differentiator. But their best and highest uses are as brand landmarks. A tagline can be one way of reminding people of your brand promise. The tone, content and how you use your tagline all can act as brand landmarks. For example, Microsoft's 'Where do you want to go today?' reflects the helpful, optimistic personality that Microsoft wants to impart. Some companies use their tagline everywhere; others use it more sparingly. Sakson & Taylor (technical communications contract firm) uses its 'for the perfect match' tagline in many places, but particularly on the toys it hands out at trade shows to demonstrate its personality attribute of playful. 3M uses the simple tagline 'Innovation' to communicate its brand principle. Volkswagon's 'Drivers Wanted' tagline reflects the company's historic sense of humor. And Coca-Cola's 'Life tastes good' ad campaign reflects the company's brand meaning, which comes from a set of values and storytelling around enhancing the special moments in people's lives. [10]

NAMING

One key component to using names as brand landmarks is to choose names that work well with existing brand nomenclature. For example, any Microsoft product name must carry the Microsoft name in front of it, which means the words must sound good when joined. In addition, Microsoft has a clearly defined brand any name must complement. Microsoft brand attributes include inviting, so any product-naming effort must consider this. Thus 'Microsoft Barricade' would probably be deemed an off-brand name.

Companies that name themselves whimsically let consumers know a little about the personality of the company, such as Loudeye (formerly encoding.com). Onvia.com, an online procurement site, wanted its name to reflect its 'optimistic' brand personality. And Lexant, a wellness-information company, wanted to convey its brand personality of 'high-end service.'

RESPONSES TO CRISES

A brand is ultimately about believability and credibility. One external brand landmark that is closely watched by customers and the general public is how a company handles a crisis. How well prepared you are, how much you talk and what you say, how your customers, investors and the general public rate you afterwards are all brand related. It's essential to lay the foundations for this landmark before you are in crisis by asking, *'Which aspects of our brand should we demonstrate during a crisis?*

The Ford Motor and Firestone/Bridgestone tire-tread separation crisis illustrates the impact of crisis management on a brand's credibility. Confusing comments by both companies, a lack of coordination, and mutual mud-slinging left consumers with little faith in either company.

As a result, Ford suffered a 17% drop in brand value, as measured by Interbrand Corp. and *BusinessWeek*.[11] According to an article in *BusinessWeek*, 'To see just how much - and how fast – a mismanaged brand can lose value, take a look at No. 8-ranked Ford. Everyone knows that Ford Motor Co. has had a tough year. Between the Firestone tire fiasco and a series of embarrassing quality gaffes, little has gone right for the Detroit carmaker. Investors certainly have been hurt: First-half earnings from continuing operations are down 91% from a year ago. But what does the blow to Ford's reputation really cost? When a brand is tarnished, its power to attract customers and command top prices diminishes – and so its value drops. That's what the numbers show for Ford. By Interbrand's calculations, the carmaker's name is worth U.S. $30.1 billion today – U.S. $6.3 billion less than last year.'

Says Jack A. Gottschalk, author of *Crisis Response*, 'Some attorneys are too wary of the legal ramifications of telling the truth to the public or the press, and damage the organization's long-term reputation as a result. Individuals familiar with the Firestone case,' he observes, 'believe the corporation relied on the cautious counsel of its lawyers instead of the advice of crisis counselors, who proposed a proactive plan for restoring consumer confidence.'[12]

Both companies appeared to ignore or deny the facts, delayed taking action, and did not reassure people that they were doing whatever they could to alleviate the situation.[13] 'Reestablishing faith in a mature brand such as... Firestone and Ford can be challenging but not impossible,' says Larry Avila, in an article in the *Chicago Business Ledger*. Demonstrating a core value of 'trustworthiness' needs to be at the heart of the crisis-response brand landmark.

One company may believe staying close-mouthed is the best reaction to tainted meat at its fast food restaurants; another may be forthcoming with apologies and immediate procedure changes – which is what Jack In the Box did in response to an e.coli outbreak in 1993.

Which will foster the better long-term brand? To keep one's brand promise, even after it is accidentally broken, companies must act quickly, address perceptions (whether they are accurate or not) and make necessary changes. Our brand research indicates companies that take care of their customers during and after a crisis end up with stronger brand loyalty and equity than they had previously. This 'taking care' landmark positively impacts sales and long-term company valuation.

Questions to ask if you face a crisis:

- *'What is the most customer-friendly response we can take in this event?'*
- *'What do people need to know about this crisis?'*
- *'What do our brand values and principle say to do now?'*
- *'What tone of response is indicated by our personality?'*
- *'What actions will convince the public of our trustworthiness?'*
- *'What is the downside risk for not taking these actions?'*

While you can have many more landmarks, both for employees and outside audiences, these examples give you the idea. A brand needs to be reinforced through brand conveyors that consistently get the message across again and again. Practically everything, from your building, to your organization structure, to your product design, can convey brand meaning. And everyone, no matter what department or role they have, can identify places where landmarks are needed, or suggest ways of changing processes or conveyors to more clearly reflect the brand.

How to Create a Brand Landmark

Point of Interest

If you've already defined your brand, how do you determine where to create brand landmarks? The litmus test is that they must make the brand experience more compelling for customers and employees. A compelling experience builds emotional loyalty, intellectual rapport or both – it captures the hearts and minds of customers and employees. You can start this process by answering the following questions:

- 'Do customers and employees understand what's most compelling about our brand?'
- 'What's our greatest challenge in creating brand awareness? Brand understanding? What landmarks could solve this?'
- 'What areas of brand awareness and integration will suffer if we don't develop landmarks?'
- 'Are any of our current company practices, brand assets, cultural norms or communications landmark-worthy?'
- 'Do our facilities reflect our brand?'
- 'Which landmarks would give us the greatest return for our money?'

GEARING UP

Part of creating landmarks is ensuring you have the right gear – resources, training and tools – to enable everyone to focus on creating landmarks and living the brand. Your gear will vary depending on what your employees need to both understand the brand for themselves and create compelling customer experiences.

Every company needs to have the right tools to conduct their business, from espresso machines to airplanes. Gear can include a wide array of devices, tools and systems. The point isn't having the most advanced systems but to ensure an on-brand customer experience consistently, by delivering something that customers value.

E*TRADE Financial, for example, promises customers they can access their accounts virtually anytime, anywhere, around the world. The company has built a brand landmark around customer touchpoints that offers expanded customer access to financial services and personal, one-on-one assistance from licensed financial services associates.

These include any of five E*TRADE financial centers across the United States. The company's customers can also access accounts via its network of thousands of E*TRADE financial ATMs and kiosks.[14] In this example, communications technology applied as a customer benefit is the gear that lets E*TRADE Financial demonstrate its customer touchpoints landmark.

Here's an example using the airline industry. Airline 'A' has a brand principle of offering convenience to its travelers. Airline 'B' has a brand principle of comfort. Each company sells seats and cargo space on airplanes in hopes of turning a profit and returning value to its shareholders. They differentiate themselves on their ability to run their business and execute upon their brand. Each thinks its brand will appeal to the largest customer base, hence winning them the largest market share. The gear each will need to help them on their journey to living their integrated brand will be different, because their brand promises are different. Below is a brainstorming list of some gear each company may consider. There are potentially limitless ideas for how to gear up to live each brand. It is a given that both will need airplanes, maintenance facilities, and passenger terminals. This list reflects possible gear that will enable them to specifically create landmarks and demonstrate their brand promises:

Airline A	Airline B
Brand principle = Convenience	Brand principle = Comfort
Provide for extra storage space on board or more options for gate checking bags.	Covered curbside
Offer additional benefit to employees of on-site uniform cleaning. Employees do not have to wash uniforms at home.	Site managers can award spot bonuses of first class travel upgrades to employees for something extraordinary they did to make travel for a customer more comfortable.
Provide self-serve, check-in kiosks.	Offer shoulder massages, first-come, first-served at the gate.

Airline A

At each arrival gate, provide phone lines where travelers can direct dial to hotels and ground transportation.

Airline B

At arrival gate, provide concierge to book fine hotels in the area or offer a cold drink.

EXECUTIVE LEADER LOG

I love to tell stories, they help break the ice, they help people laugh together and mend fences, when that's what's needed. I never thought about telling stories as a way to strengthen the brand, though it makes sense – stories are a very useful social glue. My best stories are short, a little funny and always about one person or maybe two – and they spread faster than wildfire. I've even had a story of mine told back to me once – the teller had no idea it had originated with me – when one of our sales guys saw a colleague do something really nice for a customer and it reminded them of the story they'd heard about what another of our salespeople had done from way back. That's powerful communication.

HUMAN RESOURCES LEADER LOG

When I take new employees on tours of our headquarters, it's usually right after a full day of orientation meetings. I've kind of wondered about the funny frowns on their faces by the time the tour's over, but I think I get it now – we just spent seven-plus hours drilling it into them that everyone here – from the executives to the janitors – have open-door policies and any employee can drop by anytime to chat, discuss a problem or brainstorm ideas. But the last thing on the tour is a swing through the executive office wing – at which time you have to leave the building and enter through a separate, outside door. No wonder they're puzzled.

SALES LEADER LOG

I don't know what it is about Eliot, our bookstore's unofficial feline mascot, but most of our best, long-time customers look for her as soon as they enter the store (if she's not sunning on top of a pile of books in the window when they arrive). Lots of small bookstores have resident cats, but our store specializes in used and antique books, the classics, mainly. Eliot really seems to strike a chord with our quiet but fastidious customers. She's a great conversation piece and she's helped turned some of our best customers into more than that - they're friends of ours, because we all share a common bond with Eliot.

Notes

[1] Rodriquez, Robert, (14 January 2001), 'Company Culture Can Help Determine Compatibility', *Chicago Tribune*, C1

[2] 'Samantha's Got a Brand New Bottle!', (21 November, 2001) PR Newswire

[3] Paulson, Ed, Inside Cisco: The Real Story of Sustained M&A Growth, John Wiley & Sons, 2001, p.92

[4] Moore, Linda, (29 May 2002), 'FedEx name to Adorn Football Game In Tennessee', KRTBN Knight-Ridder Tribune Business News: Memphis Commercial Appeal

[5] Wells Fargo 2000 Annual Report

[6] Foster Brewing Group, Profit Report Six Months to 31 December 2000, highlights

[7] Virgin Web site, www.virgin.com, Welcome to the home of Virgin online

[8] Dell, David, and Ainspan, Nathan, and Bodenberg, Thomas, and Troy, Kathryn, and Hickey, Jack, 'Engaging Employees Through Your Brand,' (2001) *The Conference Board*, p 14

[9] Schultz, H and Jones Yang, D (1997) *Pour Your Heart Into It*, Hyperion

[10] Coca-Cola press release, April 20, 2001, 'Coca-Cola Launches New Advertising Campaign Reclaiming Brand's Roots and Values in Everyday Life'.

[11] (6 August 2001) 'The Best Global Brands', *BusinessWeek Online*

[12] (December 2000) 'How to Keep a Crisis from Happening', *Harvard Management Update*

[13] Ibid.

[14] https://us.etrade.com/e/t/home/aboutus?gxml=hpc_disc_story_c.html

CHAPTER

MEASURE YOUR
BRAND'S EFFECTIVENESS

Hey Yogi I think we're lost.

–Phil Rizzuto

Ya, but we're making great time!

–Yogi Berra

This chapter shows how to measure brand value and evaluate brand progress – a compass check, as it were. It will help you answer the important question of, *'Are we heading in the right direction?'* Checking your compass allows you to:

- make sure you are on track for living your brand, both internally and externally;
- make the process of building brand value a regular part of doing business, through alignment of practices, brand assets, culture and communications;
- initiate a process for continually fine tuning and building on previous steps;
- encourage senior management, departments and work groups to include brand measurement metrics as part of what they evaluate, value and invest in.

Measuring brand value is rapidly becoming a 'must-have' tool for senior management. In a *BusinessWeek* article, Neil Gross states: 'As any business-school professor can tell you, the value of companies has been shifting from tangible assets – the bricks and mortar – to intangible assets, such as patents, customer lists and brand…You won't find balance-sheet entries for these assets except in rare cases, even though at some companies they may account for the bulk of the overall value.'[1]

Lacking good accounting measures, what can you do? This chapter will give you both simple, short-term measurements combined with more comprehensive long-term benchmarks to achieve your brand integration and reporting goals.

Metrics are like mileposts on a winding, mountain road that give you a good idea of how far you've gone, and how far you still have to go. Without them, you have no idea if you are making good time, stuck at a rest stop waiting in the line for the bathroom, or being towed back to the last town where the mechanic informs you 'that part will take three weeks to get here.' You won't fully support your integrated brand unless you have some way of ensuring you are building brand value; and knowing that the brand value is translating into bottom-line benefits.

Every leader is responsible for measuring the effectiveness of living the integrated brand. Why? Measurable results are the basis for ongoing investment by senior management as well as a morale booster for employees. If senior management sees that improvements in how the company is living the brand turn into profit and price-premium benefits, they will be a lot more interested in continuing to fund brand-building efforts.

This chapter provides a variety of measurements from which to create your own system. Benchmarking is the process of measuring certain aspects of your brand, then comparing those same ones into the future. Keep in mind benchmarking is both a report card and a path to improvement. It is a way to measure progress and provide rewards. And most importantly, it points the way to fine-tuning your customer experience.

Aligning processes to brand is a never-ending way to build greater return on investment. For every period you've conducted benchmarking and made departmental adjustments as a result, you are that much further down the road to competitive differentiation and unbreakable customer relationships.

There are many ways to measure brand effectiveness. These include measuring brand equity and employee alignment, more customer-specific measurements such as customer retention or customer time-to-repurchase, and more bottom-line indicators such as valuation or profit margins. We will cover each of these measurements in more detail in this chapter.

BENCHMARKING YOUR INTEGRATED BRAND

Because your integrated brand is reflected in every customer touchpoint and every company practice, you have to ensure that employees are living the brand – internal measurement. Second, you must see if your customers and prospects are experiencing your brand in ways that will cause them to become committed brand evangelists – external measurement. Third, you need methods to connect increases in brand equity with return on investment – return on brand investment measurement – to keep senior management and departmental heads committed to integrated branding. There are also quick ways to see how you're doing in-between formal benchmarks – quick checks.

INTERNAL MEASUREMENTS

To get employees acting on-brand, you need to communicate, train, measure and reward. We addressed communication and training in previous chapters: Here, we address how to measure brand-based actions and reward on-brand behavior. In our experience, companies that employ a variety of informal and formal brand rewards and measurements see the biggest benefit. According to the Human Capital Index study conducted annually by Watson Wyatt, companies with clear rewards and accountability realized a 9.2% increase in market value over companies without them.[2]

Whatever your approach, make sure you seamlessly integrate it into other employee programs. For example, if you conduct yearly performance reviews, make sure some of the review focuses on how well employees manifested certain aspects of the brand personality and values, how clearly they understood and used cultural norms, or how their actions and achievements demonstrated making decisions using your brand principle. If you have an employee-of-the-month or other internal reward program, make sure part of the selection criteria is based on demonstrating your integrated brand in everyday activities. If promotions are based on a set of criteria, add brand-based criteria to the list.

It's a psychological truth that those behaviors that get rewarded are those we continue to manifest. So it's important to build in rewards for desired behavior, and to articulate what on-brand behavior is. Otherwise, you could have a problem faced by many fast-growing companies, where, due to a lack of corporate norms around the use of brand tools, employees think the corporate brand doesn't apply to them. When we asked an employee at a large retail company how well his division was manifesting the corporate brand, he answered, 'Oh, we don't pay attention to the brand.' This behavior will weaken customer relationships – negatively impacting the bottom line.

REWARDING ON-BRAND BEHAVIOR

To get employees to act on-brand, it's better to use a brand carrot, rather than a brand stick. This doesn't mean you shouldn't identify off-brand actions, but focus a much larger percentage of your time on rewards versus punishments.

Continental Airlines is very good at focusing on rewards. All 50,000 plus employees (with the exception of management) receive either a U.S. $65 or U.S. $100 bonus when the airline posts good monthly on-time performance (as measured by the U.S. Department of Transportation). Within three months of starting the program, the airline went from one of the worst in on-time performance to the nation's first. Since instituting the program, Continental has spent more than U.S. $100 million in on-time bonuses.[3]

One consulting firm instituted a brand-reward system called 'The Brandy.' Employees win the monthly Brandy Award by acting on-brand: By demonstrating the organization's brand value of being a great team member, and by demonstrating its *customer-centric* and flexible personality. The Brandy Award is different every month, ranging from hula-hoops to ice cream parties, demonstrating another personality trait of creativity. The brand is reflected both in the brand-reward process, and in the actual rewards offered for living the brand.

MEASURING INDIVIDUAL AND GROUP ACTIONS

Rewards, however, first require measurement. If you have created your job areas and descriptions based on delivering your brand promise, you'll have a head start on measuring employee brand actions. (See Chapter 9: Hire, Train and Organize to Live the Brand.)

But it's just as important to measure group activities as it is individuals.' Groups are the focal point for company practices, cultural norms and brand asset activities that have a significant impact on your customer experience. You'll want to develop cultural norms where employees look forward to brand measurement activities as a way to improve their individual and group success. (See Chapter 5: Brand Strategy: Turn Customers into Committed Champions for more information on developing a culture that supports brand growth.)

Ways of measuring brand action include:

- performance reviews;
- brand equity scores;
- conducting brand skills tests on your intranet;
- using customer feedback to determine if employees are demonstrating on-brand behavior;
- creating a senior-management-specific measurement and continuous improvement system for modeling your integrated brand;
- testing demonstrated sponsorship for integrated branding and department goals; (See Chapter 4: Align to Deliver a Unique Customer Experience)
- doing in-depth interviews with individual employees to see if they understand, use and model the brand. (It's a good idea to then compile the same information on a departmental level to measure group scores.)

FIRST-YEAR DEPARTMENTAL MEASUREMENTS

Typical first-year outcomes for companies include aligning departmental practices with the brand and turning senior staff into brand evangelists. The following are some department-specific practice examples in a variety of companies and how to use measurement to align them with your brand.

Sales Department Practice

Brand principle = partner

Practice: sales process

Alignment need: The sales presentation does not reflect our brand principle. We simply present product features and benefits – not a program that creates a relationship. Plus, our presentation style is not partner-oriented, and we don't even know how a given prospect would like to partner with us.

Sales Department Practice (continued)

Measurement: A presentation and style that 75% of prospects will identify as partner-like – as measured in a follow-up questionnaire.

Results and next steps: 35% graded the presentation as partner-like; 60% graded our people style as partner-like. We will continue to clarify the presentation to show our long-term commitment to partnerships. Our style issues are with specific individuals who will receive additional training in how to demonstrate empathy, friendliness and passion.

Human Resources Department Practice

Brand principle = most usable

Practice: employee accountability

Alignment need: Employees are not called out when they fail to live the brand promise – specifically when they are not living our principle of 'most usable' when working on departmental initiatives.

Expected outcomes: Creation of a managerial practice that holds employees accountable and a 25% increase in employees demonstrating our brand principle and employees making suggestions about how to improve the customer experience.

Results and next steps: All top-line managers in marketing, sales and human resources are now trained in how to keep employees accountable and we've experienced a 50% increase in employees demonstrating the brand principle based on Web feedback. We will now train line managers and work to establish the practice in all departments.

Product Management Example

Brand principle = hassle-free

Practice: product improvement

Alignment needed: In general, product managers have focused on developing new features and functions to meet the most prevalent customer wants, rather than ensuring that all new features are hassle-free.

Expected outcomes: Through interviewing our best customers, we will define what hassle-free will look like, feature-by-feature, in the next product revision. The goal is 90% of customers saying we are hassle-free.

Results and next steps: 40% of customers characterize the product as hassle-free. Feedback indicates the hassle-free bar has been raised by expectations customers carry over from other parts of their lives. Our next step will be to create a hassle-free measuring system and use it to help test new features. We will focus on changing our entire feature set to meet this new challenge.

QUICK CHECKS

Here are some fast ways to get feedback on how well your company is set up to deliver your promised customer experience.

Check yourself. Ask yourself, *'How well am I living our brand in my area?' 'Am I making decisions using our brand principle?' 'Am I demonstrating the brand personality?' 'Am I demonstrating conviction and staying in connection with other employees?'* If you are a department head or part of the management team, part of your job is to consciously use brand tools to make course corrections whenever you see something that is off-brand. It's equally important that you label your actions as being on-brand so that others can model their behavior on yours.

Check your employees. Online feedback can keep you abreast of how well employees are living the brand. The first step is to create intranet Web sites that encourage employees to tell stories relating to brand success or failure. You can help bring both complaints and testimonials to the surface through home-page reminders, with banners such as *'Got a great company story?'* or *'Unhappy about something?'* as well as through paycheck stuffers. These quick checks are great for creating continuous improvement opportunities as well as reinforcing the positive aspects of your brand.

You can also use 'management by walking around' to ask employees questions like, *'What principle-based decisions have you made recently?'*

Check your department. You can also conduct periodic departmental course corrections.

The questions you want to ask as a department leader include:

- *Are all of our practices, cultural norms and communications supporting the brand?'*
- *'Are we taking on-brand actions in support of practices that originate elsewhere in the company?'*
- *'What specific actions in the past x months support our brand principle, personality, values or other tools?'*
- *'Are we building our brand assets?'*
- *'Are managers and other leaders acting as brand evangelists?'*
- *'Are all staff members using the brand principle as a compass for making decisions?'*
- *'In our interactions and communications with others, are we reflecting the company's brand personality?'*

You can also field a brief questionnaire to other departments to determine if their experience of you is on-brand.

THE BRAND SUGGESTION BOX: MONITORING BRAND PROGRESS

Another way to catch great brand ideas is through using a brand suggestion box. It's easy: Just create a small form listing your brand tools, leaving a space for employee feedback about what's working and what isn't or what they'd suggest adding. Give these suggestion box forms to new employees at orientation, and make suggestion boxes available in common areas around the office, and online.

There are many benefits to turning employees into brand watchdogs. When employees give feedback on living the brand, they become brand champions. Employees build their convictions, while getting practice applying brand tools. They feel listened to and see management's commitment to the brand. And management gets valuable input for new brand strategy. Through brand suggestion, leaders can spot trouble spots, or know which issues require more communication or training. You can also use the brand-review process to report back to the rest of the company on top employee concerns, brand weaknesses and new solutions. One caveat: The appropriate manager needs to respond to employee ideas and enact ones that make sense.

Brand Suggestion Box

Point of Interest

Suggested practice change: _____

Mission: (insert yours) _____

Values: (insert yours) _____

Principle: (insert yours) _____

Personality: (insert yours) _____

Association: (insert yours) _____

Other comments: _____

_____

_____

_____

EXTERNAL MEASUREMENTS

Annual benchmarking is one of your most important tools, because it provides senior management with success measurements that tie to revenues, profits and valuation. You can train your senior management team to use benchmarking as a way to evaluate the success of your integrated branding initiative by tying brand results to the bottom line. Once you've done this, you'll have a much easier time of justifying new brand investments. You'll also want to integrate employee brand alignment into this success measurement for the same reasons.

It's often easier to measure how well customers are experiencing your brand than employees. Customers and prospects will typically tell you what they think, unlike employees who may fear repercussions. That makes it easier to analyze which customer beliefs influence their behaviors. You can then make the link between customer behaviors, financial results and long-term business sustainability.

We recommend conducting brand-awareness benchmarking annually, using aided and unaided questions (aided is where you give them a list to choose from; unaided is where you see what answers they come up with on their own). It's to your advantage to continuously monitor some customer behaviors – such as complaints, positive comments, customer retention, types and quantities of purchase and referrals, and repurchase intervals.

ANNUAL BENCHMARKING

Annual benchmarking measurements include:
- unaided and aided awareness of the company and its products and services - including unaided first mentions;
- unaided and aided awareness of company brand concepts including principle, personality, associations and messages;
- customer brand equity scores – company-wide, by market segment, and by customer experience;
- customers' willingness to pay a price-premium over a generic product or service and size of price-premium;
- number of competitive product or service choices customers will review when replacing their current product or buying a similar new product or service.

For prospects you will also want to ask:
- the likelihood of including your products or services in their next purchasing review.

You will want to compare all of these benchmarks against previous years' measurements and against your competitive peer group.

The most effective format for external research is a combination of in-depth phone interviews, supported by a larger sample of Web-based surveys to provide statistical legitimacy.

While focus-group testing has gotten a bad name in recent years (mostly because of its misuse), it remains a viable method for digging deep into people's emotions and behaviors. Focus-group testing is a good way to test how people are responding to brand-based actions and communications.

Another way to conduct ongoing checks is to create customer councils that are representative of your customer base. You can regularly solicit information and test ideas to get a good idea of how your customer base will respond.

THE BRAND EQUITY CHECK

You can gauge the depth of your customer relationships and the effectiveness of your customer experience with just a few simple questions. The Parker LePla Brand-Equity Check™ allows measurement of customer awareness, preference, loyalty and commitment using a numerical scale that ranges from a –5 to +5, where +5 equals an unbreakable customer relationship.

Brand-equity measurement allows you to quantify the depth of customer relationships. A good rule of thumb says that the deeper the relationship, the greater the return on your brand investment. Companies use the Parker LePla Brand-Equity Check™ as both a diagnostic and reporting tool. It can predict customer retention, customer referral rates and price-premium elasticity from quarter to quarter or year to year. Brand equity scores also allow you to adjust pricing of existing products or services, set pricing for new services and determine return on brand investment.

Brand equity scores help predict both company profitability in the short term and how well you can sustain your market and financial-leadership position over time. In our experience, companies that have average brand-equity scores in the three-to-five range have a very loyal and committed customer base. As a result, these companies can charge a price-premium of 10% or more for their products and services, and typically realize up to a 25% greater valuation than peer-group averages. They also lose fewer customers, experience a faster time-to-repeat purchase and garner a greater number of word-of-mouth recommendations.

FIGURE 12.1: BRAND EQUITY PYRAMID

Company X learns from its brand equity pyramid that its customers are at the mid-preference level and its employees are at the mid-loyalty level.

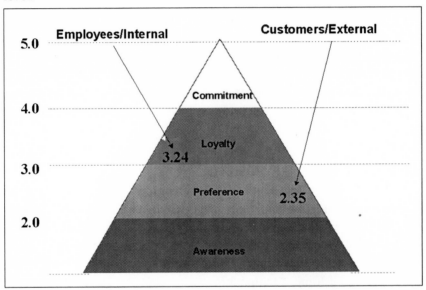

One other benefit to high brand equity is the 'wow' factor. A strong brand creates great word of mouth among your target audiences and puts your company in a more powerful position in all of its business dealings. Based on your reputation, other companies will seek you out for alliances. Prospects will experience a type of brand-awe based on what they've heard about you and be predisposed to like the way you do business.

How can you use brand equity information to fine-tune company practices? If an equity reading shows a dramatic up or down spike, you can then review the previous period and determine what caused it. What caused the drop or increase? Is it something that needs correcting or should you stay the course? While some negative events can cause a downward spike in equity, we've found that companies that thoroughly communicate their strategies and actions often can mitigate negative news and hence are more likely to keep their base of customer champions. Examples of this are Tylenol after the poisoning scare and Jack in the Box (fast food restaurant) after the e.coli outbreak. Both companies acted in ways that reassured their customers. Since its well-publicized experience with e.coli in 1993, Jack In the Box has become a crusader and food-safety resource for higher standards across the entire food service industry.[4]

Often, downward spikes can be avoided by addressing issues before they become problems. For instance, Starbucks is actively working to provide Fair Trade coffee to its customers – pre-empting a major customer and general public reaction to perceived exploitive business practices in third world countries. Seattle City Light and other utility companies around the United States are offering sustainable, electric-supply options to customers – recognizing the desire of many customers to move from unsustainable oil- or nuclear-based electricity.

Positive spikes should also be traced to their underlying causes. You can do this in the customer-interview process by asking if the interviewee's opinion has changed and why, over the past year. Was the spike a result of a change in company practices, communications or product or service offerings? If so, was the change due to an enhancement in a brand asset or was it related to something new that you haven't yet considered part of the brand?

The following are examples of activities that negatively impact brand equity, and what to do about them to maintain customer relationships.

Avoiding Brand-Weakening Actions

Employees

Action: Lack of company-value definition or follow-through by management

Mitigation: Have management identify, buy into and use values as boundaries for actions

Action: Unnecessary lay-offs

Mitigation: Staff and plan for downturns rather than economic booms

---

Avoiding Brand-Weakening Actions

Employees

Action: Lack of stated, realistic mission, vision and goals

Mitigation: Have management identify, buy into and explain mission, vision and goals

Action: Large pay-, perk- and social-status gap between management and staff

Mitigation: Encourage first-name basis with managers and eliminate perks that create symbolic barriers – such as executive parking spots

Action: Lack of both compensation for high achievement and penalties for low achievement

Mitigation: Create ways to measure and compensate achievement

Customers and prospects

Action: Lack of zero-fault complaint system

Mitigation: Develop a feedback system that catches off-brand customer experiences and follows them to resolution

Action: Product- or service-problem cover-up actions

Mitigation: Create a crisis-management system that promulgates fast, full disclosure and resolution of problems

Action: Perceived unethical company behaviors

Mitigation: Create a trends and ethics analysis function that applies current and potential societal ethical standards to all company activities

Action: Unfounded rumors

Mitigation: Develop a rumor-control function that actively addresses all rumors as they are uncovered

Action: Quiet-company syndrome

Mitigation: Create a communications program with both customers and the general public that explains company vision and publicizes company actions in all areas

Action: Poor service and lack of bonding with customers

Mitigation: Employee training and testing on service and brand tools.

BRAND REPORT CARD – CUSTOMERS AND PROSPECTS

You can create a simple brand report card to evaluate a customer's and prospect's experience with your brand. By comparing annual brand report cards, you can quickly see whether you are improving the customer experience and relationship. The research will also allow you to see how well your brand tools are being lived and communicated.

Annual brand report card			
	Current year	Previous	Five years ago
Unaided awareness-customers			
First mention			
Unaided awareness-prospects			
First mention			
Aided awareness-customers			
Aided awareness-prospects			
Unaided awareness of brand concepts			
Aided awareness of brand concepts			
Customer brand equity			
Willingness-to-pay premium			
Generic			
Company Product A			
Company Product B			
Number of choices in product review			
Time to make purchase decision			
Number not buying again			

OTHER EXTERNAL MEASUREMENTS

The amount a customer will pay for a product in comparison to other comparable products is a basic indicator of brand strength and an important brand report card line item. You can determine your price-premium (or price deficit) by asking customers comparative questions – such as, *'Which would you pay more for, Brand X or Brand Y?'* and *'How much more would you pay?'* In one brand seminar we conducted recently, people said they would pay up to 50% more for their preferred brands, in such diverse markets as recreational equipment, guitars and coffee.

You can also measure customer segment revenue based on specific brand actions where a change has occurred. For instance, several brands ranging from British Airways' *At Your Service* to Sony's *Cierge* are offering concierge services for a customer segment defined as "spends the most money." While this is an innovative customer experience extension, it is also something where the pre- to post-program change can be discretely measured. In a six-month study, the Carlson Marketing Group, a provider of concierge services, says that revenue from concierge customers grew 16%.[5]

We also recommend that you collect complaints and testimonials from customer email feedback. You can glean important information by comparing this unsolicited feedback with your other research – particularly when it's negative. For instance, if something is showing up frequently in research, but you rarely see it unsolicited, it may be the type of problem that is irritating, but not to the point that customers are willing to tell you about it. These are hidden brand detractors that can slowly erode customer and employee loyalty over the long term. Catching them in the symptom stage can allow you to correct them before you lose a large number of customers or employees.

BRAND ROI MEASUREMENTS

There are a number of methods on the market for creating brand ROI. Parker LePla works with its clients to customize general ROI tools to specific companies. As we mentioned earlier, one of the components of any brand ROI is the brand-equity score. We have correlated a company's brand-equity scores with its ability to charge a price-premium, and have discovered that for every point of brand equity, a company can charge significantly more for its products or services while creating greater customer retention. Thus, you can tie broad-based company brand investment with margins, market share and cost of new sales. With new accounting practices that will be established based on new FASB rules for valuing intangible assets, we expect to be able to tie brand investment more closely to company valuation in the future.

Harris Research offers a brand-equity measurement tool, called EquiTrend Online. This measurement of brand equity uses Internet technology to conduct an immediate, in-depth survey of 30,000 Internet users about their perceptions of the quality of more than 1,300 brands in 17 industry categories. The interesting thing about EquiTrend Online is that, according to the company, it has predicted the effects of brand equity on such bottom line corporate financial results as sales, margins, market share, price elasticity and the stock price of flagship brands. The survey demonstrates that brand-quality perceptions by consumers are excellent indicators of a brand's probable sales and profitability. [6]

As a result of four years of brand initiatives at Continental Airlines, the company achieved a return on brand investment that resulted in 23 consecutive profitable quarters, six straight years of profitable performance, after multiple years in the red and two bankruptcies. The company's brand focus also resulted in:

- sick leave down by more than 29%;
- turnover down 45% to an all-time low rate of 5.3%;
- worker's compensation down by 51%;[7]
- JD Power & Associates bestowed its top customer-satisfaction award four years out of five;
- ranked number one in on-time arrivals among all U.S. airlines;
- fourth-straight Freddie Award for delivering the best frequent flyer program;
- Continental employees earned bonus checks in 11 out of 12 months (U.S. $785 per employee) for on-time performance as measured by the Department of Transportation;[8]
- four-years-in-a-row placement on *Fortune*'s '100 Best Companies to Work For' (the only passenger airline on the list in 2002);
- Airline of the Year by *Air Transport World*, 2001.

How can you budget for brand expenditures when you're just getting started? A good rule of thumb is a strong, integrated brand will allow you to realize a 25% or greater price-premium on your products and services. You can use this as a target to build a multi-year budget – assuming an increase in company revenue that is the difference between your current price-premium (if any) and your target price-premium of

25% or greater. Of course, many brand actions will simply require a change in the focus of current budgeted items, resulting in no cost increase at all.

Do a Brand Check Now...

Assuming that your company has defined its brand in some form, you can do a general brand check right now to help determine how well the company has integrated its brand into all practices and employee actions. Ask yourself:

- *'What is our company's current brand?'*
- *'Do we charge a product or service price-premium over market average?'*
- *'How many competitive offerings do your customers look at prior to repurchasing?'*
- *'Do I make decisions or take action based on our brand tools?'*
- *'Which company practices, departments and employees are aligned with our brand?'*
- *'Do all our customers have the same, consistent brand experience?'*
- *'Are all communications based on our brand?'*

Point of Interest

MEASUREMENTS ABOUND

Here's a summary of all the possible ways to measure how well your company – both employees and groups or departments – is living the brand. While you won't want to do it all, you should be performing some kind of regular measurement to ensure your investments in your brand are paying off.

Internal measurement possibilities:
- measuring and rewarding on-brand actions;
- during employee performance reviews;
- as part of criteria for internal reward programs (for example, the employee of month);
- as part of promotion criteria;
- brand integration score– averaged and tracked year to year;
- brand equity measurement – tracked year to year;

- alignment report card for departments and company;
- alignment stories from departments;
- audit of internal communications (newsletters, intranet, company meetings);
- employee focus groups;
- rules of the road (cultural norms) alignment report card.

External measurement possibilities:

- brand awareness benchmarking;
- aided and unaided awareness research;
- brand equity pyramid measurement;
- customer satisfaction;
- price-premium comparisons with the competition;
- customer focus groups;
- customer retention rates;
- customer time to purchase;
- revenue share by customer segment;
- customer speed to repurchase;
- market share.

At this point, you're nearing the end of your journey. You've learned the process of how leaders can help their organizations better deliver on a compelling customer experience. The next few chapters are specialized side trips for people in particular situations: Read them if they apply. If you have any questions about the information in this book, please contact us at www.parkerlepla.com.

EXECUTIVE LEADER LOG

This chapter would be a good handbook for our annual brand strategy – starting with the end in mind. Our corporate communications department – both public relations and employee communications – would be a great focal point for gathering and publicizing our company's on-brand stories. I think I'll point our CFO to this chapter first – she'll be more excited about brand, knowing it can be measured and that the benefits will directly impact our bottom line.

HUMAN RESOURCES LEADER LOG

Collaboration and cooperation are central to our brand promise. But HR feels too isolated from other departments, to me. Maybe a brand-communications task force -- consisting of a combination of PR and HR -- would be a good first step for us.

SALES LEADER LOG

Our sales efforts are very successful; we exceed our targets quarter to quarter, year in and year out. Obviously, sales needs to be very well-represented in the brand research (customers, employees and managers) and on the brand-tools development team. That way, what's good about sales' contribution to customer experiences will be incorporated into our brand tools.

NOTES

[1] Gross, Neil, 'Valuing "Intangibles": A Tough Job, But It Has To Be Done,' *BusinessWeek* (6 August 2001), p 54

[2] Watson Wyatt Worldwide (2001/2002 survey report) *Human Capital Index*™

[3] Brelis, M (3 June 2001) 'I've Got The Trust For CEO Bethune, The Key to Continental's Turnaround Is An Empowered Work Force, Not Slash-and-Burn,' *The Boston Globe*

[4] (Spring 1997) *SafeFood News*, 1 (3), SafeFood Rapid Response Network, Colorado State University

[5] Lisser, Eleena De, 'How to Get an Airline to Wait for Your Plumber,' (2 July 2002), *The Wall Street Journal*, D1

[6] Harris Interactive Website, http://www.harrisinteractive.com/solutions/equitrend.asp

[7] Bethune, G (1998) *From Worst to First,* John Wiley & Sons, Inc.

[8] Ibid.

NEXT STEPS: THE JOURNEY ACTION PLAN

Your next step is to apply what you've learned. We've included this chart to help you take a next step. It includes each step in the process, what each step requires in terms of tactics, and a check off box for when you've done that part of the action plan. The rest is up to you.

Processes	Tactics	Complete?
ID Strengths and Values	In-depth interviews with stakeholders	
Reveal Tools	Mission, Values, Story, Principle, Personality, Association	
ID Company Activities	Current Practices, Assets, Culture, Communications	
Create Compelling Customer Experience	Proposed Practices, Assets, Culture, Communications	
Create Alignment Plan	One year action plan	
Perform Alignment Actions	Create fix it teams, new job descriptions, etc.	
Measure Results	Benchmarking, Awareness, ROI, Brand integration score, Alignment report card, Communications audit, Brand awareness, Brand equity, Customer satisfaction, Price-premium comparisons, Focus groups, Customer retention rates, Repurchase speed, Market share	
Reap Benefits	Profit margins, Time to purchase decision, Increase in WOM, Repeat purchase rates, Stock price, Employee morale, Employee productivity.	

CHAPTER

13

Revitalize An
Existing Organization

REVITALIZE AN EXISTING ORGANIZATION

What, then, is the true Gospel of consistency? Change. Who is the really consistent man? The man who changes. Since change is the law of his being, he cannot be consistent if he is stuck in a rut.

–Mark Twain

Along the road, companies get stuck. Sometimes they become complacent. Sometimes they start believing their own myths (e.g. 'we're the best in the market and no one can touch us'). Sometimes they let competition dictate their actions. Sometimes their day-to-day busyness prevents them from looking at the long term. And sometimes a new generation passes them by.

Whether marketplace changes or a loss of vision are making your customer experience less compelling, rerouting your brand needs to be a part of every leader's journey. If a company doesn't look at revitalizing itself by continually fine-tuning its customer experience, then it is in danger of being left behind by the marketplace.

A 50-year-old non-profit industry association was losing its way – with factions and chapters at odds with each other and with the charter of the organization. All of this dysfunction was eroding the brand that the organization had worked so hard to develop. And the younger generation was not joining at the same rate as earlier generations. The group was in danger of losing its relevancy in the market.

The integrated branding process helped bring this organization's board of directors back to the central benefits and value the organization offered its members. Then, by applying the brand, the organization found new ways to communicate, new products to offer, and new ways to make itself relevant to its membership.

A brand principle of creating opportunity led the organization to shift its focus from reactive to creative action. This principle gave the staff a better compass for guiding its programmatic decisions. New programs were added, such as a mentor program that connected older members with younger ones that let members and prospects know that they would have *more* opportunities in their field if they participated. What's more, in the past, every member request was treated with the same priority, with the result that staff members were scattered and overworked. The brand principle and mission gave the staff a way to prioritize requests. Focusing on creating opportunity has resulted in higher member retention, while the group has been able to increase new member rates by 5% in the first year.

Does Your Organization Need Revitalization?   *Point of Interest*

The following questions can help you determine if your organization needs to revitalize itself:

- When you do something new, is it mostly reactive or is it based on proactive initiatives?
- Have you defined a strategic role and do you consistently explore new ways to fulfill it with your customer base?
- Has the number of customers who define themselves as 'loyal' or 'committed' been dropping? Is their average age increasing? Are annual purchases as determined by revenue or profit margin decreasing?
- Do you use the same customer profile year in and year out, or do you consider what matters most to customers right now?
- Do you spend most of your research and development budget on trying to improve the features of existing products or to beat the competition?
- Do you identify innovative ways for solving the same customer needs that your current product solves?
- Has it been a long time since you took a significant investment risk on a new product or service line?

As this example shows, you can use the integrated branding process as a lever to get unstuck. Companies that lose their way find that brand development and brand alignment refocus them on their true value.

They use the brand development process to gain market insight and refocus on what matters to customers. They also find that the brand integration process sparks new employee action and raises morale.

SIX WAYS TO REVITALIZE

According to W. Chan Kim and Renée Mauborgne, 'Most companies focus on matching and beating their rivals, and as a result their strategies tend to converge along the same basic dimensions of competition... As rivals try to outdo one another, they end up competing solely on the basis of incremental improvements in cost or quality or both.'[1]

Is your company stuck in the doldrums? There are six ways that living the integrated brand can help revitalize a company. These are:
- identifying what's valuable to customers;
- revealing self-defeating beliefs;
- overcoming inertia;
- improving decision-making;
- decreasing complacency;
- encouraging long-term thinking.

IDENTIFYING WHAT'S VALUABLE TO CUSTOMERS

One of the problems well established, mature companies have is that they are inundated with data, and can't identify which data are meaningful. Often, the collective history of the company is what drives it forward. Companies that are set in their ways too often conduct research to justify an existing point of view, not to discover how the company is perceived, how the market or economy is changing or what it could do to meet customer needs in new ways.

The research conducted at the beginning of the integrated brand development process (Chapter 2: Bring Your Brand Into Focus) is of a different stripe, because its questions are constructed to identify what's important to customers. Companies that practice integrated branding conduct annual brand measurement research and keep brand report cards that identify the changing issues that are important to customers (Chapter 12: Measure Your Brand's Effectiveness). This style of research leaves room for customers to express their real needs and for researchers to explore new product and service concepts.

General Administration (GA) is an agency of the State  of Washington. It provides services to over 100 other agencies in the areas of product or service procurement including office supplies and surplus purchasing, and tenant improvements, car rentals, space leasing, mail services, cleaning and grounds keeping.

While GA was successfully providing these services, it faced several issues typical of an organization that is organized along divisional lines. There was very little cross-selling and customers who used multiple divisions were frustrated by the need to work with multiple GA

representatives. GA also wanted to understand what customers valued about it so that it could further meet customers needs.

Our research determined that GA had assets around not only a depth of experience in each area, but also understood how to navigate its agency customers through government-mandated accountability processes—such as the bid process. These processes tended to divert agencies' valuable time into managing operations rather than meeting their charters. GA also provided customers with one-stop support, further simplifying each agency's operations management.

Based on this, General Administration developed a strategic role of "essential operations partner for state agencies" and began immediately to offer cost-effective services packages that have covered many agencies' total operations needs. Employees use a brand principle of "responsive and responsible" to set the bar for service standards. GA has also built ongoing brand improvement into its business plan through annual brand strategies.

Brand research can also be effectively used to pinpoint how the company can serve each new generation. As companies age, their customers tend to age with them. As each new generation reaches its teens or twenties, it presents the same marketing challenge the company faced at its inception – what kind of experience can the company create that will be compelling? The trick is to create a compelling story for these new customers while staying relevant to older generations of customers.

In April 2002, in recognition of the need to stay relevant to old readers and appeal to a new generation in light of declining readership, *The Wall Street Journal* introduced a redesigned paper. In an attempt to be more reader-friendly, the new look included color, an overhauled page one and a new section called 'Personal Journal.'

FIGURE 13.1: THE WALL STREET JOURNAL: PERSONAL JOURNAL

According to Robert Samuelson of *Newsweek*, 'A paper that once catered to a narrow business and investing class with stock tables and exhaustive reporting must reach a larger crowd with new anxieties and, given its affluence, new demands. It's not that younger customers are better than older customers. But they're necessary customers, and whether the Journal succeeds in capturing them will be the decisive test of its redesign.'[2]

While a lot of writing has been done on the faddishness of teen years, great consumer brands use strategies that build long-term relationships with each new generation. Pepsi and Coke are both masters at 'evergreening' their brands. Pepsi focuses on teens through its *'Pepsi Generation'* strategy that features young people and up-and-coming young performers. It stays relevant to older drinkers by implying that they are 'with it' if they drink Pepsi. Coke inserts its distinctive labeling and symbols into happy family experiences – kids just see it as a fixture in their lives from an early age.

Disney has a program called 'Disney Dimensions,' a nine-day executive orientation course designed to help executives understand and live the Disney brand. Part of the course includes donning a Pluto or Mickey suit at one of the theme parks. It's a key component that ensures Disney executives remain in touch with the customer experience. For Anne Sweeney, president of the Disney Channel (www.disneychannel.com), having kids swarm all around her opened her eyes to the importance of creating good characters and stories and the impact they have on Disney's brand. She says that direct contact with consumers is the best way to figure out what's missing in Disney Channel programs.

'You need a lot of different things to stay in touch,' she says. 'Having the ability to dress up as a character was a piece of it. It all boils down to listening.'[3]

The National Geographic Society was founded in 1888 for 'the increase and diffusion of geographic knowledge.' The first magazine was a studious, scientific journal with a nondescript, dull-brown cover. Over the years, changes in color, typography and imagery have allowed it to reflect the sensibilities of new generations. More importantly, now in its third century, the society has managed to stay relevant to subsequent generations by extending the medium: 'After more than a century the National Geographic Society today is propelled by new concerns: the alarming lack of geographic knowledge among our nation's young people and the pressing need to protect the planet's natural resources. As our mission grows in urgency and scope, the Society continues to develop new and exciting vehicles for broadening our reach and enhancing our legendary ability to bring the world to our millions of members.' [4]

Today, the Society is the world's largest nonprofit scientific and educational organization and those vehicles include not only the original flagship magazine, but also books, CDs, DVDs, *National Geographic for Kids (Classroom Magazine), Traveler Magazine*, TV: EXPLORER on MSNBC, TV: National Geographic Channel, radio expeditions and e-mail newsletters all tied together with the familiar golden rectangle – which has been part of the magazine's front cover for over a century.

FIGURE 13.2: NATIONAL GEOGRAPHIC MAGAZINE

The inaugural 1888 issue of National Geographic magazine.

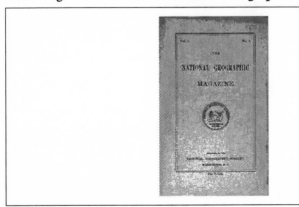

FIGURE 13.3 NATIONAL GEOGRAPHIC WEBSITE
The National Geographic Channel (www.nationalgeographic.com/tv/ channel/index.html) is an example of how National Geographic has stayed relevant to new generations.

　　While determining what is relevant to customers is important, it can leave a company facing a difficult decision – does it change based on what's currently popular, or stay with its long-term brand assets? This is a question that Jeep has been facing with the popularity of 'street' off-road vehicles. A recent article by Jeffrey Ball in *The Wall Street Journal* states '...the people behind the wheel at Jeep are beginning to think the unthinkable: The brand can safely be enlarged to include vehicles that are more like cars, don't claim to be able to survive the Rubicon Trail (a punishing off-road trail in Nevada and California) and, in some cases, don't even have four-wheel drive...Such talk is sacrilege to Jeep disciples.'5 Jeep-owner Kathleen Snyder says of these two-wheel-drive versions: 'Many Jeep owners think it's a waste of time and an insult to the Jeep name.6' G. Clotaire Rapaille, a consultant in Boca Raton, Florida agrees. Rapaille says that many consumers think rugged vehicles like Jeeps are cool but can justify paying a lot of money for them only by citing their go-anywhere capability – which he calls an 'intellectual alibi.'

REVEALING SELF-DEFEATING BELIEFS
Many cultural beliefs are invisible to senior management. For example, in a building services company with several divisions, each division thought it was the only one with quality people and practices, hence would not recommend the other divisions' services to clients. But

no one identified this as a belief, so it couldn't be resolved. Instead, people in the company bemoaned the lack of cross selling, without understanding why it didn't occur. Short-term fixes to the apparent cross-selling problem could not solve the underlying – and more foundational – cultural problem of a lack of inter-division trust.

The integrated brand process allowed the company to ask questions that had never been asked before, such as *'what is each division's biggest weakness?'* This process reveals underlying values and cultural rules of the road that can then be exposed, hence acted on consciously. In the case of the building services company, by identifying the lack-of-trust issue, the company could work on the real problem, resulting in increased multi-service sales.

Cultures can also hold two conflicting beliefs at the same time, and not know it. One company, an XML software organization, had expertise at the heart of its brand. But cultural norms that resulted from personality characteristics of friendly and approachable kept it from touting that deep expertise for fear of putting others off or seeming as if its employees were not listening. Once the conflict between these cultural norms and the brand principle was identified, the company became more intentional about offering its extensive knowledge to the market in a way that was still true to its personality.

Other self-defeating beliefs extend beyond corporate culture to a general pessimism about both a company's offerings and its customers. One such example was the Harlem Globetrotters basketball team. Started in 1926 to showcase the talents of African-American ballplayers, the team was believed to be the best basketball team in the world. In the 1980s, as the U.S. NBA league became dominant, the Globetrotters were increasingly irrelevant as a competitive basketball team – which was a key component – along with comedy routines and amazing basketball feats – to their success. Worse still, 'the people running the company did not respect the players or the product and were indifferent to the customers,' according to Mannie Jackson, chairman, writing in a *Harvard Business Review* article. Jackson challenged this self-defeating belief in his very first meeting with the team: 'I started talking about building a competitive team, being known for our contributions to charity, being good to kids, and rebuilding the quality of the organization.' The result? In 1992, the company lost about U.S. $1 million on gross revenues of U.S. $9 million; in 2001 this has turned into U.S. $6 million in profit on U.S. $60 million in revenues with attendance rising from 300,000 to 2 million in the same period.[7]

OVERCOMING INERTIA

Integrated branding results in brand tools that inject energy, direction and focus into an organization. The tools focus strategy on what is important to the customer experience, rather than on activities that are less relevant to the people who matter: those that give your company money. By focusing on your strategic role in the customer experience, which reflects changing customer needs, it's a lot easier to keep from getting into a rut in the first place. For decades, Polaroid Corporation focused on a product, Polaroid cameras, that produced instant pictures from a special film process. What would have happened if they had focused on a strategic role of providing instant images instead? If you doubt that this would have made a difference, consider the fact that the first digital cameras appeared on the market in the early 1980s, yet Polaroid entered this market only in the last couple of years.

An example of successfully overcoming inertia through branding is specialty outdoor retailer Patagonia. Founded in 1975 to serve the needs of climbing fanatics with environmentally sound equipment, Patagonia was originally staffed by those same passionate fanatics. Rapid growth ensued, and by the mid-1980s, the company found that it had sold its products into retail accounts that couldn't deliver on the brand promise. As a result, the company was eroding brand equity and disenfranchising customers. 'Sales staff often didn't understand the relative value of one fabric over another, and store managers didn't display products in a way that would help customers understand their use or value. Customer expectations were shaped on the retail floor and if the product didn't meet expectations – even if they were unrealistic – customer anger was directed at us. Some products aren't meant to be waterproof – but if the customer is told they are, then they had better be.'[8] Consequently, the company reduced its wholesale accounts by almost one-third, hired visual merchandisers to help establish on-brand Patagonia sections in key stores, ran seminars for dealers and hired sports specialists to research and determine the best shops for their products. In the mid-1990s, Patagonia moved both its mail order operations and distribution center to Reno, Nevada, putting it closer to the high Sierra Mountains and allowing it to hire more back-country athletes, once again staying in tune with its roots and staying close to the customer experience.

Today the company continues to stay focused by hiring outdoor and environmental fanatics who use, test, and evolve the company's products. The result is that Patagonia is designing and selling innovative, standard-setting clothing and equipment. And the phone at the company's headquarters is answered by an 11-time world champion freestyle Frisbee player!

Once you're clear about your strategic role and what customer experience you are providing, ongoing research can keep you on track by telling you how customer needs are changing, or how they may need to change. Replacing a product-driven strategy with one that is customer-driven is a very powerful revitalization step.

Brand research can also help you handle sticky political problems. One high-tech service company had a division that was very different than the others, and not performing well financially. The owner of the company was personally attached to the division, so it was allowed to drain resources from the company. After conducting research, the entire management team could see how this division was not manifesting the company's brand tools, and instead of being a brand asset, detracted from the company's overall brand promise. This information gave the management team the ammunition to convince the owner to make some hard decisions, ultimately dismantling the division and deploying its staff elsewhere in the company.

IMPROVING BRAND-BASED DECISION MAKING

Because one result of the integrated branding process is a set of tools individuals use to make on-brand decisions (Chapter 3: Tools to Live Your Brand), people start to make better decisions with less need for micromanagement. For example, Newhall Land, a community planner in Los Angeles County, has always been committed to making its planned communities more valuable. But once it identified its brand principle as responsible community perspective, it had a better way to make decisions. Now, when it makes choices about planning, charitable giving or communications, the decisions are focused in a way that demonstrates a responsible community perspective to its audiences. For instance, for planning a new community, it teamed up with a local conservancy to ensure that the local wildlife habitat was preserved. The company can hold its head up, knowing that it is acting on brand and that, ultimately, its customers will appreciate the additional community value those on-brand decisions result in.

Focusing decisions on what customers value about your brand is the way to get out of the ditch and back on the right road. Eighty-two-year-old clothing retailer Eddie Bauer lost its outdoor roots over the last decade – instead it featured dress-casual clothing lines with deep discounts. The once-successful company's sales were in a free fall and it went long periods without a CEO. The company is now returning to 'an authentic, original American lifestyle brand, known for our innovative spirit and a passion for creating a first-rate customer experience.' Dress-casual will decrease from about half to 15% of the store's lines and be replaced by washable suede, leather, rainwear and down outerwear. 'Versatility and innovation will be key features of the outerwear,' said Martin Zaepfel, president and CEO of Bauer parent company, The Spiegel Group, Inc. [9]

DECREASING COMPLACENCY

If a company is doing well, it's very easy for it to a) keep doing things exactly the same as always, and b) see danger signs after it is too late to do anything about them. The problem with the first mindset is that innovation and staying ahead of the market in that environment become impossible. The problem with the second is that if the market changes rapidly, the company has very little time to overcome its inertia.

Campbell Soup Company is a company that failed to see some warning signs. With a 100-plus year history of marketing soup as a convenience food (made into a cultural icon by Andy Warhol), its 70% market share lulled the company into a false sense of security. The company failed to recognize that for generations raised on fast food, convenience had a different definition. Consequently, despite market trend indicators such as yogurt in a tube, pop top containers, peanut butter slices and drive-through coffee stands, the company was late entering the ready-to-serve segment. Earnings slipped and unit sales declined. At the same time, sales of the uncondensed Progresso brand rose 18%. [10]

In July 2001, the company announced a series of investment initiatives focused on improved product quality, increased marketing, including advertising, and accelerated innovation. In a press release, Douglas R. Conant, Campbell's president and CEO said: 'This plan represents the single most comprehensive commitment to revitalization ever undertaken in the 132-year history of Campbell Soup Company. Bold action is required. Bold action is being taken.' [11]

Conant also said, 'Soup is our middle name. We know more about soup products, packaging, and manufacturing processes than anyone else. And from a consumer perspective, we know the soup category inside out. We just haven't used our knowledge to full advantage. We have been slow to innovate. We have not kept pace with competitive quality moves. And we have been inconsistent in our advertising messages and spending. Change is underway. This year we have been encouraged by a 5% increase in consumer purchases of soup. As we have invested behind our franchises, we have seen growth. However, we have more to do to reassert our leadership position in the face of aggressive competition.' [12]

New initiatives include soups in a sippable, single-serving, microwaveable container, adding 'pop 'n pour' lids on its Swansons broths and easy-open lids on its condensed soup. As of press time, it was too soon to tell how customers were responding to these new initiatives and what the net effect would be. In February 2002, the company reported lower shipments and a weak quarter for condensed soups. According to Conant, 'Although we are not satisfied with this performance, we are confident that as our transformation plan unfolds, we will revitalize this important franchise.' [13]

A clear brand and ongoing measurement of that brand can provide the impetus for jump-starting change. That's because an integrated branding focus forces companies to stay in close contact with its customers. Another way to build in anti-complacency action is through your brand team. Part of the ongoing mission of the brand team should be to ask the 'what if' questions that are a part of conducting annual measurement research. Assuming your brand team and brand manager include senior management and are reporting to the CEO, this group has the opportunity to continue to keep the company embracing change – when changes in your marketplace warrant it.

ENCOURAGING LONG-TERM THINKING

Because integrated branding starts a thought process that encourages increasing differentiation over time, people also get in the habit of thinking long-term. And long-term thinking provides companies with sustainable, rather than fleeting, advantage. When employees start to think about everything they do from a *'how can I act using our brand principle to continuously set us apart in the market?'* point of view, in addition to '*how can I increase sales or profits for the short term?*' then the entire company is set up to prosper for both short- and long-term.

Long-term thinking is visionary, because it requires people to predict what customers will want from you in two, five, or 10 years, then plan for those scenarios. Vision based on what you do well is something that customers like to see. It sets you apart as a leader, and creates greater customer commitment.

One company that has done this well is Intel. When the company first began branding its processors, the industry was skeptical. Intel has sustained its brand investment, making Intel Inside one of the few technology ingredient brands to have a dollar value at the cash register.

CREATE A BRAND STRATEGY THAT KEEPS THINGS FRESH

Given that change is necessary, how does one stay true to one's brand? The answer is to know what is immutable about your brand, and what can be safely refreshed. The brand manager's mantra should always be: 'What should we keep? What can we safely update?'

In answering these questions, first, keep your core brand consistent. What's unique about your approach to customers shouldn't change, the way you express it should. If you consistently use your strategic role, brand principle, personality and values over a period of years, you'll build defensible differentiation.

EXECUTIVE LEADER LOG

They've just hired me as COO to come in and make some much-needed changes in how this company does things. But every change I try to make is met with 'that will never work,' 'we'll never be able to do that,' and 'no one will really buy into that and make it happen.' Maybe integrated branding's the key that will unlock the potential I see all around me. I think I can advocate this brand thing – no one would expect something so 'feel good' from a hard-liner like me, so they just may go for it – and use the results to fuel the changes I think we have to make if this company's going to survive long-term.

HUMAN RESOURCES LEADER LOG

Our managers are being brow beaten by the executive team for their complacency and slow-mo inertia. They, in turn, are punishing their direct reports and department workers with vague (but loud!) demands for initiative and action. Perhaps integrated branding could help put the 'leader' back in all our company's 'leadership initiatives,' by giving us a way to set clear direction and motivate (vs. punish) people to work together towards exciting goals. I think if I proposed this as a solution to each group based on the pain they're feeling, I could get buy-off pretty quickly (especially since it will take the pressure off them).

SALES LEADER LOG

If integrated branding could get the board off our backs about short-term quarterly revenues and let sales do the job it's so good at – relating to our customers' long-term, deep-infrastructure needs and providing great consulting (even if it means sacrificing a short-term sale here and there because it's the right thing to do for the customer) – I'm all for it. We really need something that helps the board and the company see eye to eye. Note: draft a memo about the 'seeing eye to eye' need and send it to the CEO.

NOTES

[1] Kim, W. Chan, and Mauborgne, Renée, 'Creating New Market Space,' (January-February 1999), *Harvard Business Review*, p 83

[2] Samuelson, R (22 April 2002) 'How the WSJ is like Jell-O,' *Newsweek*, p 45

[3] Kelley, J (1 February 2002) 'Trading Places: To truly learn about customers, executives are taking roles on the front lines of their businesses,' *Context*

[4] National Geographic Web site: www.nationalgeographic.com/birth/nfor7at. html

[5] Ball, Jeffrey, (24 April 2001) 'Will Watered Down Version of Jeep Lure Consumers or Affront Loyalists?' The Wall Street Journal, p B1

[6] Ibid.

[7] Jackson, Mannie, ((May 2001), 'Bringing a Dying Brand Back to Life,' *Harvard Business Review*, pp 53-61

[8] Excerpted from 'A brief description of how we got here,' on Patagonia's Web site: http://a248.e.akamai.net/f/248/2630/1h/www.patagonia.com/pdf/defining_ quality.pdf

[9] Tice, Carol, (21-27 June, 2002), 'Bauer hears call of the wild,' *Puget Sound Business Journal*, pp 1, 76

[10] After 100 years of condensed soup, Campbell's looks to get hot again, Hope Yen, Associated Press Newswires, 20 August 2001

[11] Campbell Soup Company press release, July 27, 2001

[12] Ibid.

[13] Campbell Soup Company press release, February 13, 2002.

CHAPTER

START-UPS: BRAND DRIVEN CHALLENGES

Success is a journey, not a destination.

–Edmund Burke, British statesman

How do you live your integrated brand when you don't have a customer experience or brand promise yet? Revealing a brand for a start-up is something like answering the question of *'which came first, the chicken or the egg?'* The challenge the start-up faces is to create its brand with little of the customer or cultural data of a more mature brand. On the positive side, a start-up that seriously considers brand direction early will make faster and more lasting inroads with customers than the competition and, if desired, be better poised for a liquidity event than its non-branded competitors. A start-up also has more leeway to explore what it wants to be when it grows up, versus revealing what's already there. The question start-ups need to answer is how to maximize the likelihood that prospective customers will embrace its unique customer experience.

Building a start-up brand is a group effort. To create the most effective brand tools, everyone in a small start-up should be part of the branding process. We recommend your very first discussions about company strategy focus on the customer experience you want to deliver and what company actions will help you do that. Then fine-tune the preliminary brand experience and preliminary brand tools by testing your assumptions in the marketplace over time.

If your company thinks that it should focus on product or service development only and considers brand only as something 'nice to have,' you are already missing the boat. If you understand that profitability is based on meeting a need through a compelling customer experience, then you're ready for integrated branding.

An integrated brand can give you a huge competitive head start. Companies that create a strong brand and use it in all decisions will create products and services that beat the competition. Also, due to the cumulative results of integrated branding over months and years, your initial focus on a compelling customer experience will drive market share dominance.

There are other advantages to beginning the integrated branding process while you are still a start-up. The first is creating an understanding of the best product or service direction you can head in. Ironically, identifying *what* customer experience need you want to fulfill, rather than what product or service you are going to produce, will keep your offerings on the right track. You'll avoid a series of traps – that we've termed me-too, short life span and insufficient experience offerings.

'Me-too' are products or service offerings that look nearly identical to the competition's and so become subject to price discounting.

'Short-life-span' products are those that make little market impact because they aren't effective at addressing a customer experience need.

'Insufficient experience' offerings don't fulfill enough of a given customer experience to compel the customer to keep using the product.

Defining your strategic role in meeting a customer experience need early will allow you to position your product or service for a current sweet spot while maintaining a clear direction for the long term. Placing your product or service in the context of a strategic role that meets a major customer need will allow you to flexibly respond to changing customer preferences and/or new technologies while creating high-demand products in the near term. Do you define your business as selling insurance products? Your strategic role is probably closer to providing financial security. Do you think your business is building faster and better computers? Andy Grove, chairman of Intel, who has more of a claim to this business than perhaps anyone, says, 'We need to look at our business as more than simply the building and selling of computers. Our business is the delivery of information and lifelike interactive experiences.'[1]

In an article by Rochelle Burbury titled 'Meet the New Marketing Manager,' she brings home the influence your strategic role will have on

244

how you define your business: 'Virgin's trick has been to — in the terms of Global Foresight marketing futurist Nick Marsh — reinvent its own industry. Virgin Blue considers itself more in the hospitality industry than transport. Passengers are treated more like guests. 'The last thing we want to do is be benchmarked on the transport industry,' says David Huttner. 'We're run not much differently than hotels or a restaurant. It's the concept of having guests in our home for a few hours.'

In fact, Virgin has taken a whole lot of transport industry best practices and turned them on their head. For example, it doesn't use air bridges but allows passengers to walk across the tarmac, re-creating, says Huttner, a 'Casablanca ambience' to flying. It has no lounges, in-flight meals or frequent-flyer program. 'Service,' it says, 'is not about a boxed meal.'[2]

Another benefit to branding early is determining a rationale for brand naming and structure. Most companies create brands haphazardly – either based on each new product or service they offer or using the company name as the umbrella brand for all products or services. This can confuse customers through too many different brands or too many different experiences under the same brand name. Mapping a consistent brand structure at the onset will provide you with both significant economies of scale and brands that are customer-experience appropriate.

A third benefit to branding early is that it gives you the ability to identify and manage brand assets. Brand assets can be tools, strategies, practices, the company's reputation, cultural norms or associations – anything that your customers would pay more for as part of their experience with your brand. One example of an asset would be a building management company's unique building services such as a concierge and valet parking, resulting from a brand principle of people-friendly buildings.

Identifying brand assets also allows you to properly value them. By investing in assets that enhance your customer experience, you realize significantly higher company valuations should you decide to sell or go public. Brand assets are also indicators of what differentiates you from the competition and are key into figuring out your brand tools. Over time, you may want to add additional brand assets in response to changing customer needs. Brand assets are one fruit of living the brand and an important factor in developing unbreakable customer loyalty and premium prices.

Another benefit to developing integrated branding early is hard wiring living the brand into your culture. It's much easier to develop an employee base that uses brand tools (essential to realizing the payoff from integrated branding) when you are dealing with just a few people. New hires will then automatically receive brand training as part of their orientation and consider living the brand just another cultural norm – 'the way we do things around here.'

WHEN TO BEGIN BRAND WORK

The process of defining your brand building blocks of strategic role and unique customer experience should begin when the new company is just a concept on the drawing board. But, the company must have certain basics in place to create an integrated brand. When should you think about creating brand tools? Usually in the first three-to-12 months of operations you'll have done enough work around a role, your unique approach and customer experience to begin seeing where your company value lies.

How do you know you're ready to brand? Questions you can use to help determine this include:

- *'Have we committed to a product or service direction?'*
- *'Have we done the research to ensure that there is a sufficient market to meet our growth projections?'*
- *'Have we tested the role and product/service direction with potential customers?'*
- *'Are we able to deliver on our proposed customer experience?'*

Another question is how much influence start-ups should let financial partners have over their concept. We've seen many instances where getting financing becomes the sole driver of company direction. The worst-case scenario is to create a company around what Wall Street is rewarding today. By the time your product is at market, Wall Street will have moved on to something else, and you'll be stuck with a less-than-optimal concept. It's better to stay the course on delivering customer value, while focusing financial communications and road shows into telling a simple but compelling growth story.

Another pre-requisite for determining brand tools is to have at least part of the senior management team in place. Management – particularly the president, CEO, founder and other executives – will set the company's unique approach to its business including its strategic role, customer experience, brand tools, and general culture. The management team's focus and passion will determine the company's unique strengths because it's their combined experience that determines what's valuable.

Consider two start-up companies that meet golfers' needs for carrying their golf clubs around a golf course. Company A's management team may have a passion for meeting the golfer's every need on the course – not just carrying their clubs. They might create a brand principle of experience breadth and use it to answer the question of how clubs should be moved. The result might be a non-motorized golf cart that has a cup holder, insulated storage area for hot and cold drinks and a computer that not only acts as a scorecard but also analyzes and suggests improvements to a golfer's game.

Company B's management team has a passion for creating healthy exercise experiences. They create a principle of mental and physical improvement and use it to identify that the act of pulling a golf cart puts great strain on the arm and back muscles and could result in back problems. Further, the act of constantly righting a two-wheeled cart adds to the potential for harm. They create a healthy exercise experience by designing a cart that is meant to be pushed rather than pulled, with a three-wheel base for greatly increased stability.

By focusing on brand tools that mirror senior management passions, these companies will be able to innovate in ways that continue to enhance the value of their brands, products and services over time. Of course, they would also use market acceptance and feedback as a guide for improving and fine-tuning their brands. Company B, for instance, may find that its business is not confined to golf but may include many other repetitive physical activities. A thorough understanding of your focus will help guide the types of products and services that make the most sense for the company to be involved in – our experience is that senior management's passion for a type of product, service or experience is the best determinant of brand direction.

After you've created your initial brand, how do you know when to revisit and finalize your brand tools? We recommend that you conduct benchmark research when you have at least a few customers that know you well, which could be as soon as three to six months after your initial product or service launch. Following that, we recommend that you conduct an annual measurement and brand review process where your team creates a brand report card. See Chapter 12: Measure

Your Brand's Effectiveness for more information on measuring brand strength and awareness.

START-UP MYTHS THAT ARE SELF-DEFEATING

All entrepreneurs believe that their start-ups are unique. Many will also think that what they've thought of is so good that they don't need to do anything to be successful apart from the product. They ask, '*Who cares about unique approach or differentiation when we're in a totally new market?*' The answer is that if they're successful, they will soon have competition. And there are almost always other ways of solving the same problem currently. By differentiating from the start, they will create a greater defensible advantage and have to rely less on a product/feature horse race to stay ahead. Additionally, because people are solving the problem somehow without their product, the start-up has to break through current marketplace beliefs. The branding process provides the start-up with more direction for educating the market on its differentiation, as well.

We thought we would include a few myths that you can use to test whether you are creating a strong, sustainable brand or a one-hit wonder:

- **Myth 1:** 'If we have a good product/service, sales will propel us to long-term profitability.'
  Debunked by: A good product or service may result in short-term sales if you have a good sales force. Competition, lack of differentiation, customer experience knowledge and product direction makes the long-term outlook uncertain. Terry Drayton, the former CEO of Homegrocer.com knows this first hand. Drayton built the online grocery store into one of America's largest before it was sold to The Webvan Group. A year later Webvan declared bankruptcy. According to Drayton in an interview with the Seattle Post-Intelligencer, 'Webvan's demise did not mean shoppers disliked the service. Webvan failed,' he said, 'because of poor management decisions, costly marketing campaigns and an inability to connect with the customer.'[3]
- **Myth 2:** 'We'll succeed because we need only a fraction of the market to buy from us.'
  Debunked by: It doesn't matter how big the potential market is. If you don't have a core customer group that completely

identifies with your approach to solving their problem or meeting their needs, you will not get a large enough customer base to succeed.

- **Myth 3:** 'The quality of our product or service will attract and keep customers over the long term.'
  Debunked by: Quality is essential – but it can't sustain sales without help from the rest of the customer experience. In the past, quality products or services have lost for a litany of reasons ranging from delivery channel problems to the wrong brand image. *In Differentiate or Die*, authors Jack Trout and Steve Rivkin cite a Gallup poll that found that only 28% of executives had achieved significant results in either profitability or market share from their quality initiatives.[4]

- **Myth 4:** 'In time, all products and services become commodities.'
  Debunked by: Non-commodity products abound in mature markets. Southwest Airlines demonstrates this in passenger air travel, for instance. Coca-Cola gets a premium for sugar water and Morton does the same for table salt. Several companies have successfully branded even the most plentiful substance on earth, water — enabling branded versions such as Perrier to be sold for a higher price.

- **Myth 5:** 'Customers repeat purchase mainly because a product or service worked.'
  Debunked by: True with some customers. Others – particularly your loyal and committed customers – buy for a litany of reasons including: they like the experience or the people they are buying from, feel more taken care of, feel the future development direction is better on one product more than another, or due to the company's reputation. Around 70% of the U.S. population admits they buy using brand as a key criteria. Given subconscious motivations, the real number is probably much higher.

- **Myth 6:** 'The only important bottom-line measurements are revenues, margins and net income growth.'
  Debunked by: Strong financials are the result, not the cause. Strong customer relationships and customer experience are what drives the bottom line. It's these factors that create higher margins, increased sales and sustainable profitability.

- **Myth 7:** 'We can manage our offering better and more cost-effectively in-house rather than by partnering or co-branding.'
Debunked by: The most effective way for a young company to grow its brand is through sharing the equity of established brands. Partnering also allows you to fill customer experience holes. In the early 1990s, the Harlem Globetrotters basketball team was in restart mode – with very little brand awareness. Chairman Mannie Jackson observes, 'Our relationship with Disney has worked out very well. When commercial partners or others hear that we're aligned with Disney, it locks us into their minds as family entertainment.'[5]
- **Myth 8:** 'Our future will depend on how well we execute on our product or service.'
Debunked by: That's half the battle. The other half is delivering the customer experience. You need to consider how you can make your customer experience unique and compelling in every interaction customers have.

CREATING A BRAND-BASED BUSINESS PLAN

When it's time to move from scribblings on a cocktail napkin to a formal business plan, where do you start? Begin by creating a business plan focused on defining your strategic role and delivering a differentiated and compelling customer experience. Most entrepreneurs spend so much time making the numbers work that the whole point of the exercise – creating a compelling, unique and sustainable business – can be lost in the process.

That's because most start-ups consider only three success factors when creating their business plans. They typically start by seeing an unmet need – this then generates enough passion to create a company. The second factor that most consider is potential market size and the likely market percentage that will purchase their product or service first year, second year and on out. The third is making all of the numbers work – from R&D to customer support.

As we covered in the myths section, the unspoken assumption is that a successful company is based on successfully selling the first product or service. While it's essential to have a successful product or service offering, it won't guarantee company longevity or profitability. And even if you are looking for a liquidity event short term, having a brand foundation will create a significant valuation premium when you go to sell. The truth is management teams that focus on customer experiences that build unbreakable customer relationships, and the whole bundle of actions that make them up, have a better result regardless of their long-term objective.

Take, for example, Amazon.com, which succeeded where other online stores failed. In a column written by Stewart Alsop for *Fortune* magazine, Jeff Bezos, CEO and founder of Amazon.com, was asked, 'When are you going to know that Amazon needs to make a profit, rather than putting growth first?' Bezos replied, 'Customers come first. If you focus on what customers want and build a relationship, they will allow you to make money.' That perspective creates a long-term sustainable advantage that is not captured by the quantitative analysis performed by most Wall Street analysts.[6] Amazon.com opened its virtual doors in July 1995 and subsequently turned its first profit in January 2002, primarily by *lowering* prices to customers.[7]

It isn't as difficult as you might think to approach your new business from the customer-experience point of view. If you have already envisioned a new product or service, you can start by extrapolating to the type of strategic role you want to play and the customer experience you would want as a result. Your goal is to get more excited about meeting the unmet customer experience need you've identified than creating a new product. If you can't, you will severely limit the amount of success you will experience.

HOW TO DEFINE YOUR CUSTOMER EXPERIENCE

How do you determine what your strategic role and customer experience should look like? Start by doing your homework. Spend significant time defining current strategic roles and experiences in your industry area and determining what would cause customers to switch to your company in both the short and long term.

Follow up your customer analysis by reviewing your management team's approach – what strengths it brings to its chosen industry others don't. What types of successful brands, products and companies were the management team members involved with in the past? What did they do that made their companies successful? What is your team's management style? A management team that really understands how to drive costs down will do better with a price/performance brand than one that focuses on relationships, for instance. Other management teams are very service and support oriented. Others are interested in a particular product category and creating the very best product they can. Still others seek to add more meaning to their work and focus on finding ways to be socially conscious. These are all seeds from which you can grow a compelling customer experience. Your particular set of strengths, backgrounds and beliefs will help determine what the start-up brand should look like.

A related question to explore is why you decided to start this particular company. Did you see a market need? If so, what was it? Or did you fall in love with a product or service concept? A majority of companies start because someone found an innovative way to fill a customer need. The problem with this cutting-edge approach is that it's very hard to sustain. But knowing what gets you excited will help you to form a relevant brand – innovation may just be one component of a much more compelling strategy.

TARGETING YOUR CORE CUSTOMER

Next, look at differentiation based on what your potential 'core customers' value. Understanding what's important to particular segments, how that overlaps with your company's approach and how competitors position themselves in that space is essential to guiding brand development.

Who are you targeting as core customers? This group needs to be large enough to fuel growth, but small enough that group members share a large percentage of traits. Adults between 25-60 who play golf more than once a week could be the core customers for a three-wheeled golf cart, for instance. The 'everything' golf cart might appeal more to a 25-45 age group who might be more comfortable with the technological aspect of the product. You can determine all of this through focus group and product-trial testing based on your 'test' segments. Since all segments are arbitrary, you'll want to fine-tune your own segments in addition to using published research on age groups, industries, and behaviors such as VALs (values, attitudes and lifestyles).

Once you've determined which segment is your core customer and what other segments might also be good customers, you can then work on focusing your strategic role and creating the ultimate customer experience for these customers. In your offering category, what need are you fulfilling that transcends the initial product or service? (The strategic role). How do you want customers to feel before, during and after using your product or service? (The customer experience.) What combination of products, services and actions will create an unbreakable relationship between your best customers and your company?

Once you define your role and experience, you can create brand tools and use them to keep you on the right path. For instance, let's say you are creating a same-day courier service in metropolitan areas. After conducting extensive research, you discover that there are high-frequency business users who want the experience of not *ever* worrying about the package once it has gone out the door. The proposed service would let customers send packages with the peace of mind that comes from knowing they will be delivered within the time specified. When this is not humanly possible, the company would take on the job of finding out the package's status and new delivery time. In effect, the company becomes an employee of each customer whose job it is to make sure packages are couriered in a timely and secure fashion. Your company has taken on the role of 'we're your best employee' and further enhances it by using online software that intelligently fills in all of the blanks on a delivery order based on just a few key letters or words. The company might also extend the 'best employee role' to coordinating its billing system with customer budgeting systems – reinforcing the 'no worries' experience.

You have decided that the business (your mission) you are really in – the one that transcends delivering packages locally – is being a best employee for simple task outsourcing. This means that you would structure your start-up to fulfill the need of not worrying about all kinds of simple-but-important tasks that don't need to be done in-house, such as flight reservations and same-day confirmations or even receivable collections.

The ultimate customer experience you've created can be delivered through a principle of not worrying. Its benefits are peace of mind and greater productivity. The company's other brand tools – its personality, company values, story and associations – would all support and build on the 'not worrying' experience and the 'best employee for simple task outsourcing' strategic role and mission.

Contrast this approach to a typical business plan where most of the effort would be spent describing the nuts and bolts of the courier service and how much volume would be required to make annual growth and profit projections. The fact is, most business plans lack either a *short-term* or *sustainable* differentiation strategy and the only reason many do well initially is because they have accidentally redefined a category and therefore have a temporary market advantage. The company that focuses on branding a customer experience and getting everyone to live it – such as FedEx, which has a customer experience of highly reliable overnight delivery – is the one that wins.

SEGMENTING BY WHAT CUSTOMERS VALUE

Another way to target your best customer is to clearly define your basic value strategy. There are three pieces to basic value. They are price, quality and level of relationship. Price will vary based on the perceived quality of the experience and product or service. The higher the perceived quality, the higher the price you can charge. And if you charge a low price versus market average, people will discount the value of your offering regardless of its quality. In developing markets, quality drives new pricing models – as brands with less quality are forced to price themselves lower than higher quality brands.

You can (and should) create a customer experience that allows you to charge a price premium. Because customers pay more for the right brand experience, you'll also want to look at your mix of price, quality and relationship in each customer interaction that are part of your product or service offering.

There are four ways to segment quality, price and relationship in your offerings: premium quality, price/value, lowest cost and high relationship. Three of them, premium quality, price/value and high relationship, will be your preferred options if you want to create a sustainable business with the greatest profitability over the long term.

PREMIUM QUALITY

Premium or super-premium quality says that customers are paying more for the product because they value a very high level of performance, reliability and consistency, and service. The drawbacks to this segment are that there are fewer buyers in it, buyers will expect more proof of quality, and, if you make a quality mistake, you are more vulnerable to losing customer loyalty – particularly if you don't fix the mistake quickly.

A large number of companies purport high quality in both their messaging and pricing. However, independent customer experiences, such as those measured in *Consumer Reports*, often don't substantiate these claims. Start-ups aspiring for premium quality should be very sure that they understand what 'premium' means to customers in their category and be sure they can then live up to it.

PRICE/VALUE

Also known as price-performance, these brands typically offer higher-than-average quality at closer-to-market-average prices. This customer experience promises aggressive pricing – you are likely to pass cost savings from innovations along to the customer – and performance that is better than average. You want customers to get that premium feeling from using your product/service and feel they are getting a good deal at the same time. While customers are getting a lot of value for the price, you are also able to fund this by keeping the price well above the market average (10-25%). These brands often get the best of both worlds – a larger customer base and a sustained price-premium over the market average.

LOWEST COST

Often considered generic or commodity brands, these products and services appeal to buyers who have less money or are willing to compromise on quality and service to some degree. Lowest-cost brands have many drawbacks. They are highly vulnerable to price wars by their more profitable competitors or lower-cost providers overseas and are often the least profitable, with little money left over for research and development or for keeping key employees. Lowest cost is rarely a desirable category and most companies end up here due to a lack of differentiation – see 'Start-up myths that are self defeating' earlier in this chapter.

HIGH RELATIONSHIP

High relationship brands are those where the customer has ongoing interactions with the company beyond the sale and beyond basic customer support. These brands appeal to customers who are highly social while also appealing to those looking for a safer buy. High relationship brands are almost always also premium or price/value brands.

The degree of interaction necessary to be high relationship can vary from industry to industry. For companies that sell lawn mowers, a high relationship might look like online reminders for tune-ups or pick-up/ drop-off mower maintenance. For software it might be much more like a constant relationship with regular updates, tips on how to leverage all of a program's functions and a chat site for giving seminars, answering questions and talking to peers. The level of relationship depends on what meets your customer experience definition.

The costs to create relationships don't have to be prohibitive and are more than offset by being able to charge higher-than-market-average prices. If you think high relationship brands don't pertain to your category, consider Ben & Jerry's ice cream. It's just ice cream, and yet it's created a vocal and active customer dialogue. Ben & Jerry's offers seven ways to interact with the company:

> <u>Flavor Locator</u> – Our flavor locator can help you find a store near you that carries your favorite flavor of Ben & Jerry's.
>
> <u>Just The FAQs</u> – Search our database of questions and answers – you can ask us questions here too.
>
> <u>Suggestion Box</u> – You never know where our next out-of-this-world flavor (or other idea) will come from... unless you tell us here!
>
> <u>Euphoria, not!</u> – Had a less than euphoric experience with Ben & Jerry's? We want to hear about it!
>
> <u>General Comment Box</u> – Something you want to tell us about – that isn't a question, suggestion, or less than euphoric experience?
>
> <u>Contact Info</u> – How to get in touch with us when all else fails.
>
> <u>ChunkMail</u> – Subscribe to our FREE Online Newsletter.[8]

The company also features a Citizen Cool contest featuring 150-word essays from customers that are making a positive difference in their communities. This is a great way to tap into the hearts and minds of customers and widen the brand relationship. Citizen Cool has received thousands of entrants and Ben & Jerry's has created a Citizen Cool movie featuring these outstanding customers.[9]

Whatever mix of these value strategies you choose, you will want to make sure that you leverage them with senior management expertise and passion, brand tools, direct employee actions and company activities that support your core customers' brand experience.

Turning Your Start-Up into a Sustainable Brand

Point of Interest

The steps to determining your strategic role, core customer experience and brand tools are:

Step 1: Begin with focusing on and getting excited about what ultimate strategic role and customer experience you want to deliver:

- *What are all of the aspects of that experience and how does your first product or service embody that experience?*
- *Can you deliver the complete experience in-house, or are you dependent on a larger value chain?*
- *If it is a larger value chain, how can you control the quality of the total brand experience?*
- *What is the larger role you want to play in your customers' lives that is not dependent on a particular product or service?*

Step 2: Determine the unique management strengths, focus and passions you bring to this experience and role.

Step 3: Determine what customer segment(s) you will use for your initial focus in developing brand tools and the product or service value you want to represent.

Step 4: Your integrated brand is at the intersection of all of these factors. Create your preliminary brand tools based on what you have learned from steps 1-3.

Step 5: After your customers have had several significant interactions with you, conduct customer research to test and fine-tune your strategic role and experience, core customer segment and brand tools assumptions. The beauty of integrated branding tools is that they act as a compass for company and employee decisions rather than telling you exactly what to do. But if brand tools are based on inaccurate information, they will not produce the best customer experience. On the plus side, brand tools allow you to create a unique customer experience that does not feel manipulative, as is the result of many one-size-fits-all employee-training programs. Brand tools allow employees to genuinely use their creative abilities, but in a way that is on-brand.

EXECUTIVE LEADER LOG

It seems like all the venture capitalists out there these days are demanding business plans that drive to profitability within the first year. Integrated branding, especially getting articulate about the compelling customer experience we're designing our product for, would give us the direction we need to plan and talk intelligently about profitability. And it's sure to give us a leg up on the other entrepreneurs we're competing with for the VC's dollars – I'll bet no one else is thinking beyond their next product delivery deadline.

HUMAN RESOURCES LEADER LOG

We're going to have to start hiring some staff pretty soon if we have any hope of not losing market momentum. We're a great team for making product-design decisions, but I can see hiring decisions – even deciding what positions we should hire for first – really bogging us down. It sounds like integrated branding could be a lifesaver in that department.

SALES LEADER LOG

Every graphic design and product-naming firm in town is knocking at our door, and we're not even to prototyping yet! I'm afraid of what we might end up with in the way of a logo, product name and Web site if we let one of these groups loose on our 'baby' before we can clearly make them understand what's behind it – for us and for the people who want our product. I think I'll propose that we figure out our brand foundation before we invest in something we'll later regret.

NOTES

[1] Pine, Joseph II and Gilmore, James H., (July-August 1998) 'Welcome to the Experience Economy,' *Harvard Business Review*, p 99

[2] Burbury, Rochelle, (10 May 2002), 'Meet the New Marketing Manager,' *Australian Financial Review*, p 26

[3] Cook, John and Leff, Marni, (July 10, 2001) 'Webvan is gone, but HomeGrocer.com may return' *Seattle Post-Intelligencer*

[4] Trout, Jack, Rivkin, Steve, (September 2000), *Differentiate or Die*, Soundview Executive Book Summaries, p 4

[5] Jackson, Mannie, (May 2001), 'Bringing a Dying Brand Back to Life,' *Harvard Business Review*, p 58

[6] Alsop, S (30 April 2001) 'I'm Betting On Amazon.com,' *Fortune*, p 48

[7] Excerpted from a 22 January 2002 Business Wire press release on Amazon.com Web site: www.amazon.com

[8] Excerpted from Ben & Jerry's Web site: http://lib.benjerry.com

[9] Ibid.

CHAPTER

NON-PROFITS: BRAND DRIVEN CHALLENGES

A good person, striving dimly,
Is well aware of the right path.

–Johann Wolfgang Von Goethe, German poet, dramatist

It is a misconception that branding applies only to Fortune 500 companies who can afford prime-time television ads or flashy logos. Integrated branding benefits non-profit organizations by helping them clarify what their unique approach is to their service areas. Non-profit organizations have their own set of obstacles and pitfalls where integrated branding can help. But often, lack of sufficient funding and not defining the experience they are providing the community can get in the way of the journey to effective brand leadership and execution.

Non-profits can realize many benefits from integrated branding. These include:

- a much clearer focus on what the organization should and should not be doing;
- a growth in community awareness due to that focus;
- an increase in donations due to a greater emotional and intellectual identification with the organization's work and mission;
- sustained loyalty of donors and followers during times of crisis.

In this chapter we'll give you an effective approach for answering what need is being filled for the paying customer, the donor of time and money. We'll address how your non-profit can create a unique customer experience for both its clients and its donors, how you can build a non-profit brand on a shoestring budget, and, how to get boards, volunteers and staff to live your brand.

261

Holt International provides adoption and family preservation services in 13 countries throughout the world. It pioneered international adoption in the 1950s and, since then, has been a leader in helping countries build infrastructure and services to help deal with the world's homeless children while helping over 100,000 children find permanent homes.

Holt International wanted to reveal its brand because, over the years, it had added many new services beyond international adoptions—specifically in-country services that gave homeless children a better chance at becoming part of a permanent home. For example, these included developing caring foster care homes in each country—which greatly increases the child's ability to bond with an adoptive family.

HoltInternational
FINDING FAMILIES FOR CHILDREN

In addition, Holt wanted to clarify the differences in its approach from agencies that view adoption as the business of providing children to American families while dispelling the myth that Holt was more costly—many adoption agencies do not disclose the full cost and families are hit with unexpected costs when they go to get their adopted children. Holt executives wanted to make sure that it was telling the whole story to prospective adoptive parents and other constituents.

Parker LePla interviewed 117 constituents, including adoptees and people from most of the countries that Holt works in. Its adopted families and other constituents rated Holt 'off the charts' in everything from service quality to integrity. Holt developed a strategic role of 'finding families for children' which succinctly sums up all of its services. This has helped it understand what new services to develop while clearly differentiating it from for-profit adoption agencies.

Agency president Gary Gamer observes: 'The process of introspection that goes along with the branding process surfaced some long simmering questions within Holt International that ultimately needed to be resolved to enable our organization to move forward and serve more children. Branding has been important for us to both better relate to the external world, and align our internal operations for greater effectiveness and sense of purpose. Joe LePla and his staff were sensitive to our needs and allowed our staff to really take the lead in developing the brand tools so necessary for success.'

Point of Interest

SERVING THREE MASTERS: YOUR CLIENTS, VOLUNTEERS AND DONORS

While many non-profits have already benefited from adopting for-profit business models for management and marketing, integrated branding has the potential to make them even more successful. That's because it focuses management on the experience they create for clients, volunteers and donors – compelling leaders to really understand what these constituents value. At the same time, brand tools help to clarify and simplify the non-profit's message – increasing its value in its donors' eyes.

Here's how one non-profit used integrated branding to solidify its customer experience. The Seattle Children's Home (SCH) was misperceived by many donors to be an orphanage – rather than a provider of mental health and education services for Washington State's most fragile children. Volunteers and donors were aware of only a small percentage of SCH's many programs. The integrated branding process helped SCH clarify its value in a way that donors, volunteers and staff could understand and commit to.

The new brand principle (See Chapter 3: Tools to Live Your Brand, for more on brand principles and other brand tools) resulting from SCH's brand discovery process was building partnerships to improve futures. SCH used this principle to keep only services that focused on improving kids' futures in partnership with other providers. This allowed SCH to better leverage its talents while doing more of what its people love to do – helping children that have fallen through the cracks. As part of this process SCH increased its investment in the Continuum of Care, a program ensuring that a child would be continuously supported with the right services until he or she was successful.

It also created a new visual association based on the concept of transformation – as exemplified by a butterfly in the organization's new logo. In this case it's much more than just part of an attractive logo. SCH has found a myriad of ways to extend the butterfly throughout the organization's activities. The Home's annual fundraiser was renamed the Butterfly Ball and debuted in 2000. It was the biggest fundraiser in the Home's history and more than doubled previous amounts that had been raised. A Lalique butterfly was given to those who donated U.S. $5,000 and above, and a Waterford butterfly to U.S. $2,500-level donors.

In this example, the client experience was improved by the brand—changing from the offering-specific focus of receiving mental health and educational services—to one where every action was designed to improve the child's future. The donor experience changed from writing a check to help severely emotionally disturbed or (incorrectly) orphaned children, to the satisfaction of knowing that they are making a difference in fragile children's futures. And the volunteer experience changed from a micro-view of what SCH did in one or two areas to the big picture – creating more of a head and heart connection that encouraged greater volunteerism.

The Crisis Clinic: A Case Study

Crisis Clinic – a safety net for anyone in King County, Washington in a crisis – began in the 1960s as one family's answer to a crisis that could have been avoided. As a result of this experience, the group founded America's second-oldest crisis phone service or crisis line where people could turn for counseling and intervention whenever they needed it – 24 hours a day, seven days a week. Today, Crisis Clinic is a focal point for crisis resources. These include training, outreach and a bridge to community resources in the greater Seattle area through its 24-hour Crisis Line, Community Information Line, Teen Link help line, Survivors of Suicide support group and other referral programs. In addition, Clinic staff train the general public and therapists on suicide prevention and understanding mental illness.

THE CHALLENGE
As with most non-profits, Crisis Clinic staff and volunteers are mainly drawn to their work by a strong sense of identification with the organization's mission. Crisis Clinic knew it had a highly loyal team, but suspected that staff members' and volunteers' morale could be higher. The staff and volunteers were valued, but they didn't necessarily know that, or hear it often or loud enough.

THE SOLUTION
Crisis Clinic developed and promoted its brand. After in-depth interviews with clients, staff and community partners, Crisis Clinic

developed a principle of effective answers. This principle clarified the unique approach Crisis Clinic provides in delivering community services – i.e., answers that effectively solve people's problems.

During the process, Crisis Clinic developed a common set of brand values that staff and volunteers could adhere to and communicate to clients and community partners. Crisis Clinic now recognizes and promotes its values of universal access, and consistently communicates the worth of its volunteers, employees and partnerships. Crisis Clinic also identified its personality traits of compassionate, flexible, expert, responsive and trustworthy to guide the tone and style of its external communications.

Given that it touched the community through many different programs, Crisis Clinic created two brand associations, lifeline and caring, as focal points to further deepen the emotional tie clients and community partners had with the Crisis Clinic brand through its many programs.

INTEGRATING CRISIS CLINIC'S NEW BRAND

Crisis Clinic went beyond communications-level brand-integration to the level of customer-touch-point branding (See Chapter 4: Align to Deliver a Unique Customer Experience, for more information on brand levels.) Using its new personality traits and building in guidelines on how to give effective answers, Crisis Clinic created a universal response script to ensure that its staff and volunteers answered the phone consistently across services. Crisis Clinic also has used the brand to hold more open staff meetings and discuss the organization's values and mission – helping to remind staff and volunteers why they work in social services and creating an environment where they could feel more committed to the Clinic.

Here's another example of branding the customer experience. The WSA, which is the technology industry association in Washington State, had the challenge of appealing to multiple audiences at the same time. It needed to attract the person who wrote the membership check while serving all employees within each member company. It was very successful in developing programs. But it ran the danger of being too diffuse for members to be able to easily define and, therefore, prioritize in their budgets to fund. By clarifying the mission for its organization of helping Washington State and its technology companies succeed, identifying a brand principle of sharing expertise, resources and insight, and a strategic role of being the heart of the Washington State technology community, it has been able to focus on meeting both the member check writers' and member employees' needs.

This mission and principle has caused it to focus on programs that provide technology community services and leadership, include networking, specific departmental and leadership education, investment forums and lobbying. Its messaging and corporate identity maintain this focus. As you can see in its home page – the organization demonstrates sharing expertise, resources and insight through the programs mentioned, while graphically demonstrating its people and sharing orientation through the site's photographic treatments.

FIGURE 15.1: WSA HOMEPAGE

One non-profit found particular value in determining its strategic role. Seattle Works fosters in young adults a lifetime commitment to community involvement through innovative volunteer activities and educational opportunities. Seattle Works saw itself in the important role of a facilitator of volunteer experiences that helped people become more engaged in their community. However, the facilitator role caused Seattle Works' constituents to feel more loyal to the organizations Seattle Works partnered with than to Seattle Works itself. Seattle Works needed its volunteers to understand the tangible benefits it offers in addition to facilitating a volunteer's community service experience.

Through the process of revealing its brand, Parker LePla developed the idea of replacing the facilitator role with the role of a community services mentor. By defining this strategic role differently for Seattle Works, Parker LePla helped the organization see itself differently. Instead of perceiving it was on the periphery of the relationship between a community service organization and a volunteer (and therefore on the periphery in other people's perceptions), the mentor role put Seattle Works squarely in a leadership position. Seattle Works is beginning to use the mentor language to describe the role of key volunteer leaders and board members, helping them understand just how pivotal a role they play in accomplishing Seattle Works' mission.

LEADING THE CHARGE WITH A SHOESTRING BUDGET

How can you make an impact for your non-profit on a pauper's budget? By making that budget work harder for you. Integrated branding is a critical process for non-profits because it focuses all organization actions and messages on what creates the most value. Imagine the things you could achieve if every action in the organization was based on delivering the same experience. Imagine the relationship depth you could build with every staff member, donor and volunteer if all communications were consistent and compelling. By understanding how to build loyal and committed constituent relationships, you can leverage any budget to many times its face value.

It's essential that organizational leaders embrace the brand and model it for staff, donors and constituents. The president of the Seattle Children's Home asks his staff, *'How are we improving kids' futures?'* before taking any action. He even sports butterfly ties and cufflinks to make the brand more concrete to other staff members!

Many non-profits recruit well-known public figures to chair their events. Such celebrities as Jerry Lewis, Nancy Reagan and Jimmy Carter have all been successfully used to support causes as diverse as muscular dystrophy, drug abuse prevention and affordable housing. While using celebrities is one of the quickest ways to create awareness and brand direction, a problem with this approach can be with the longevity of the celebrity's commitment – it should be measured in decades, not years. A problem also arises if the celebrity falls out of public favor.

USING VOLUNTEERS TO EXTEND YOUR BUDGET

One of the biggest challenges an integrated brand can help with is leveraging volunteers. Not only is the integrated branding process effective in aligning volunteer activities with brand (see Crisis Clinic example earlier in this chapter), brand can also be an effective tool for harnessing the power of volunteers to demonstrate your brand and publicly convey your message.

Many non-profits, such as Habitat for Humanity and the Salvation Army, use hundreds or thousands of volunteers. How can you harness the power of such a potent marketing force? By making sure that everyone is communicating the same message and taking the same on-brand actions. Corporate marketers would drool over the potential of having a word-of-mouth sales force that was totally committed to selling their products, because word-of-mouth recommendations are one of the most powerful influences on what people decide to do with their money. Even if your 50,000 volunteers (and donors) talk to just one person a month about your program, that would give you 600,000 impressions a year – and, most likely, with an ideal target group that has dollars or volunteer time to donate.

Your job is to motivate volunteers and donors to tell your story by arming them with the right tools and the right inspiration. The right inspiration results from understanding and communicating your brand value in a way that creates the commitment from volunteers that we discussed earlier. Additionally, part of your focus in every communication should be to move volunteers to action in the simplest way possible.

Which brand tools should you focus on with volunteers? All volunteers should be able to give a rendition of the organization's simplest story – its elevator statement – that includes its strategic role, brand principle and key results. Here's one for an art and community development non-profit called Pomegranate Center: 'Pomegranate Center helps communities utilize their unique gifts to become more vibrant and humane. We do this by integrating social, artistic and environmental perspectives into the creation of meaningful gathering spaces.' Pomegranate's complex, layered story becomes manageable when everyone knows the same story.

Volunteers should also understand how to use the non-profit's brand principle to make decisions and take actions on behalf of the organization. All of this should be part of a volunteer orientation program.

MANAGING IN-KIND DONATIONS

Non-profits frequently use a crazy-quilt set of collateral, marketing, signage and corporate identities, simply because they don't have a guide for keeping corporate partners on track. Your brand tools, particularly the strategic role, principle and personality, can be used to leverage in-kind donations so that they don't become one-of-a-kind donations.

Solidify Your Constituents' (Your Three Masters') Experience

- What do your clients perceive that you do for them?
- What value do your clients get from your product/service?
- What do your volunteers perceive you do for them?
- What value do your volunteers get from volunteering for your non-profit?
- What do your donors perceive you do for them?
- What value do your donors get from donating to your non-profit?
- What value would you like each group to receive?

Consider the answers to the above questions for each constituent group. Now examine each interaction your organization has with each group. Are you paying off the 'perceived' and 'desired value' for each group? What can you change to assure that you do this?

THE CHALLENGE AND POTENTIAL OF NON-PROFIT STRUCTURES

THE BOARD

The best boards act as a conveyor of the brand to the outside world. While their fiduciary function may be organization oversight, their greatest value comes from opening doors to opportunities, and from evangelizing and living your brand. The problem with most boards is that they spend much of their time and energy listening to too much day-to-day organizational detail. Board meetings become drudgery rather than what they should be – support sessions that motivate, invigorate and teach your board how to represent your brand.

The key to getting your board to a level where they are consistently evangelizing your organization is through a planned board orientation program that results in emotional identification with your brand, positive peer influence and focused action. With the right orientation, living the integrated brand becomes an ongoing process that builds its own momentum.

Your first job with new board members is to turn them into brand champions. To get there, you must be able to capture both their hearts and their minds. This requires multiple, positive, first-hand experiences with your brand. In addition to regular board work of reporting and planning, these experiences should include:

- a comprehensive explanation of what beneficial experience you offer clients and donors;
- first-hand interactions with both clients and donors where both groups demonstrate the benefit of your brand;
- a board-member mentor or buddy who models brand action and then explains what they modeled and why;
- fun, social activities and individual recognition that bond the board together and enhance everyone's self esteem; and
- the new board member evangelizing your brand successfully to other peers.

Program results, if you have the right raw material, will be a board member that moves to the committed level of the brand equity pyramid (see Chapter 1: Why All Leaders Need to Be Brand Driven).

Another non-profit issue is that many non-profit boards experience a complete turnover every two years or so. While one board may have signed on to do the brand development work, the next may consider it frivolous or irrelevant. While one board was integral to the development of the brand tools, the next may not fully understand them or know how to roll them out to staff and volunteers in a meaningful way. A new board may argue with the conclusions of the last. A strong board may overrule staff's implementations; a weak one may not do anything.

Therefore, the organization's strengths and brand tools must be driven by staff and championed by the president – but with deep participation from the board. We recommend that a staff member becomes the brand manager, and that every new board member go through brand training as part of his or her board orientation process. This approach offers several benefits: the brand's health is husbanded by the staff, so that they get ever better at living it, and the new board members become much more effective at brand-based leadership from the start.

Some boards have a greater impact on their organizations than others. While some merely do what the staff tells them to do, others are always in conflict with staff. The integrated branding process will identify and resolve a lot of these issues while helping determine the best volunteer, donor and community experience and strategic role. Once decided, brand tools can help continue to keep boards focused because of their ability to guide decisions and actions.

When the Dispute Resolution Center (DRC) of Kitsap County (WA) embarked on branding to guide its decisions and actions, it discovered that new group dynamics came into play. The DRC wanted to create some momentum for funding and volunteerism, so came together to discuss such topics as *'Who are we?'* and *'What do we do that's of real value to our constituents?'*

When coming together as a brand team is the first time the organization's staff, board and volunteers have ever discussed important issues as a group, it may present unique group dynamics challenges. Powerful people often clash and where a group lacks experience, it may not have established truce behaviors to fall back on. Leaders, accustomed to assuming certain roles or levels of participation, may need to become less or more dominant than they are accustomed to being. People who are typically followers may suddenly find themselves expressing the strongest convictions, and may struggle with being effective. Because most non-profits rarely have the time, resources or extra energy to coalesce group dynamics, it's important to have a facilitator who can help you separate content from behavior both through ground rules and on-the-spot mediation.

STAFF CHALLENGES

Typically, non-profit staff members are very committed, enthusiastic and values-driven. This bodes well for living the brand, because they are already disposed to using brand tools, such as values. But just as likely, they will have trouble coming to consensus on brand tools they haven't discussed in the past – such as their strategic role, principle and mission. Strong opinions live in non-profits about why they are there, and how they want to project that to the world. You need to make sure that you've got the right tools and process to support all of these people coming to consensus.

In the case of Pomegranate Center, a non-profit that helps communities create gathering spaces that incorporate artistic, social and environmental perspectives, the mission was a stumbling block. It took almost no time to agree on its brand principle, uniting beauty and justice. It was obvious to the group members. The group spent six full hours, however, arguing about what the mission was. It ended up being: 'Helping communities utilize their unique gifts to become more vibrant and humane,' but could have easily been: 'Promoting sustainable communities;' 'Increasing civic perspectives;' or 'Merging environmental, economic, design and community perspectives.' The fact is, they do all of that and more, and different people were attracted to Pomegranate Center for these differing reasons. A brand development process with an experienced facilitator was essential to helping this diverse board come to consensus. Prior to integrated branding, twenty different versions of what Pomegranate did were floating out in the community, making it more difficult to focus and deliver results.

Board members had a hard time asking for corporate donations, primarily because they couldn't succinctly discuss the benefits or mission of Pomegranate. They knew it was cool, that it was necessary, that it was positive. But they couldn't articulate the key premise of the organization. With a mission in hand, board members started asking for corporate grants, with the result that corporate grants, which accounted for 10% of the budget in 2001, rose to 23% the following year.

CULTURE AND YOUR INTEGRATED BRAND

It's also important to know what type of culture you have and the personality and cultural norms your organization uses. This will allow you to identify brand actions that will be more difficult for your staff to do, or what messages may not resonate with all audiences based on your past staff communications.

Many non-profits are characterized by a charismatic leader with a strong, 'just do it,' cultural norm. Others are more mature organizations with long-time legacies. More mature organizations are often more cautious about putting a stake in the ground about brand behavior, and use a cultural norm of 'how will it play with all audiences, including donors?' as a stumbling block to decisive brand action.

And finally, it's important to select a brand manager. While you could hire from the outside, a more cost-effective way is using an existing staff member. But turning a staff member into an effective brand manager can be problematic – but not impossible. For one thing, the brand manager needs to have the ear of the president and have the power to effect change. They must also be a good negotiator, to work around the landmines that can occur when you are trying to change the behavior of staff, volunteers and your board. Finally they will have to handle this new role when they are probably already overworked. See more on job clarity in Chapter 9: Hire, Train and Organize to Live the Brand.

EXECUTIVE LEADER LOG

As executive director, this sounds like a great way to get us more focused. I worry, though, about getting board buy-in. We've got some pretty opinionated folks on the board, people who I think might see brand as too 'fluffy' and consumer-ish. On the other hand, board recruitment's always been difficult because we make them personally commit to fundraising goals. If we could show how brand makes that much easier, it might just turn the tide.

HUMAN RESOURCES LEADER LOG

Wow, one of our biggest problems here has been staff and volunteer turnover. People come in all passionate and excited about what we're here to do, but the bureaucracy disillusions them. Brand tools would give us a way to weave the inspirational aspects of our work throughout all our operations – and maybe we'd hold onto our great volunteers longer.

SALES LEADER LOG

As development director at a small community service non-profit, I can really see how integrated branding could help our fundraising efforts. Nobody here is a marketing professional, but using brand tools would help us be better at marketing our organization, even if it was just at the way we conduct ourselves with the people we serve.

CHAPTER

HEALTHCARE ORGANIZATIONS: BRAND DRIVEN CHALLENGES

*Give a man health and a course to steer; and he'll never
stop to trouble about whether he's happy or not.*

–George Bernard Shaw

In the early 1990s, 125-year-old Vanderbilt University Medical Center, long known for its leading-edge research and specialization in organ transplants and trauma, had a rude awakening. It was losing business to the competition. Worse still, market surveys revealed Vanderbilt was rated last in customer preference of the region's four major hospital systems. 'Consumers thought we were smart, but not very caring,' explained Joel Lee, executive director of communications. In response, Vanderbilt conducted an 18-month brand makeover in hopes of winning back most-favorable ratings and keeping up with or surpassing the competition.

Understanding and keeping a brand promise is important for any company that wants to be a long-term leader in its field. This is even more important in the healthcare industry, where people's lives and well being are tied to their relationships with their insurance and healthcare providers. In the case of Vanderbilt, the organization had organically grown its brand strengths over a long period. The problem was leaders weren't consciously aware of what those brand strengths were or how to manage them to create a better patient experience. They were also unaware of their weaknesses. The result? Prior to revealing and managing its integrated brand, the organization's revenues and market share plummeted.

In an article titled 'Marketing,' published in *Healthcare Business*, July 2000, Sara Selis reported that as part of the brand-development process, Vanderbilt adopted personality traits of friendly and warm, and a value of being efficient. All hospital staff received eight-to-12 hours of training on how to treat patients as customers, and Vanderbilt made each employee personally responsible for solving problems. Within two years of launching its revealed brand, Vanderbilt moved from fourth to second place in consumer preference studies, and increased its reimbursement and market share significantly in several areas.

The State of Healthcare Branding

With the exception of a few healthcare providers and research organizations, such as Vanderbilt, Mayo Clinic and the Blues (Blue Cross and Blue Shield) most consumers and employers have a difficult time differentiating one organization from another. In addition, patients have less incentive to be loyal to their providers because their choices of insurance plans and care facilities are limited by their employers' decisions. Finally, creating loyal customers has been hampered by a mistaken customer belief that most healthcare providers – from physicians to hospitals – deliver the same quality of care.

This lack of patient preference directly translates into lack of sustained revenue growth. It also contributes to the inability of many healthcare providers to realize good margins on their services. Any company or industry that doesn't know how to make its customer experience different and compelling will end up in the bargain basement. Simply put, since a brand that's perceived to be a commodity has no customer loyalty, it can keep customers only through discount pricing.

Such practices can plunge healthcare providers into a never-ending price war, inhibiting both innovation and quality. If customers don't care about their healthcare providers, they won't be willing to pay extra for a service, or won't protest when their insurer or employer stops or limits certain coverage. Hospitals, clinics, physician groups and vertically integrated medical systems have become commodities by substituting sound-alike advertising campaigns for a unique and compelling customer experience. Others have tried using medical specialties, such as birthing centers or cancer treatments to be different. The problem is that these generic specializations aren't a competitive barrier to entry.

One healthcare segment has been using branding to effectively stimulate demand. Advertising campaigns have spurred patients to ask for specific medications by brand name, such as Celebrex, Claritin and Lipitor. This is a great example of the power of consumer pull in creating a brand and brand name. In an article titled, 'Lazurus at Large, How about a vodka chaser for that purple pill? Purple pill ads are strangely effective' that appeared in *The San Francisco Chronicle*, December 19, 2001, David Lazarus reported that while the cost of direct-to-consumer promotions get passed on to patients in the drug prices, U.S. $2.5 billion in the year 2000 – they also perform a valuable function by creating more product and company investment demand.

Case Study: Moving Customers to a Commitment Level

MONISTAT 1 Combination Pack from McNeil-PPC Inc., the number-one-recommended vaginal yeast infection product, is a good example of successful healthcare branding. This campaign asks women to take a test that identifies their attitudes towards their health and healthcare. Based on an initial survey of 500 women (ages 18-49), the company was able to come up with two patient profiles – the impatient patient and the patient patient. The company then created a sponsored Web site, www.fastsymptomrelief.com, and based on which profile you fit into after questioning, gave you tips on how to deal with health-related issues using the advice of stress experts Wayne and Mary Sotile.

According to the survey, more than three quarters of the women surveyed fell into the impatient patient category who want immediate access to fast relief – something that the MONISTAT product is designed to do.[1] By identifying the aspects of the product that were designed specifically for impatient women patients, the MONISTAT product is building patient's emotional loyalty and intellectual commitment.

THE ANTIDOTE TO COMMODITY HEALTHCARE BRANDS

What steps can a healthcare provider take to effectively use integrated branding?

Start by revealing and living your integrated brand. Every healthcare organization has strengths that contain the seeds for consistently delivering a unique and compelling customer experience. The first step to differentiation is to understand these strengths. WellPoint Health

Networks has a brand based on selling people choice – what each individual wants and needs. In an article titled, 'WellPoint Makes a Strong Recovery: Six years ago its prognosis was poor. Today its expansion is being cheered by investors and challenged by consumer advocates,' in the *Los Angeles Times*, December 12, 2001, Ronald White reports that chief executive Leonard D. Shaeffer cites the options his company offers small businesses, 'We offer them a plan that allows every employee to choose the right plan for them, so those small companies get to choose nine different health plans and four dental plans. We offer them more options.'

Selis in her July 2000 *Healthcare Business* article also stated that Washington Hospital Center discovered that its unique cardiac expertise allowed it to vault into high-profile brand awareness in the Washington D.C. area. It used a unique educational program around women's cardiac health, because it had determined through a Gallup poll that most surveyed doctors incorrectly identified some symptoms of heart attacks in women. The hospital's free cardiac-health information kits generated U.S. $2.4 million in cardiac procedures, boosted business for other areas of the hospital and significantly increased consumer awareness.

Understanding your organization's strengths begins with asking the right questions. '*What does the patient, employer, broker, insurance user or benefits administrator experience with your organization look like? What role do you play in each group's work or personal life? What's consistently good or bad about your experience? What would they say about you to friends or family? How convenient is it to use your services? How effective are the results?*' As healthcare leaders begin to answer these questions they will start viewing their services from their customers' point of view. Getting an organization to see itself through its customers' eyes is the key to revenue growth and increased market share and the first step to living an integrated brand.

Leaders at every level of the organization can play a role in revealing their organization's integrated brand by making the customer experience central to action.

THE CHALLENGES IN HEALTHCARE BRANDING

Developing an integrated brand will require you to respond to some challenges that are unique to healthcare:

- decisions need to be relevant to the life-long needs of your customers.
- patients need to care about your healthcare offerings and trust you to deliver them.
- the relationship with the primary care doctor must generate patient loyalty.
- you must understand and build your defensible difference.
- you must fix every mistake.
- you must address the needs of every customer group.
- you must implement trends that improve the customer experience.

MAKING DECISIONS BASED ON LIFE-LONG CUSTOMER NEEDS

Everyone needs healthcare services, insurance and products, from birth until death. And healthcare services, products and medicines tend to be used more consistently and for longer periods than other consumer offerings.

Whether you are a direct or indirect healthcare supplier, if you look at your patient relationships from the point of view of lifelong partnerships, you may find many ways to adjust your offerings to something closer to what patients want. Ask yourself, *'How can we improve the patient relationship not only tomorrow, but next year as well?'* and, *'What are the repercussions of a patient using a particular product or service over and over again?'* Answering these questions may cause you to periodically reinforce warnings to patients about the interactions of different drugs, for instance.

Often, patients aren't even given context for why you are doing something. An example of this is the explanation of benefits statement that you receive from your healthcare coverage providers. Most patients either mistake these for bills or consider them worthless and throw them away. But one purpose for them is so patients can tell their insurers if they didn't receive such services. This would then prevent fraudulent claims from healthcare providers. Without context, these forms detract from the patient experience and don't do what they were intended to do. The leaders' job is to walk in the customers' shoes – so that his or her organization's healthcare offerings truly meets customers' needs.

GETTING CUSTOMERS TO CARE

Give your customers a compelling reason to treat your offerings as more than a commodity – something they value enough to not go elsewhere to get. This is the central issue addressed by an integrated healthcare brand. 'The challenge of marketing healthcare is that it is rarely defined as a desirable product,' says R. Scott MacStravic, Ph.D., author of the book *Creating Consumer Loyalty in Healthcare.*

Besides the traditional lack of a customer focus, a healthcare brand is hard to execute perfectly because it involves coordinating the activities of many people, services and reports. Healthcare organizations often make the mistake of trying to communicate the benefits of their system in all its complexity – a practice research has shown to be both confusing and meaningless to consumers as reported by Emily Wolf in a January 1, 2001 *Healthcare Executive* article called, 'A new way to approach healthcare marketing.'

How can you eliminate the complexity from your customer experience?

Put the relationship with patients at the center of what you are providing. The last thing a customer wants from any healthcare partner is to feel like a number or a statistic. That means anyone who deals with customers must be given guidelines for behavior that allow patients to get an authentic, personalized experience.

Second, you'll build the level of trust necessary for a successful healthcare brand only if you keep your brand promise. Walking the talk is important for any organization that aspires to be a strong brand, but in the case of healthcare, following through on your promises is a make-it or break-it proposition. When patients put their and their families' health in your hands, you really want to make sure you do everything humanly possible to deliver as promised. A big part of delivery for a patient is feeling that you care. This is true whether you are a physician, an insurer or a medical-products provider. If you act like you don't care about patients' best interests, they will react more from the emotional and survival level – typically negatively – than in any other industry.

GENERATING PATIENT LOYALTY THROUGH THE PHYSICIAN RELATIONSHIP

No matter what advances happen in healthcare technology, the primary doctor relationship will continue to be at the core of successful healthcare brands. Most patients greatly prefer to have a physician-centric healthcare experience. In a recent study by NFO WorldGroup,[2] of 2,514 respondents representative of U.S. households, respondents clearly wanted healthcare decisions in the hands of their physicians, not their healthcare insurance providers.

All companies in the healthcare field need to focus on how they can positively impact the patient experience through primary care and specialist physicians. For instance, if you are a medical-products supplier, it's in your best interest to help physicians improve their patient relationships – because patients will judge your product based on whether it was prescribed correctly and whether the hand-off from the doctor to them was done in a timely and convenient way from the patient's perspective.

Healthcare products that treat potentially life-threatening problems, such as CPAP machines that treat sleep apnea, require a fast handoff between the time the doctor makes a diagnosis and the equipment provider gets approval from the patient's insurance company. Because of the many steps in this process and the fact that no partner takes credit for it, patients frequently experience delays of days or weeks in getting treatment. The result is patient dissatisfaction with all involved – a situation that the medical-products company could completely remedy.

Sometimes the positive effect would be as simple as avoiding potentially life-threatening circumstances resulting from a patient-doctor interaction. There are many examples of doctors writing prescriptions for the wrong medicines and the wrong dosages or having unintelligible handwriting that the pharmacist misreads. Imagine the damage that this can do to your brand image Once again, if one or more of the groups involved were to take responsibility for the patient receiving the right dosage information, this problem could be solved.

Another way to positively impact the patient relationship is by stopping the practice of basing patient visits totally on financial metrics and what you can be reimbursed for. If your organization tries to cut costs by measuring its doctors on a patients-seen-per-day metric, you are missing the opportunity to create loyal patients and brand champions. If you are a healthcare provider, we recommend creating a senior management task force whose role is to continuously improve the patient experience in the doctor's office or hospital room, while still keeping the organization fiscally healthy.

Washington-based Group Health Cooperative under its Welcoming Environment initiative, has tied 20% of every physician and executive's compensation in part to customer-service metrics. California-based WellPoint Health Networks has done something similar. As noted by White in his *Los Angeles Times* article, WellPoint Health Networks rewards health-plan physicians for patient satisfaction and treatment outcomes rather than for cost-containment and economizing. Since initiating this system, its California participant numbers have increased by 9.5%.

UNDERSTAND AND BUILD YOUR DEFENSIBLE DIFFERENCE

Ask yourself, *'What is it about our approach that is really different?'* Most hospitals, clinics, physician groups and vertically integrated medical systems have relied either on a very soft-sell 'caring' approach, or on selling their leading-edge procedures or expertise in medical specialties as their differentiating message. To patients, these are all shorthand for 'commodity brand.' Finding the answer to this through research and the brand-discovery process is what leads to long-term patient retention.

As a leader, your job is to look for those things that your customers consistently say are different (and better) about your organization. Your differences may not be obvious from just one interaction – it's the pattern that forms from watching and listening to customers over a period of time that's key. While we rarely run into organizations that don't have unique strengths, we occasionally see companies where they are very minor. If you find yourself in such a company, your job is to identify those small differences and weave them into a distinctive fabric that customers care about and often experience.

FIX EVERY MISTAKE

Mistakes by healthcare businesses – whether in delivery, insurance or products – are more visible than in any other business. Due to the sheer number of patient interactions, mistakes happen frequently. Creating a system for correcting every mistake and learning from mistakes is as important to the customer experience as the physician relationship. According to Alec Appelbaum, in an article entitled 'The Constant Customers' in the *GMJ,* 'When customers experience problems – say, a service glitch or a faulty product – a funny thing happens. Companies that deal quickly and thoroughly with customers' problems tend to arouse passion [loyalty] in their customers just as sure as companies that never create problems.'

So how should a healthcare company respond to mistakes?

The first response is to adopt a brand value of *learning organization*. A learning organization seeks to pre-empt mistakes by devising systems that keeps them from happening. A learning organization also sinks its teeth into mistakes with the tenacity of a bulldog, not letting go until a mistake is resolved or the patient acknowledges that all that could be done has been done.

At the same time, in any high-transaction industry, it's important to not let complaints become the only thing your staff hears about. It's equally essential to not create a culture of blame. This is one place where the brand research process can help you. Through this process you will get a truer picture of how customers feel and can then spread this typically good news among fellow employees.

ADDRESS THE NEEDS OF EVERY CUSTOMER GROUP

Healthcare brands need to address both differing types of customers and differing customer demographics within a specific group. How you do this and the level of attention you give each flavor of customer needs to be an integral part of your brand strategy.

When it comes to customer demographics, you will want to segment customer messaging by age. In his book, *The New Rules of Healthcare Marketing*, Arthur C. Sturm, Jr. suggests lifecycle management as a way to grow unbreakable brand relationships in healthcare: 'Lifecycle management involves educating an individual on what to expect as each stage of the lifecycle approaches and then guiding that person through that stage and into the next through appropriate interventions, education, and therapies.'[3]

We believe that the best way to keep your brand refreshed and relevant is to make it meaningful to each new age group. The question to ask is *'How does your brand meet the unique needs of this age group?'* You will want to pay particular attention to entry-level age groups to make sure you capture each successive generation. Entry-level for healthcare really begins when patients enter the workforce, but prospects can be influenced much earlier through brand-awareness programs for teens and college students.

Clarifying Customer Demographics

Answering some of the following questions will help you with clarifying demographics issues:

- Are your chosen customer segments helpful in making product/service and marketing decisions?
- While staying on brand, are you giving the right messages to each group?
- Do you try to create loyalty with every patient age group?
- How do you prioritize your employer, broker and insurance company relationships?
- If you are an insurance company, do you primarily focus on brokers and employers, and pay little attention to patients?
- If you are offering a medical product or drug, do you focus on physicians or do you also focus on the insurance company and patient experience?
- How effective are your customer feedback methods?
- How do you get customers to care about the same things you do?

Group Health Cooperative is one organization that is looking at lifestyle needs. Group Health calls itself a coordinated care organization, and backs this up with a physician-as-partner approach to healthcare delivery. The organization puts power into this partnership by creating easy access to primary care doctors and specialists. As part of this program, it provides same-day access to primary care doctors. The organization also hires specialists who practice in focused areas within the disciplines of pediatrics, surgery, gynecology and gerontology – turning them into better-informed personal health advisors and coordinators. This allows Group Health physicians to help patients intelligently manage their own health at every stage of their life.

USE CURRENT TRENDS TO STRENGTHEN CUSTOMER RELATIONSHIPS

If you keep your eyes open, trends are easy to spot. For instance, the authors regularly look at general-interest and business periodicals such as *Time, Newsweek, The Wall Street Journal* and *USA Today* to see the number and types of healthcare stories that are making news. You will also see the seeds of trends in healthcare-industry magazines. Why is trend-spotting important? By keeping an eye open for the latest trends, you'll think about how they might impact your customer experience and be able to form a plan to address them.

Among hospital bed reduction, managed care and quality and productivity improvement, one of the major healthcare trends in healthcare over the past two decades has been that of cost control. The latest coda to this trend has been shifting more of the responsibility for healthcare from employers to employees. According to William M. Mercer, a benefits consulting firm, as reported by Steven Styre and Charles Stein in *The Boston Globe*, Boston Capital Column, December 13, 2001, 'The trend among companies, big and small, is to push more cost and responsibility for healthcare bills onto workers.'

Whether you are on the insurance- or the care-delivery side, you need to be aware of the growing importance that cost will play in patients' lives and find ways to help patients save money. If you are an insurance carrier or healthcare provider, you might make sure patients clearly understand the ramifications of selecting a particular plan. One way to do this might be a Web site address or information hot line to give them comparative plan answers during open enrollment periods. Or you might give patients advice throughout the year that will help them reduce the number of doctor visits they need to make. You might help them get questions answered or get prescriptions more cheaply over the phone or via email. By consistently helping them keep costs down, you'll inevitably build patient loyalty. The wellness movement is another trend that healthcare organizations can use to drive down costs.

Making patients pay for a portion of their healthcare represents an opportunity for strengthening healthcare brands. It takes healthcare out of the after-thought category for patients – thereby making it more important to the patient. Customers taking more control over their healthcare experiences will allow healthcare companies with compelling brands to shine. In this new world, where the patient's experience and value-for-services-rendered matters more, providers that think only in terms of the bottom line and reducing costs will be less successful.

Tipping Points: Building Brand Momentum

Strong brands, revenue growth and sustained profitability aren't achieved in a day. For consistent brand results, you'll need to develop a multi-year, integrated brand improvement plan. If your starting point is no competitive differentiation, it will require a number of years to create a strong brand – even after you have defined a unique role and focused everyone's actions to deliver a unique and compelling patient experience.

But the rewards can be huge.

How can leaders ensure their company's branding process will be accepted by the entire organization? By using your brand tools to guide staff actions and communications. (See Chapter 3: Tools to Live Your Brand and Chapter 4: Align to Deliver a Unique Customer Experience for more information on creating and using brand tools.)

In any integrated branding project, there are tipping points, places in the organization where early action will significantly impact larger group change. Some tipping points include upper management, physician executives, human resources, and sales and marketing buy-in and brand action modeling. Insurance companies need to add brokers to this list and healthcare delivery systems must also add physicians and other clinicians influencers to their buy-in and modeling list.

Leaders, starting with the CEO, whose actions can make the difference between everyone living the brand or just giving it lip service, play the starring roles. CEOs who task themselves to be brand evangelists will be the ones who bring the organization online quickly and completely by demonstrating brand actions and evangelizing brand successes to others. (See Obtaining Sponsorship to Achieve Integrated Branding, in Chapter 4: Align to Deliver a Unique Customer Experience for more information.)

One of the major problems in building brand momentum is in organizations that use outside contractors to deliver some or many of their services – such as with physicians in community hospitals. You will also need to bring these contracted employee groups into the brand fold as well. In these cases, you need to treat these contracted employees in much the same way you would any other employee group – from hiring them based on brand values to compensating them based on how well they live the brand.

A marketing campaign is another tipping point that can play a significant role by introducing the brand to internal and external audiences. An integrated brand that is introduced through a compelling marketing campaign is a very powerful inducement to employees to start living the brand. That's due to the pride of being part of a fun, successful and exciting endeavor. In designing your first campaign after brand discovery, look for a current customer benefit that your brand approach addresses particularly well, and communicate that.

While you're focusing on tipping points that communicate and model the brand throughout the organization, it's important to keep brand coordination in mind. We recommend you retain an outside brand counsel – much like you would legal counsel – to ensure everyone is moving in the right direction. Such counsel pays for itself by providing a third-party perspective and allowing you to access the experience of other companies who have been through the process.

The Ten Steps to a Sustainable Healthcare Brand

You will build an effective, integrated healthcare brand if you follow these ten steps:

Step 1: Look at everything from the customer's point of view.

Step 2: Understand your unique healthcare role and approach, and create a compelling customer experience around it.

Step 3: Make the physician/patient relationship the center of your healthcare offerings.

Step 4: Create patient relationships based on emotional loyalty and intellectual commitment to your healthcare approach.

Step 5: Adjust all processes that are not aligned with your brand.

Step 6: Create lifestyle and life-cycle hooks to promote wellness behaviors.

Step 7: Prevent and/or correct all mistakes to the patient's satisfaction, if it's in your power to do so.

Step 8: Make your brand relevant to every customer.

Step 9: Benchmark and fine-tune your brand practices.

Step 10: Adjust your services based on current healthcare trends – while keeping your brand promise.

EXECUTIVE LEADER LOG

Good point about using current trends to strengthen customer relationships (I think healthcare executives are more accustomed to looking at trends as threats, rather than opportunities, hmm...). Our annual (even two to three years out) planning process sometimes gets in the way of our ability to be as nimble or as flexible as we'll probably need to be, given the speed of market changes these days. What kinds of mid-term adjustment periods can we build in so we aren't watching trends from behind a glass wall, without the ability to react?

HUMAN RESOURCES LEADER LOG

I would love to see integrated branding help turn us into an employer of choice. Not only would we be better at attracting top clinician talent (for reasons other than just compensation), I can see it eventually improving our labor-relations efforts. Imagine – nurses and physicians vying to work here, versus across town.

SALES LEADER LOG

When I present different plans to my business customers, they always want to flip directly to the charts that compare costs and areas of coverage. Sometimes I can see them wanting their 'favorite' plan to be the lowest-cost one, so they can justify it in their own minds. Clearly defined brands and truly differentiated patient experiences would sure help move these decisions beyond the 'purely cost' basis. What can I, as an insurance broker, do to help employers make better-informed decisions?

NOTES

[1] (11 December 2001) 'Impatient Patients Seek Fast Relief and Empowering Relationship With Doctors,' PR Newswire press release

[2] (11 December 2001) 'Healthcare Decisions Belong to Patients and Their Doctors, Not Insurance Companies,' BusinessWire press release, NFO WorldGroup, US Healthcare Survey

[3] Wolf, E (1 January 2001) 'A new way to approach healthcare marketing,' *Healthcare Executive*, pp 12-16

CHAPTER

BRANDING ISSUES FOR
MERGERS AND ACQUISITIONS

Nothing worth learning is learned quickly except parachuting.
–Scott Chou, Kauffman Fellows III, Onset Ventures

If you have merger and acquisition leadership responsibilities, why should you care about integrated branding? For several reasons, including to get the most value from each transaction. Understanding the brand value of companies you are acquiring will help you more accurately set a buy or sell price and not leave money on the table. That's because brand equity has a significant upside effect on company valuation. This can represent a significant bargain for buyers and boon for sellers when the other party isn't considering the brand value in their due diligence.

Beyond short-term financial gain, understanding integrated branding will also help you understand how a potential merger or acquisition's practices can improve your customers' experience. On the down side, customer-experience and corporate-culture mismatches are two of the biggest reasons mergers and acquisitions fail.

Exactly, how important could recognizing brand value be to both parties in the sale? Here's one example: In 1988, investment bank KKR paid U.S. $25 billion, nearly twice its book value, for RJR Nabisco.[1] The clarity and familiarity of such Nabisco brands as Winston Salem and Oreo cookies were valuable assets for the sellers in this transaction.

In a 2001 study by Interbrand of 'The World's Most Valuable Brands,' brand value as a percentage of market capitalization averaged 30%. This totaled U.S. $817 billion.[2] For a number of well-publicized acquisitions in the 1980s including Nestle's purchase of Rowntree and

Grand Met's purchase of Pillsbury, payments for intangible assets ranged from 66-88% of the total purchase price.[3]

Besides improving the financial upside of the transaction, understanding how brand works also increases the likelihood of long-term success. That's because integrated branding allows you to quantify and manage your organization's practices, assets, cultures, communications and people as well as those of organizations you wish to merge with or acquire. The success of doing a merger or acquisition depends on how well the acquirer understands both the other company's and its own culture and intangible brand assets.

Microsoft is one company that has taken this approach. Through its Integration Framework, the company looks to all the value drivers of a target company – including the target company's practices, brand assets, communications and culture. The company intentionally looks at how it integrates companies to ensure that all the value it seeks to retain is integrated effectively. For example, work practices (such as development methods or customer service practices) may be left alone or slowly integrated over time to ensure that the acquired company's valued customers' brand experience would not be unintentionally altered as part of the acquisition.

Integrated branding can help leaders by providing a context for comparison, valuation and outcomes that allows them to effectively merge company cultures, or, not enter into transactions where cultures are too different to be merged.

A great example of a mismatch was the Snapple purchase by Quaker Oats in 1993 for U.S. $1.7 billion. Quaker Oats, fresh from its success building the Gatorade brand, expected a repeat performance with Snapple. But by 1997, Quaker had sold Snapple to Triarc Beverages for U.S. $300 million with the additional result of both the chairman and president of Quaker Oats losing their jobs. According to John Deighton, the Harold M. Bierley Professor of business administration at Harvard Business School, '...Quaker's failure can be put down to a fatal mismatch between brand challenge and management temperament. ...There are factors beyond economic analysis to take into account if the process of brand management is to cohere. What we call brand identity is actually a form of meaning, made at least as much by small, impromptu managerial acts as by grand designs precisely executed.'[4] Even if a merger or acquisition is not on your company's immediate horizon, you should read this chapter. 'Preparation has the greatest positive impact on M&A success,' explains Deloitte Consulting's Patrick Kager and Jan J. Malek. '…and the timing and likelihood of participating in a merger or acquisition is unpredictable.'[5]

The hard truth is that the road is littered with mergers and acquisitions that either failed or did not live up to their potential:

Here are the facts:

Most experts give M&As a 50-50 chance at success.

A global survey of 540 large companies across all continents by Deloitte & Touche suggests that almost 70% of companies that undertake a merger or acquisition fail to achieve their stated goals.[6]

According to a report by The Conference Board, *Managing Culture in Mergers and Acquisitions*, 'Only half of surveyed executives perceive their recent M&A experiences as successful.'[7]

Finally, a survey of 1,000 organizations by human resources consultant Watson Wyatt found that less than 33% of companies attained their profit goals after tie-up; only 46% ever met their expense-reduction goals and the mergers failed to produce the expected benefits 64% of the time.[8]

Does this mean you should avoid such opportunities? No. There are many successful companies that use an acquisition strategy as a way to stimulate growth or cut costs. For sellers, they are the most used method for creating liquidity. But you *should* find ways to make success more predictable. 'Understanding how brand impacts value should be in every CEOs play book, especially if you're a seller,' says Byron McCann, founder of Ascent Partners Group, an M&A advisory firm specializing in information technology. 'You should think in terms of how to get bought, not about whether you are going to sell. It's important to be ready to sell when the planets line up for you.'

This excursion along the integrated brand journey will help you do just that.

THE PROBLEM WITH MERGERS AND ACQUISTIONS

To understand how integrated branding can help improve the likelihood of success for your merger or acquisition, you first need to identify where problems occur. According to The Conference Board report, the most difficult issues to resolve are:

* leadership style;

- systems of management;
- decision making;
- communications.[9]

A 2000 Towers Perrin study of company executives (two-thirds of whom had been involved in three or more mergers, acquisitions or joint ventures over the previous five years), cites six obstacles to success:

- loss of productivity;
- incompatible cultures;
- loss of key talent;
- clash of management styles/egos;
- inability to manage/implement change;
- objectives and synergies not well understood.

And the seventh obstacle, the inability to sustain financial performance, can be viewed as a result of not executing on the other six. The good news is that integrated branding can solve all of these issues. We'll examine some of the ways integrated brands overcome these obstacles in the following sections.

THINGS TO CONSIDER WHEN DESIGNING A MERGER AND ACQUISITION BRAND-BASED STRATEGY

It's a myth to believe that a successful merger or acquisition is solely determined from financial criteria. A strategy focused on the financials ignores where value is created in all organizations – at the customer and employee levels.

Traditional merger and acquisition leaders value 'hard' assets (such as real estate, patents, capital equipment and revenue) and fail to fully appreciate the so-called 'intangibles' (such as reputation, brand assets, work practices, communications and cultural norms). Even when management does value some of these activities, it rarely uses a system that gets the most value out of them; thus, when it comes time for integration, it leaves value on the table.

The obstacle faced by most merger and acquisition leaders is that they have only a vague understanding of what their companies do well (brand assets) and what compelling customer experience (resulting from the brand promise) their companies are trying to create.

And probably the least understood impact of a merger or acquisition is its impact on the customer experience. Acquirers often give only lip service to the brand promise of the acquired company – so they don't adequately understand the ramifications of what new assets and practices they are bringing into their organization. Sometimes the power struggle that ensues and the high level of distraction engendered by a merger also impact the acquiring company's customer experience. Tig Krekel, president and CEO of Hughes Space and Communications, a subsidiary of Hughes Electronics, says, 'in the drive to complete a deal, it's easy to lose sight of the concerns of customers. There's almost never any detailed analysis in due diligence of how the customer will react to the pros and cons of the deal from their point of view.'[10]

Lloyd West, president of Professional Life Underwriters Services, a wholly owned subsidiary of Comerica, says, 'Keeping clients is one of the toughest and most enduring challenges following an acquisition or merger.'[11] This is particularly true for the company being acquired. Says West, 'To break through clients' fear and cynicism, you must present convincing arguments – through tactics such as letters, newsletters, seminars and face-to-face meetings – that your agency will not only keep its special qualities, but will deliver new advantages.'[12]

To understand the real value of a transaction, you need to keep customers, employees, culture, practices and what customers value beyond products and services (your brand assets) – all integrated brand components – at the heart of any valuation and integration strategy. Thinking of company valuation in terms of brand components enables acquisition teams to accurately assess value and create plans for integrating that value into the acquirer's organization as well as being in a position to grow it.

It's rare for an acquiring company to add practices, brand assets, culture or valuable marketing programs from an acquired company, due to the 'not invented here' syndrome. For acquiring companies that know their own value and recognize what they could acquire to generate even more value, this represents a great opportunity. For sellers, this represents a barrier that they must overcome in order to get full value out of the sale.

While this synergistic potential is more difficult to achieve, it's frequently worth doing. Acquirers often discard easily attained value to be had from merging best practices of companies. This is the case in the following three popular – but in our opinion, not-fully-leveraged-acquisition and due diligence strategies. While many of these deals were financially successful, a brand component focus would have helped each create even more value.

Acquire for talent. A well-known software company tends to value only the engineering talent it can gain from an acquisition. Its first step after acquisition is to move all the talent to its main campus and integrate it into its current operations.

Acquire for products and services. Software giant Symantec is a good example of this type of acquirer – with such acquisitions as Norton Utilities and WinFax. Valuable practices may not be fully integrated into the acquiring company.

Acquire for predictable revenue streams. Sungard, a U.S. $2 billion in annual revenues Wayne, Pennsylvania-based provider of IT solutions for financial services firms, focuses on adding revenue streams to its bottom line. It has successfully undertaken almost one hundred acquisitions since 1986 and tends to keep them relatively independent.

Another piece of brand value that acquirers often ignore is brand name equity. Think about a scenario where you are purchasing a company that is much better known by the general public. *If you're the acquirer, why should your brand name be the one that survives when the acquired firm has stronger brand equity?* Acquirers leave value on the table when they consume a popular brand name and don't either assume its brand name or transfer its brand name in a managed process over a period of time.

One transaction that effectively kept valuable brand-name equity was Minneapolis-based Norwest's purchase of Wells Fargo Bank in 1998. Even though Norwest was much bigger, the Wells Fargo brand had very positive equity based on a 'heritage of financial services' and the Wells Fargo stagecoach association. The stagecoach is the visualization of Well's Fargo's brand promise, and represents the company's values of speed, reliability, service, safekeeping, innovation, trust and 'coming through' for customers.[13] In this union, Norwest not only adopted the Wells Fargo name but also moved its headquarters to San Francisco. This 1998 merger marked the beginning of a series of successful acquisitions. Since taking the helm in 1998, CEO Richard Kovacevich has completed more than 200 acquisitions. Today the Wells Fargo brand has 117,000 employees, and 6,000 stores in 35 states, and is ranked seventh in the nation.[14]

Washington Mutual, which specializes in retail banking and mortgage originations, conducts extensive communications with each acquisition's customers prior to bringing the other company into the fold and changing its name. By the time they become Washington Mutual customers, these customers understand what Washington Mutual stands for and how that positively relates to the promise of their former bank. The company transfers brand-name equity through a carefully orchestrated campaign that also focuses on bringing the other bank's employees into the Washington Mutual fold.

GETTING THE MOST VALUE OUT OF AN M&A

How can you get the most out of your merger or acquisition?

Historically, the scope of due diligence has been too narrowly defined to maximize brand value. The problem starts with conducting a due-diligence process that does not take all brand factors into consideration. Byron McCann observers, 'The due diligence mindset is a defensive, risk identification and avoidance process. It is not tuned to the upside potential that would result in leveraging company brand and culture.'

In a December 2000 *Harvard Business Review* article, Robert J. Aiello and Michael D. Watkins state: '...acquirers have wiped more value off their market capitalization through failures in due diligence than through the lapses in any other part of the deal process. Smart acquirers approach a $1 billion acquisition with the same attention to detail they would apply to investing $1 billion in building a new plant.'[15] KPMG's head of M&A Integration, John Kelly, says too often companies are concentrating on the hard mechanics to extract value from an acquisition; 'The research has shown it is the soft issues, such as people, that are key in achieving the realization of value.'[16]

There are many things you can do to enhance the effectiveness of your M&A due diligence process.

ENLARGE THE SCOPE OF YOUR DUE DILIGENCE

First, enlarge the scope of your due diligence to include an analysis of integrated brand components including the customer experience. The first step to success is to understand the due diligence process is much more than just a go/no-go on the deal. The due diligence framework should include an analysis of customer fit and brand fit, and the identification of all the alignment activities necessary to make this fit happen. The team will also need to summarize the customer experience each company delivers. The new brand should create a customer experience that is superior to the previous one.

You also should look at brand structure very early in the process. You will want to identify the dominant brands from a customer-experience perspective. You'll also want to determine if your brand name should replace the acquired brand's or co-exist with it. It's essential to create a focus while harvesting the equity of all existing brand names.

EVALUATE BRAND EXTENSION LIMITS

You'll also want to ask yourself if the acquisition represents a brand extension – where your brand represents new kinds of products or services. The basic criteria for a successful extension are: *'Do our strengths lend themselves to this new business? Will our existing or prospective customer base trust us to be the source of these products or services?'*

The degree of match between your strengths, what customers perceive you can do, and the acquired product or service line is critical.

SECURE SPONSORSHIP

Secure sponsorship for the project with senior management. (See Chapter 4: Align to Deliver a Unique Customer Experience for more on effective sponsorship). 'You need to make sure that the top people on both sides want to do it,' explains Kevin Oye, vice president of business development for optical switching company Sycamore Networks. 'If the desires of the people are different, no matter what you do, it all fails.'[17]

It's a given that the deal must work financially and must have financial benefits for both sides. The real question is, *'What is our goal beyond immediate top-line or bottom-line improvement?'* Once you answer this question, you'll have the basis for securing sponsorship for getting the most possible value out of your merger or acquisition. This requires restructuring on two levels. The first is to change your initial perspective as an acquirer or seller from *'How much money are we going to get out of this?'* to *'How will this help us create sustained profitability?'* The second mental restructuring required is to change how you think about this activity – moving from a merger or acquisition to integration mindset.

DESIGN THE INTEGRATED CULTURE

As we mentioned earlier, realizing the need for and actively managing cultural change is one of the keys to success. There are three possible ways to deal with merging cultures. It's critical to decide which one you are aiming for before starting the process – and your guide should be, *'What strategy will best serve our customers and enhance our customer experience?'* All three strategies rely on your understanding the cultural norms of both companies to be successful. (See Chapter 7: Are Your Cultural Norms Supporting Your Brand? for more on identifying and working with cultural norms.)

The three cultures include:

Assimilation. In this scenario the acquiring company assimilates the other company's culture. Employees learn to adopt the cultural norms of the acquirer in order to be recognized and rewarded moving forward.

Hybrid culture. This is partway between assimilation and an integrated culture. The two companies map out the post merger customer experience in predictable situations such as sales calls, customer contact, product development, corporate communications and vendor management, that identify best practices that best serve the customer from both companies. They then can establish rules of engagement. This approach doesn't necessitate cultural change, but creates a consistent customer experience. For this approach to work, senior management needs to demonstrate and actively reinforce these rules of engagement.

Often, hybrids begin their marriage by emphasizing what they have in common. One of the most successful M&A players, Cisco, uses the value of employee ownership as a cultural norm that it shares with potential acquisitions.[18]

Integrated culture. This is an option that takes the most effective cultural norms from each company to create something new. Cultural norms answer the questions of *'How does work get done?'* Beyond understanding what type of culture the merged company will have, it's also essential to understand the cultural norms that will add the most value to ongoing company decision-making.

Two venture capital firms that merged decided to define an integrated corporate culture. It worked because they had complete agreement from all senior partners that a competitive advantage would result from an integrated culture – one that encompassed new and integrated cultural norms. Partners reviewed each other on how well they were promoting and living their integrated culture, and assigned a full time employee to be the culture keeper until norms became fully established.

In addition to determining how to integrate cultures, leaders must be sensitive to the insecurity that the merger or acquisition process brings up in employees and prepare to spend significant time in the seemingly non-productive culture-building activities of defining, coaching, persuading and listening. The integration team should also be assigned the role of ensuring that key influencers in both companies are on board early in the process and are also demonstrating leadership. Kerry Killinger, CEO of Washington Mutual, spends significant time 'on the ground' at new acquisitions. During a recent 12-month period, he met face to face with all 12,000 employees of acquisition Great Western. Washington Mutual's approach is that the best mindset for both buyer and seller should be that this is a great opportunity to make something much greater than either party had alone.

UNDERSTANDING BRAND ASSETS

Understanding the brand assets and structural fit of both parties can make a huge difference to how you choose and prioritize candidates and how well you glean value from the resulting acquisition or sale. (For more on brand assets see Chapter 4: Align to Deliver a Unique Customer Experience). For example, a profitable regional bank (let's call it Personable Bank) with a strong brand based on customer service (personable tellers and bank officers, and ease of doing business) was purchased by a large national bank (let's call it Big National Bank). Over a period of time, Big National Bank changed the business practices of Personable Bank's staff to ones that were less personable. Then, in a few hours on a Friday night, Big National Bank dropped the Personable Bank name and changed every bank sign to its name, so that one of the most obvious outward manifestations of Personable Bank's brand, its name, literally disappeared over night. Big National Bank did nothing to transfer Personable Bank's customer-service equity through either its actions or communications – in fact the quick changeover had the effect of cutting the equity off at its knees. Subsequently, Big National Bank shortened banking hours and made everything from getting loans to waiting for tellers less convenient.

While the financial and product side, such as distribution of offices and types of financial services, made sense, Big National Bank lost

Personal Bank's valuable customer-service equity – which it paid a premium for due to the strength of the regional bank's reputation – but the value of Personal Bank's intangible customer-service asset wasn't measured so Big National Bank didn't realize that it had lost anything. Valuing brand assets in its due diligence might have led Big National Bank to the conclusion that another regional bank that had fewer brand assets but the same financial and marketing components would have been a much cheaper and more successful buy. Conversely, brand due diligence could have caused Big National Bank to create an M&A brand strategy for transferring this valuable equity from the acquired bank.

Contrast this with Washington Mutual, which not only looks at the customer experience of each of its acquisitions, but also launches a

FIGURE 17.1 WASHINGTON MUTUAL PUBLICATION FOR NEW CUSTOMERS OF ACQUIRED DIME BANK
When Washington Mutual acquired Dime Bancorp Inc. in 2001, it created 15 issues of Dime Connections to align Dime Bancorp employees to the Washington Mutual brand.

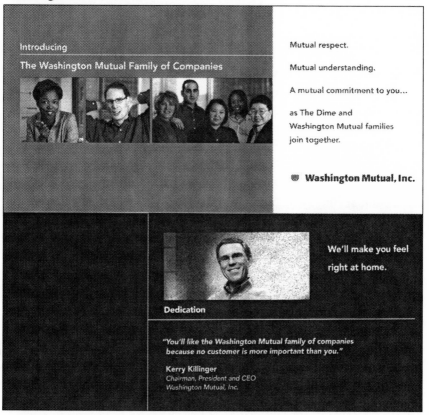

301

communications campaign to let employees and customers know with whom they will be doing business – and how it shares the important values of the acquired company. These campaigns typically include letters, billboards and advertisements over a six-month time frame. Internally, the campaign introduces the acquisition's employees to Washington Mutual's brand with a transition newsletter called Connections, and leads employees step-by-step through the acquisition process. At the same time, the company brings in 'buddies' from established Washington Mutual offices that have been through past acquisitions to be on-site before and after the official public transition. These buddies sometimes arrive as much as one month prior to the transaction and stay for up to two weeks after the conversion.

Washington Mutual also closely tracks certain post-acquisition metrics. The attrition rate of customers is one of the metrics it considers most important, because it's key to how well the company is delivering its customer experience. The immediate post-acquisition period represents a great opportunity to reinforce brand value with existing customers while building more business with new ones.

IDENTIFYING OTHER VALUABLE ACTIVITIES IN ACQUISITION CANDIDATES

Company practices and brand assets are building blocks of the customer experience. However, they are usually ignored in due diligence. Besides the obvious processes that keep every company running, the acquired company might also have unique practices that would greatly benefit the acquirer. Personable Bank might have had a highly successful system for turning depositors into mortgage holders that would have helped expand Big National Bank's business, for instance. Unless the company being acquired has recognized and built its brand assets, the buyer may miss them. Although brand assets vary from company to company, typical assets are activities that benefit customers. Brand assets may include a unique company approach, type of company reputation, industry leadership position, quality-control systems, employee experience and training, company culture, customers, compensation and rewards, and delivery systems. Brand assets are *any* practice that contributes to a compelling and distinctive customer experience.

A study conducted by Interbrand and Citibank shows that *only* one third of the value of Financial Times Stock Exchange (FTSE 100) companies is accounted for by net tangible assets.[19] One of the reasons for not spending too much time looking at brand assets has been the difficulty in valuing them. Howard Stock of *M&A Reporter* says, 'the problem with companies' current reporting of intangibles is that it is largely subjective, which makes it difficult for an investor to compare apples with apples.'[20] This is now changing as the issue of valuing brand assets is receiving attention from the Financial Accounting Standards Board (FASB).

In one FASB Statement, intangible assets must be recognized as assets apart from goodwill, with examples including marketing-related, customer-related, creative-types, and contract- and technology-based assets. Another FASB Statement governs the treatment of intangible assets on the balance sheet as either amortizable, as an expense or as a write-off. While these rules will cause more attention to be paid to brand assets, they will not impact other, more people-based assets of an acquisition.

REVIEW AND ALIGN COMMUNICATIONS

A final due diligence consideration is corporate- and product-based communications. How have you represented your brand in past communications – both externally and internally? How does this compare to the company you will be integrating with? You cannot assume that your new communications will look or feel like one brand, either to existing or prospective customers. Failure to address this issue will result in communications that are at cross-purposes and missed opportunities to build brand equity.

You can create a communications program that lets customers of the acquired company know who you are and the advantage of your brand promise. At the same time, you can provide your customers with new value learned from the acquired company.

How you handle internal communications is also very important as the following story illustrates.

Like many companies, the IT consulting firm where Sandy Smith used to work had a mission statement full of high-minded values such as 'trust' and 'openness with employees.' Everybody pretty much believed it – until the company sold out to a bigger company without bothering to tell employees first.

'Workers had to learn the news from a co-worker who heard it on her car radio at lunch,' said Smith, a quality control and training manager. In the 18 months until the sale was completed, morale and output plunged.

Employees grew so cynical they ignored directives from headquarters and ran for the exits even faster than usual in a merger.

'Nobody ever trusted the company's communications again,' Smith said.[21]

According to Craig Tall, vice chair, Corporate Development and Specialty Finance Group of Washington Mutual, 'If there is one key to a successful merger, it is over-communication. We make sure everyone hears and understands the story.' Over-communication will keep people from filling in the blanks in an information vacuum while creating consensus for change. Over-communication is also essential to set employee expectations and eliminate surprises and disappointments.

FIGURE 17.2 WASHINGTON MUTUAL PUBLICATION FOR EMPLOYEES

It's important to introduce newly acquired customers to your brand promise.

Adding brand-based considerations to the process switches the emphasis for doing mergers and acquisitions from perceived financial gain to the customer experience, and from the deal itself to the impact the deal has on your company after closing. It doesn't end when the papers have been signed, the logos have been changed, employees have new business cards, and you think you've dotted all the i's and crossed all the t's.

The best companies understand that these transactions need to serve the brand. Even those companies with extremely successful track records give such deals a back seat to delivering on their brand promise. At its 2002 annual shareholders' meeting, Washington Mutual's Killinger told shareholders the company would be spending the next year focused internally on improving customer service. Killinger acknowledged the company's rapid growth [through acquisitions] meant service levels 'have not been where I expect them to be' and that 'it would take something very special for us to pursue a major transaction.'[22] This statement was made while the company was also announcing record first-quarter results and an increased dividend for shareholders.

THE PARKER LEPLA BRAND-BASED DUE DILIGENCE MODEL

The purpose of this model is to give companies a step-by-step schematic for how brand considerations integrate into a typical acquisition process. The process has five steps: 1) due diligence; 2) pre-acquisition; 3) negotiation; 4) foundation building; 5) integration. This brand-based due diligence process allows you to add integration and synergy potential to short-term financial-return deal benefits.

Assumptions: Our Brand-Based Due Diligence Model assumes that the acquiring company wants to get the most value out of each transaction – rather than solely looking at value as ongoing revenues or tangible assets. It also assumes that this purchase represents a significant change or augmentation for the acquirer, and that the acquisition is friendly.

TABLE 17.1

Due diligence *	Pre-acquisition

• Customer experience assessment and comparison. Decide who are the best customers and what are their current experiences.
• Brand tool and brand integration assessment and comparison.
• Talents and strengths (business and function leaders), and weakness assessment and comparison.
• Company practices assessment and comparison.
• Brand assets and liabilities assessment and comparison.
• Communications assessment and comparison.
• Cultural norms assessment and comparison (including decision-making style).
• Financial models.
• Product and distribution modeling.
• Government considerations.
 	
* Some elements of this model are also talked about in more detail in earlier chapters. See Chapters 1-5.
	• Set up your integration team with clear marching orders and measurable outcomes that include creating a new performance level, using existing best practices and producing optimal performance from employees.
	• Identify critical must-haves for integration success.
	• Identify synergies between the companies. You are looking for four main effects:
	  – determine who the best customer is;
	  – enhance the customer experience for the long term;
	  – make the merger of the two brands believable to both core customer bases;
	  – synthesize the company actions (practices, assets, communications and cultural norms) to enhance the new firm's abilities and shore up its weaknesses.
	• Identify barriers to integration in each area. You are looking to minimize:
	  – customer experience confusion based on overlapping offerings and inconsistent brand principle, value, personality and employee practices;
	  – employee confusion about roles and taking action;
	  – employee alienation (due to resistance to change or poorly communicated change) resulting in work that either meets only minimum performance requirements or actually descends to the level of sabotage;
	  – slow or stalled integration.

Negotiation	Foundation building	Integration
• Use the assessment, comparison, synergies and barriers to determine the value and structure of the deal. This will give the acquiring firm and its integration team a huge advantage in the negotiation process because they will have a more complete understanding of how the proposed acquisition should be valued. This will give them the flexibility to accept a valuation that the acquired company will think is reasonable, but may still be a deal from the acquirer's point of view. It will also allow them to play hardball on the downside, because it lets them bring up the true barriers to integration.	• Use the integration team to determine and clarify new senior management roles. • Use an extended integration team, including combined senior management (which now includes key players from the acquired company) as the vehicle for setting direction for the new company. • Use a facilitated integrated-branding process to create a new and improved customer experience through analysis and agreement on brand tools, brand strategy, cultural norms, ongoing brand-asset resource allocation, and company practice alignment and integration. • Create both an internal and a public communications plan. • Augment performance measures-of-success and annual goals based on new analysis and planning efforts.	• Implement the internal and public communications plans. • Create an online resource center that includes an integration coordinator and staff for quality assurance, feedback, problem solving and measurement. • If the acquisition will remain a separate division, initiate a short-term management exchange. • Use feedback to continually improve the integration process. • Hold annual meetings of the integration team to course correct and measure outcomes until goals have been achieved.

SOME EXAMPLES OF DOING IT RIGHT

In February 2000, an unusual merger between Earthlink and Mindspring closed. There were two things that made it unusual – first it was a merger of two equals – a process that is fraught with potential political infighting and power plays. Second, the goal of the resulting organization was to integrate some of the best brand attributes of both companies. For instance, when they went to merge their back office and billing operations, 'company leaders found certain aspects of both to be desirable,' according to a 1998 *Harvard Business Review* article by Ronald Ashkena, Lawrence Demonico and Suzanne Francis. The authors state: 'EarthLink's system was easily scalable, while MindSpring's was flexible. Taking desires for both features into account, the company pulled off another feat of corporate triangulation: Using functions from the two legacy systems, it built an entirely new billing system from the ground up.'[23]

Brokerage house Merrill Lynch has made more than 18 successful acquisitions in the past seven years, including the purchase of Mercury Asset Management for U.S. $6.6 billion in 1997. One of its success stories is the integration of companies with varying global cultures into its organization. Chairman and CEO David Komansky talks about the philosophy that drives the company's actions, 'It's totally futile to impose a U.S.-centric culture on a global organization. We think of our business as a broad road. All we expect people to do is stay on the road within the bounds of our strategy and our principles of doing business. We don't expect them to march down the white line, and frankly, we don't care too much if they are on the left-hand side of the road or the right-hand side of the road.'[24]

Cisco Systems is the poster child for doing it right. The company has acquired 70 companies since 1993; 26 companies in fiscal 2000 alone. Additionally, it has retained almost all the acquired personnel, while improving revenues derived from the acquired firms' products and technologies. According to John Bayless at venture capital fund Sevin Rosen Funds, who helped in a Cisco acquisition, 'I haven't found anyone in the industry that has a process that is as tuned.'[25]

According to Ed Paulson in *Inside Cisco: The Real Story of Sustained M&A Growth*, 'Fundamental to the Cisco acquisition approach is the belief that acquiring a company's technology without acquiring the future efforts of its people is a formula for an unsuccessful purchase.

As a result of this basic tenet, Cisco spends a lot of time evaluating a company before any purchase agreement is reached.'[26]

Cisco has a list of minimum criteria that must be met before even getting to due diligence. The basic criteria are:

1. The target and Cisco must share a compatible vision of the future, from both an industry and product perspective.

2. The acquisition must produce a quick win for Cisco shareholders, preferably within 12 months of purchase.

3. The companies must share a complementary culture, or what Chambers calls 'the right chemistry.'

4. There have to be long-term wins for the four major constituencies-namely, shareholders, employees, customers and business partners.

5. For large acquisitions, the target must be geographically located close to a Cisco office. [27]

Washington Mutual grew from a small, regional player into the United States' biggest thrift and home lender through a steady series – more than 32 since 1983 – of acquisitions. Along the way, it has become known for doing it right, through many methods mentioned earlier in the chapter. And the numbers bear witness to the company's success. In 1983, Washington Mutual had U.S. $5 billion in assets and 2,000 employees. At the beginning of 2002, it had 45,000 employees and U.S. $275 billion in assets.

'If you had invested U.S. $100 in Washington Mutual common stock at the time Washington Mutual first became a publicly traded company on March 11, 1983, and in each of the S&P 500 Composite Index and the S&P Financial Index (and reinvested all dividends), the value of your investment in Washington Mutual common stock would have grown to U.S. $4,464 by the end of 2001, compared with U.S. $1,396 for the S&P Financial Index and U.S. $1,269 for the S&P Composite Index.'[28]

Since most liquidity events for shareholders occur through mergers or acquisitions rather than IPOs, managing the alignment of brand equity with a solid set of potential buyers well in advance is one of the most important jobs a CEO can do for shareholders, customers and employees. The benefit of doing this in advance of a sale will help a company position itself for its current business opportunities as well as for a successful exit in the future.

What to Ask During Brand-Based Due Diligence

Point of Interest

Discovery:
- What is our strategic role?
- What is our current customer experience?
- What are our dominant brands?
- What are the brand tools that make up our brand promise?
- What is our brand strategy?
- What are our significant company practices?
- What are our intangible brand assets?
- What do our communications look like?
- What are our cultural norms (rules of the road)?

Deliverables:
- How will this integration improve our customer experience?
- What synergies will allow us to raise the competitive bar?
- What will our new brand tools and brand structure look like?
- What will our new culture look like?
- What will our communications look like?

EXECUTIVE LEADER LOG

It could be an interesting exercise, as a precursor to planning an exit strategy based on being acquired, to look for potential acquirers based on brand similarities and compatibilities, rather than on complementary product lines. It might bring potential out-of-the-box synergistic opportunities to light preparing it to be bought.

HUMAN RESOURCES LEADER LOG

I know we're hoping to merge with a current partner, sometime in the next two years. However, I also know that many key employees are nervous about a culture clash. I wonder if proposing that both firms discover their brands and develop a two-year plan to bring them together, prior to the merger, wouldn't help things go more smoothly and help avoid the mass exodus of product developers, which is what I'm afraid of?

SALES LEADER LOG

I've been through two mergers – and both times, sales plummeted right afterwards. What can I do as sales manager given our upcoming merger, to prevent that from happening this time? Maybe pairing up our salespeople with someone from the other company's sales force would be a start. If we reward the two of them equally for sales, with an extra bonus for cross-selling, that would surely demonstrate to both customer bases how committed we are, and what value they'll get from the combined product lines plus the combined service and expertise of the sales forces.

NOTES

[1] (29 November 2001) 'Brand equity increasingly important in determining corporate value,' The Korea Herald, Financial Times Info Ltd - Asia Africa Intel Wire.

[2] Interbrand Web site: <http://www.interbrand.com/papers.asp>, p 9

[3] Haigh, D (June 1999) 'Understanding the Financial Value of Brands,' Brand Finance PLC, p 6

[4] Deighton, Jon (January 2002), 'How Snapple Got Its Juice Back,' *Harvard Business Review*, p 7

[5] Kager, P and Malek, J (1 August 2001) 'Get ready to merge or diverge,' *Pharmaceutical Executive*, pp 52-60

[6] (16 September 2001) 'Mergers & acquisitions - Is it good for your company's health?,' *Investor Digest*

[7] Radzin, J, editor, 'Managing Culture in Mergers and Acquisitions,' *The Conference Board*, p 7

[8] Yoon, S (11 October 2001) 'Career Review: Pay Attention to People,' *Far Eastern Economic Review*

[9] The Conference Board, Managing Culture in Mergers and Acquisitions, John Radzin, editor, page 7, sponsored by The Continuous Learning Group

[10] Carey, D, moderator (May-June 2000) 'Lessons From the Master Acquirers: A CEO Roundtable on Making Mergers Succeed,' *Harvard Business Review*, pp 145-154

[11] West, L (19 November 2001) 'Keeping clients not easy after a merger,' National Underwriter Property & Casualty - Risk & Benefits Management, p 14

[12] Ibid.

[13] Kovacevich, RM, *The Vision & Values of Wells Fargo*, How we intend to be one of America's great companies, p. 18

[14] Prince, CJ, (01 May 2001) Cool hand Kovacevich, Chief Executive

[15] Aiello, B and Watkins, M (November-December 2000) 'Special Report, Managing M&A Magic, The Fine Art of Friendly Acquisition,' *Harvard Business Review*, pp 99-116

[16] 'Human Resources—Ensuring there's life after mergers,' *Post Magazine*, 4/26/01, p 32

[17] Weber, T, (27 August 2001) 'Lessons learned from last year's M&As: Whether acquiring or merging, cooperation between companies is key,' Telephony, p 20

[18] 'Special Report, Managing M&A Magic, The Fine Art of Friendly Acquisition,' Robert J. Aiello and Michael D. Watkins, *Harvard Business Review*, November-December 2000, pp 99-116.

[19] (2001) FASB Statements No. 141 & 142, 'The impact on intangible assets including brand, a special report by Interbrand,' Interbrand

[20] Stock, H (10 September 2001) 'FASB Assesses M&A's Intangible Aftermath: Financial Accounting Board Awaits Comments on Two Proposals,' M&A Reporter

[21] Shellenbarger, S (16 June 1999) 'Companies Declare Lofty Employee Values, Then Forget to Act, Work & Family,' *The Wall Street Journal*, p B1

[22] Virgin, B (17 April 2002) 'Record quarter at Washington Mutual: Company says it will now turn its focus to service,' *The Seattle Times*, p C1

[23] Ashkena, R, Demonico, L and Francis, S (January-February 1998) 'Making the Deal Real: How GE Capital Integrates Acquisitions,' *Harvard Business Review*, p 167

[24] Carey, D, moderator (May-June 2000) 'Lessons From the Master Acquirers: A CEO Roundtable on Making Mergers Succeed,' *Harvard Business Review*, pp 145-154

[25] Goldblatt, H (8 November 1999) 'Cisco's Secrets,' *Fortune*, p 178

[26] (2001) 'Inside Cisco: The Real Story of Sustained M&A Growth,' Ed Paulson, John Wiley & Sons, p 30

[27] Ibid.

[28] (2001) Washington Mutual Summary Annual Report, p 33

CHAPTER

THE BRAND MANAGER EXPERIENCE: IN THEIR OWN WORDS

When we wrote *Brand Driven* in 2002, we believed that tapping into our clients' experiences was essential to providing our readers with practical advice for living their brands. So most of the strategies in this book are practical and proven processes for taking your brand to the next level. This time, we're pleased to offer a chapter where we've taken practicality one step further. The following represents the experiences and "aha's" of brand managers in their own words.

We define a brand manager as someone who has either titled or de facto responsibility for building and protecting the company's brands. In some organizations this means everything in the organization including setting annual business strategies and in others is more narrowly defined within marketing or human resources.

We wanted brand managers to tell us what worked or didn't work on the road to integrated branding. What motivated them? What was most effective? Where did they feel that they'd failed? This brand manager "forum" includes people from many different departments – senior management, marketing, human resources and legal at organizations that range from community not-for-profits, to business-to-business, consumer, healthcare, high-tech and government. Finally, they range in size from local institutions to the Fortune 100.

We've gathered their answers into a Q & A format to highlight the differences and the themes faced by all brand managers.

Jim Kessler is Vice President and General Counsel of Health New England (HNE). HNE is a managed care organization serving western Massachusetts since 1985. HNE employs more than 200 associates and serves nearly 100,000 members and 5,000 employers. HNE's brand principle is personal and accountable service, and it is building an association around local healthcare provider. Parker LePla began working with HNE in 2002 and supplied it with a brand environment assessment that measured the perceptions of employers, members, insurance brokers, physicians and HNE's own associates. From this the organization created its brand tools. Parker LePla has also helped it with annual brand strategies, tagline direction and developing a deeper understanding of its relationships with physicians.

Jamie Gier is the senior director of marketing for IDX Systems Corporation, Carecast Operating Unit, now part of GE Medical. IDX Systems Corporation provides information technology solutions that maximize value in the delivery of healthcare by improving the quality of patient care, enhancing medical outcomes, and reducing the costs of care. Core to IDX is Carecast™, an enterprise-wide clinical software solution that creates a comprehensive lifetime electronic patient record by automating the workflow of physicians, nurses, pharmacists and other users while supporting clinical, financial and administrative processes. IDX Carecast is used at many of the top healthcare networks and hospitals in the United States, Canada and the United Kingdom, Its brand of Advancing Fail-safe Care™ emphasizes high system reliability, speed and clinical excellence. Parker LePla conducted an initial assessment and benchmarking study in 2001 and recently completed a 2004 brand report card, which measures specific brand equity gains and competitive brand strength.

Rob Fukai is the former executive director and Steve Valandra is the communications director for the General Administration Department of the State of Washington (GA). General Administration's strategic role is the essential operations partner for state agencies. It supports more than 100 agencies' day-to-day operations so that each agency can focus on what it does well. GA helps agencies navigate business and government processes and stretch their dollars. It provides such services as procurement, space leasing, project design and construction, maintenance, office supplies, motor pool and mail services individually or as part of a cost-effective services package. Employees use a brand principle of responsive and responsible to set the bar for service standards. Parker LePla helped the division with research and facilitated its management team in developing several brand tools including the strategic role, principle and story. We have also helped it set annual brand strategies and consulted on ways to enhance employee acceptance of the brand.

Jennifer Brandon is the executive director of Community Voice Mail National. CVMN partners with community-based organizations to empower people in crisis and transition by distributing free, personalized 24-hour voice mail access nationwide – directly linking individuals to jobs, housing and stability. Community Voice Mail helps people avoid long-term unemployment and homelessness, to escape domestic violence, and to become more productive and self-sufficient. It also helps social and health workers who distribute its numbers to do their jobs more effectively. CVMN has successfully replicated the Community Voice Mail program in 37 cities to date. One of the most important brand principles at CVMN is valuing partnerships, which is how it uniquely delivers on its mission.

Stephanie Ferguson is a director in the People & Organization Capability Division within Human Resources at Microsoft. Her group works on a wide variety of projects, all aimed at developing and organizing Microsoft's people to successfully move toward the mission of enabling people throughout the world to realize their 'potential,' while living by their tenets and values. 'Living their brand' is a guiding principle for Stephanie and her group. Her customers are internal Microsoft employees and leaders. Her groups help employees better realize their potential, as these leaders are Microsoft key corporate assets.

Adrienne Gemperle is the former vice president of Human Resources at Shurgard Storage Centers. Shurgard Storage Centers, Inc. is one of the world's largest owners and operators in the self-storage industry with 620 properties under management across the United States and Europe. Of these storage centers, the company owns 496 properties, representing approximately 32.4 million net rentable square feet. With more than 1,800 employees, Shurgard acquires, owns, and manages its own storage centers. After determining that the company's brand promise was expect more, the company went through an employee branding process with Parker LePla that looked at how each employee was delivering expect more to the customer and with each other internally, culminating in an all-managers' meeting where the results were disseminated and discussed.

Courtenay Chamberlin is the former communications director and brand manager of Tacoma Art Museum in Washington State. The

80-year-old Tacoma Art Museum, boasting a new U.S. $22 million facility, has the mission of connecting people through art. Museum collections and educational programs are dedicated to art of modern and contemporary periods, with an active commitment to art and artists from the Northwest. Tacoma Art Museum is part of a regional economic development effort focusing on a cultural renaissance in Tacoma. In preparation for a big public relations campaign coincident with the opening of its new, world-class building, Tacoma Art Museum undertook the integrated branding process to help communicate its new image. The result? Tacoma Art Museum knows its focus should be on stretching people's minds, and in a personality that is approachable and inviting. Its public relations, ads, programs, fundraisers, educational efforts and marketing reflect and reinforce this brand reality.

How do you use your organization's brand to guide your decisions? Can you give me an example?

Kessler (HNE):
The first thing this has meant for us is that it has helped us to understand what Health New England's (HNE) character really was. We *felt* it but didn't have any shared way to *talk* about it. Having the brand put into words helps us with decisions: we've put a name to our brand identity and can use it to think about whatever comes up and that has been really useful.

We have not done as much as we need to or applied it as consistently as we would like to. That's because our brand concept is so much rooted in how we normally behave that people will often kick back and assume they don't have to think about it. People say, "Why should I take time to apply the brand? Isn't 'personal' and 'accountable' how we do it already?"

It has been useful in helping us to think about things like our member service function. Even though we live our brand as part of our culture, it helps us value our service qualities of being *personal* and *accountable*. It stops us from being tempted down a path that might seem good for our bottom line in the short run, but bad for our future. In order to be more efficient, many companies are making their service functions less personal and less friendly. It's been a competitive advantage to us to have a customer service function that *is* really personal. Thinking about our brand helped us to avoid the trap of automating our way into the next generation of customer service, but paying a big price we weren't really contemplating.

Gemperle (Shurgard):

We use our brand promise, *expect more*, and our values to give our store managers a framework for making decisions. We don't have a lot of rule books here. Our store teams work largely independently and have a lot of discretion in the day-to-day operations of their stores. If a prickly decision crops up and a manager isn't sure what to do, he or she can turn to our brand promise for a guideline as to what is right for the customer and our company.

Our brand promise is deliberately lofty – something we aspire to. It is also dynamic; we don't ever expect to fully achieve it because we want to continue to strive for something better. We're a service business, which means we can never do enough to please our customers, or better yet, anticipate their needs.

At the same time, we knew we needed to make our brand promise meaningful in the here and now. How is it relevant to a store manager— and his prospective customer – today? So as a first step, we translated our promise into four specific 'proof points' – four very tangible reasons a customer should store with us rather than the place down the street. These have become very helpful sales tools for our managers. Better yet, they are setting new standards for the storage business.

Valandra (GA):

One thing we've done initially is to integrate our brand into our strategic plan and into all of the division business plans. It is written into every division's annual plan. The question we pose is, "How are you going to honor our brand promise?" and then we ask our people at the top, our assistant directors and program managers to come up with answers. Part of the strategic plan is to develop better ways to reach customers and provide service. Our goal is improving customer commitment, which we believe we will reach through everything from employee training to revamping our web site.

Fukai (GA):

At this stage, it gives the employees actionable things that they can do to respond to all of the changes that are occurring. Changes like reduced budgets and increased competition will potentially have a very negative impact against performance. We've created a framework for customer organizations to be successful in this environment. And the key difference is integrated in performance management and employee selection as well as day-to-day with customers.

Ferguson (Microsoft):

We have a great brand. Realizing potential is applicable to everything we do. We are looking at cultural aspirations and our employee value proposition in a way that will help us build an integrated brand. We don't want to do something to our culture that doesn't support our external facing brand and goals.

We look to our mission, tenets, and values to guide our decisions. For example when we built the leadership competencies for Microsoft we looked through the lens of what we need to do for our business, as well as our brand, our values, and our tenets. These are very important lenses for all the work we do.

On a tactical level, we have looked at how our brand shows up visually internally as well as externally. For example, on our HR intranet.

We also think about how our brand is communicated at our Executive Briefing Center. Important visitors talk to us about HR practices. Now they see these non-product communications in a branded template. We talk to lots of companies and we want the message and image to match what they are hearing from other Microsoft groups.

We've used our brand to guide decisions about our succession planning program and how we manage our talent.

To help prioritize decision making, we have done real research with employees to substantiate their opinion of our brand value.

Gier (IDX Carecast):

In marketing, we use brand to help develop our message platform and we incorporate it into all communications to all key constituencies. The brand guides all content for advertising and public relations down to what we pitch and how we pitch it. For example, we review editorial calendars for all of our targeted trade publications and identify story opportunities that we can match up with customer examples that best communicate our brand. Maybe a magazine is doing a cover story on medication error reduction, for instance. We will look at customers that have tangible results in using information technology to improve patient safety and the value it delivers to their hospital or clinic users. We are allowing our customers to be the voice of our brand. Through them we communicate our brand's values and attributes.

From a global viewpoint, we use the brand to guide all areas of the business – for instance, in product strategy, we make sure our product road map aligns with what our customers value in information technology. It is the value customers get from our product and organization in addition to new brand value from ongoing development – ensuring that any development work we do is aligned with our brand. Because *reliability* is a brand attribute, when we make enhancements to our product, our development team ensures we are not compromising reliability. And now seeing the impact our brand has made in customer loyalty and satisfaction, and employee loyalty and satisfaction, we are using that information to drive our strategic imperatives going forward. So our brand not only guides our daily decisions but our long-term business strategy as well.

Brandon (CVMN):

Partnerships run through our structure: We partner with community-based agencies, which in turn partner with peer agencies in their communities. We do not just hire people and place them into a community to run Community Voice Mail. We choose to work through local agencies that know each community because they have already established connections.

We have an application process that local agencies go through in order to become a CVM site. In the application we ask for a number of standard things such as their business plan and funding information, but we have also decided to ask them for evidence of partnerships since that is our unique way of achieving our mission. Evidence of partnerships runs through the application as an important criterion we look for. Applicant agencies must show intention by at least 10 other organizations within their community that will use their voice mail service. This helps all of us assess need and promote the community-wide value of the service. CVM sites partner with organizations that do not just service homeless individuals, but a broader range of individuals in need within the community such as low income, healthcare, job services, domestic violence, etc.

We also have created a memorandum of agreement (MOA) which can be found on our website. This MOA helps establish our respective roles and expectations of the partnership as well as what some of the standards are. The agreement is reviewed annually. Our goal with this document is to establish standards, but also remain flexible enough to allow for localization and to partner effectively with many different organizations that have many different missions.

We invested in designing a strong, user-friendly website that includes information on each CVM site. This makes it easy to get information out and connect with people. It also helps us control the message in a cost effective way. Our service as well as our national federation model and approach are interesting to funders as well as people in need of local information.

Chamberlin (Tacoma Art Museum):

We use our brand as an input to our strategic planning process. We check our goals against the brand: We ask ourselves such questions as "Is it mind stretching? Is this goal civic minded?" For our day-to-day operations, our brand has become a component for how we choose exhibitions and then, how we display them. For every potential exhibition, we ask ourselves: will the community be able to align themselves with this exhibition? Is it mind-stretching? Are there core themes we display through the art? And how do we convey them to visitors? It has helped us to have a common language to talk about things and when I ask, 'Does it support the brand?' everybody knows what I mean. This in turn has helped us all be on the same page.

Branding in Action at the General Administration Division, State of Washington

Point of Interest

When General Administration (GA) revealed its brand, one thing that became immediately clear was that its strategic role of essential operations partner meant that it needed to change the way it did business. Rather than selling each of its many services individually, it now made sense to develop a one-stop service for its agency customers.

Phil Grigg, information systems manager for GA, saw this as an opportunity for change. "I had already thought that GA should market its multiple services and along came this branding initiative talking about a similar kind of a thing. And we had an empty building so there was an opportunity to benefit the State at the same time.

Coincidentally, one of GA's customers, the Governor's Office of Indian Affairs, was looking for space and talked to Grigg about its horror stories around both not knowing the procurement rules and how lack of bandwidth caused them to spend too much time on operations.

'We walked them through a needs assessment which covered everything from computer support to an affordable and measurable office supply system. Our ability to provide all of these services in one package, with one contact person and one bill, represents a huge savings for them,' explains Grigg. 'For us, it's a good deal because we are doing this stuff anyway – what difference does it make if we have a few more people calling our help desk?'

GA helped this agency buy its way out of an old lease, realize economies of scale through co-locating the agency's staff from different sites, and follow the correct procurement procedures for accountability. It also provided a complete suite of other services including tenant improvements, utilities, janitorial, security, recycling, computer desktop support, training, network access, motor pool, contracting for surplus, access to conference rooms, telephone system, software licenses, and periodic reporting to the State. Most importantly, GA is helping this agency save both time and energy, which the agency can now redirect in the form of additional service and support to its constituents – the tribes throughout Washington.

'As with any change there are challenges. We have had to develop a new kind of billing program and in some cases we are asking a division to provide more services than they might normally – in order to meet the customer's need for a complete package. And of course we have some people who haven't gotten with the brand yet and say that we really don't do business that way. Having the support of the executive director and the fact that this brand is factually based on what we do well, helps with these issues.

'A lot of our strategic role is about listening to the customer instead of us describing how we do business. Being an essential operations partner requires active listening.'

Where do you see living your brand paying off the most for your organization?

Valandra (GA):

I'll see it paying off when we get the proper things in place to be able to retain our current customer base. In the State of Washington, competitive contracting will allow agencies to go to the private sector if they don't like what they are getting from us. In the past, our customers have had a problem with our consistency of service as well as with our project progress communications. Our greatest potential for improvement is to increase the level of communication and follow-up in the work we are already doing – this really stood out in our original brand research.

Fukai (GA):

Every day in every way. Most difficult for me personally is finding a way to move this through the organization – because any large organization has so much momentum and inertia against new ideas. Then there is the culture piece. We need to figure out ways to energize the organization itself. The other piece is to resist the urge to mandate things. I sit in a meeting and employees talk and talk and we kind of drift off. Why don't we just decide it will be "mail services"? (A new division name) But people will not do it unless they can impact the implementation – and what that looks like will be different for every organization.

Ferguson (Microsoft):

Integrating our brand throughout people and internal organization practices, systems and research we do is fairly new to us. The ultimate payoff is yet to come. Thinking ahead it helps clarify our goals to our employee base and executives. If there is a difference between an external message and an internal message we have to explain it and show the links. When these messages are aligned they are more compelling and require fewer resources on our part to justify and explain our actions and decisions. We don't have to point out where there is alignment – if they are aligned – people just get it.

In HR, we can make real progress toward living our brand, which will help us make progress to be a successful company. We're not just thinking about it.

Gier (IDX Carecast):

There are two areas – number one is business alignment and direction. For several years after the acquisition of our operating unit by IDX, our product lost significant identity in the marketplace. We weren't sure how we were perceived in the market as defined by customers, analysts and consultants. This allowed our competition to step forward and reposition our product. We knew we needed to determine what made us distinctive based on what our customers valued about our product.

We got our top management involved in creating our brand. We started by identifying strengths, weaknesses and what our customers identified as unique. We then used that information as a compass for knowing where we needed better alignment across the entire organization. The brand is our compass. And our compass is focused on "fail-safe care" – we develop and implement software for mission critical environments within the healthcare enterprise. If patient care is going to depend on technology you need to make sure the technology helps support a fail-safe system. This compass ensures that all we do helps advance fail-safe care.

Fail-safe care can be further broken down into three components. First, the technology must be reliable – it can never go down. Second, if you are going to get clinicians to use technology, it must have sub-second response time to support efficiency. The technology must operate at the same pace as the mind – otherwise clinicians will not embrace using technology. The third is promoting an institution of safety. It's equally important that our technology supports safe patient care across the enterprise, reduces medical errors, improves physician productivity and eliminates time consuming administrative tasks.

The second aspect of brand pay-off is focused on customer success. In our business, our partnerships are like a marriage – they last 20-plus years. In many cases, our technology solutions become the backbone for how customers deliver quality patient care. So we need to make sure customers are successful in using the technology, achieving value and getting the most out of their partnership with IDX. These are multi-million dollar investments – our brand was built on the successes of our business as experienced by our customers.

Today, we are seeing the impact our brand has made on customer loyalty since its inception. As an example, our customers, repeat purchasing is a key indicator – would they recommend us to others? From a recently completed brand audit, we had a 30% increase in the number of customers who would repurchase our product. This is particularly important because in our business, peer-to-peer word of mouth is essential to those purchasing software. We need to ensure customers are benefiting and satisfied with the service we provide as an organization.

Point of Interest

IDX Carecast: The Brand Report Card

IDX Systems Corporation's Carecast Operating Unit wanted to track the strength of its brand and determine what actions, messages and sales strategies had resonated with customers. They hired Parker LePla to create a brand report card that benchmarked its brand in 2004 with previous research conducted in 2001.

The report card provided IDX Carecast with an at-a-glance picture of brand equity growth, buying criteria as well as how well brand messaging had resonated with customers. Report card sections included numeric brand equity scores for specific customer experiences, numeric product criteria importance ratings, perceived market value over average market price, the top three vendors in the consideration set, unique brand approach and brand attributes cited.

IDX Carecast discovered that it had realized significant improvement in many areas that reflect brand equity and that customers considered it to have a great value-vs.-competitive-products premium. Customers also had heard and valued its core brand attribute of advancing fail-safe care.

According to Jamie Gier, director of marketing communications for IDX Carecast, 'Seeing the impact that certain brand attributes have made in customer and employee loyalty and satisfaction has allowed us to use that information to drive our strategic imperatives going forward.'

326

Gemperle (Shurgard):

In taking care of our customers. One of the challenges of a business such as ours is that our leadership team too rarely comes in contact with our customers. Our store teams are the face of Shurgard, and we count on them to present a helpful, smiling one to the public. Our brand promise helps us to attract the kind of people to our organization who will deliver extra-mile service to thousands of customers around the country. On a corporate level, it also reminds us that if we expect our store teams to go the extra mile for their customers, we'd better do the same for them – and for each other.

Kessler (HNE):

We had a lot of activity in our community that was not bringing concrete benefits to us – such as interactions with our brokers, who are our major sales channel, and other relationships with people all over the community because we are a local company. But we weren't seeing these relationships clearly or consistently, and we weren't getting all of the benefit from them that we could have. We can now see how those relationships were a tremendous part of our company strength and a reason for our survival. A lot of smaller health plans like ours have not survived, but our strong relationships with members, employers, brokers and others have kept us going. Because of our brand focus, we are building on those relationships. We have reached out to brokers we had less contact with and developed new relationships. We began adding relationships with practice managers in our provider offices. We've also done a good job of getting more involved with the local chambers of commerce. The brand has also helped us make the best use of our limited advertising budget. In the past, our advertising didn't have a clear, consistent message. The brand work has really helped us to have a clearer sense of who we are.

In many ways we still haven't gotten the benefit from branding we really should—we have been slow in moving forward on some projects. That may be a result of failing to apply the brand to decisions and pushing brand projects out of the way for the crisis du jour. The biggest challenge I've had is making sure the brand stays connected to people's perceptions of the work they do every day. People will say, of course, 'I am all about personal and accountable,' but sometimes you have to go the extra step, roll up your sleeves and ask, 'Am I really doing everything I need to do? Will my actions make a difference to my underlying business objectives? Will these actions ultimately lead to new business prospects and new business in a powerful way?'

Where we have succeeded in making these connections, our brand focus has worked well. When we looked at some key prospects instead of focusing on standard sales points for HNE's health plans we asked ourselves, 'How do our personal relationships and localness play into this discussion?' We just landed the City of Springfield, MA account in part by focusing in on the personal relationships—we thought about areas where our relationships were not as strong as they should have been. We started thinking about that a long time ago and it has really paid off. Before we began the brand work, we would have said 'We have a great health plan – how come we aren't in the account?' And now we realize that sometimes building the relationship with the prospect comes first, because the relationship allows people to see how well our plans work. We will continue to focus on things about the brand that make a concrete difference.

Another thing we were completely ineffective on was public relations—part of it was how we were or weren't using our relationships in the community to make ourselves better known. The more we thought about this, the more we realized we could benefit from these relationships. One of our employees knew a lot of people in TV and radio stations but never made them aware of Health New England as a source of news or information. We've now connected those dots and we've gotten more press on community activities in the past year than in the whole previous history of HNE. We are still learning and struggling. But at least we now have the concepts and are making progress where we never were before.

The great thing is we are beginning to see questions and possibilities where we never saw them. Because of what we have done at our associate (employee) meetings people really have an idea and an image that they can put words to. This will be supported by our new tagline: 'How can we help?' Having the whole company on board as to why we are special has kept morale very high. Health New England has never had a tagline, let alone one that is consciously tied to what we stand for and our competitive advantage.

Chamberlin (Tacoma Art Museum):

The staff now has the ability to differentiate our museum from any other museum in the area. We also have some common goals that everyone can identify. Best of all, everyone from maintenance person to curator can say where we fit in the industry and what we're trying to accomplish.

Tacoma Art Museum: Living the Brand at a Cultural Institution

How do you transform the curious, one-time guest into a regular museum visitor and increasingly committed museum champion? By articulating and living your unique approach and the promise to the community.

That's what Tacoma Art Museum did when it was planning a move to a new U.S. $22 million world-class museum facility. The 86-year-old institution knew it had a deeply embedded promise, but had not articulated it. Since the Tacoma, Washington community had been investing heavily in art institutions as a tourist draw, there was a lot of competition for mind space and all the museums were starting to merge together into a fuzzy undifferentiated grouping. Many people came to the Tacoma Art Museum looking for the Glass Museum, and vice versa, for example. Differentiation was becoming critical.

How to differentiate? First off, Tacoma Art Museum articulated its brand tools:

Principle:

Mind-stretching

Values:

Community, Integrity, Pursuit of excellence, Inclusiveness, Art, Art's impact on people's lives, Learning

Personality:

Gracious, Approachable, Smart, Passionate, Civic minded, Dynamic, Innovative

Positioning:

Tacoma Art Museum, at the center of the Tacoma arts community, connects people to new concepts in an inviting way.

Ad campaign theme for the opening:

'Antidote to everyday'

Secondly, to demonstrate its unique promise, Tacoma Art Museum distributed 5,000 'floaty' toothbrushes that had a visual in the handle of two girls walking into the new museum 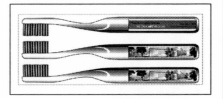 and when you tipped the toothbrush, they came out as Renoir's Two Sisters, a painting in the museum's permanent collection. These toothbrushes were then handed out at ten locations in the Tacoma and Seattle area, 'making art part of your every day' – literally.

The new building was designed to pay off the branding as well. The building enables the museum to better live its mission through offering more coveted exhibitions, more space for discussion and a more mind stretching experience overall. Security guards were trained to answer visitor questions in a mind stretching way. Curators looked for ways to connect people to art more viscerally. The result? More patrons than expected. More visitors turned into members than projected. A clear distinction from other Tacoma-area museums. A clear promise, executed well, connecting the community with art.

What's hard about living your brand?

Valandra (GA):

The thing that surprised me the most was resistance from higher level management people – there is more than just skepticism. A few of the other level managers – if you could speak to them privately – would say they don't think it is really necessary for them. In one case they believe they know the customer base so well, they know what they need to do and don't need any assistance. Our executive director has made it clear that this is something we are going to do and it's key to GA's future. Our director and deputy director are meeting with all employee groups to talk about the reasoning behind the effort and what it offers for them.

Through the brand team we hired a contractor to do a usability study on our website and it identified eight major problems. It will give us a better foundation on how to do business. There will be more of these brand building things that come along and these will be identified throughout all programs to build cohesiveness – but the director talking to all employees is key. Part of the effort is getting feedback from each employee. We ask: 'What do you need in your area and what can you do to improve the services in your area?' For example one of the truck drivers for the Central Stores Division said, 'I go out and drive around and am at different agencies all the time and often they ask about other GA services. But I have nothing I can give them that tells them about those other services or who they could contact.' This confirms what the research told us – and it's something that the brand team will work to make happen as quickly as possible. Acting on this type of feedback helps us to understand and reinforce on-brand behavior at the staff level.

Fukai (GA):

It was pretty easy because we were looking for some kind of framework to have success. We were in a new competitive environment and transitioning to a new Governor – a perfect storm for the sponsorship discussion. The deputy director, Grant Fredricks, and I believed that branding would allow us to cope but also advance the ball. Through our branding efforts we have initiatives to add to our General Administration portfolio of services that would really save the state and taxpayers a lot of money without degrading the services we provide. In order to do this, our customers have to have confidence in our ability to deliver our current services. You can't introduce new products very effectively if you are starting from a place of negative brand equity or even a 2.0 (a rating on a -5 to +5 brand equity measurement scale). You can't get there without the confidence of the customer base. We are very concerned about that. I was at a meeting yesterday and the leadership group was talking about big ideas that their teams had. One was strategic sourcing. It is about cost savings realized by intensely managing the supply chain across state government. This is a good idea, but to implement we have to overcome customer skepticism that it is an attempt by GA to centralize and control their purchasing.

Gaining internal sponsorship was relatively easy. But gaining sponsorship at my level with colleagues is not easy because of where we were starting from. We are seeing positive signs – such as the work that one of our program managers, Phil Grigg, has done to enable GA to act as an essential operations partner in many areas across divisions for agency customers. While many of these service package partnership projects are currently for smaller agencies, the biggest benefits will be realized by larger agencies. In one such case at the Department of Health, our Real Estate Group was able to consolidate them from 23 separate offices and 23 separate leases. This group got very creative to transfer those leases to one new facility and they are there today. Their director has nothing but good things to say about how at GA, we were their essential operations partner to make this happen.

Ferguson (Microsoft):

This goes to the newness of our efforts in this area. Using our brand as a lens is not yet a habit or a natural inclination for all our leaders. It is change. Change is hard.

We need to ensure that the decisions, actions and communications that come out of our group are authentic and not marketing spin to employees. We are a self critical culture. We can be very cynical of internal messages. If the message does not fit actual experience, it can get a reaction.

Our brand isn't necessarily everyone's first thought. It gets into the decision eventually. We are still working on the seamlessness and habit of using brand as a decision guide in the minds of employees.

Gier (IDX Carecast):

Surprisingly, one of the most challenging aspects is having an enhanced focus; our brand has made us realize that we can't be all things to all people. What I mean is that there is temptation to adjust messaging based on how our competitors are promoting their products instead of selling our unique brand attributes. It's easy for a sales person to come back and say 'a competitor is saying this and we need to say it too – instead of remembering that our brand was developed based on what our customers value and not on today's trend. Often times after we've presented our value proposition – our brand – to prospects, they'll say 'you're right I never thought of that before.'

Brandon (CVMN):

The most challenging part about valuing partnerships so intensely is that we are relational as well as structural, which means we don't have a cookie cutter program: We are essentially trying to share ownership in order to provide the greatest good to the greatest number. As a result we sometimes run into difficulties especially in our strategic planning process.

This is particularly challenging for our board of directors because they don't have as much exposure to the different needs of partners. They are trying to make decisions based on the needs of the partners, but the needs vary. Our role is to provide both direction and support which can get confusing at times.

One specific example is that a national conference topic may be irrelevant to one partner and just perfect to another. Another is that a service in different cities may operate in different ways, which, if not communicated clearly, can confuse outsiders. The need to be extra good at communicating can slow things down but it's critical.

Kessler (HNE):

The struggle is to connect the theory of the brand with day-to-day work—showing people how it will connect to what they want to accomplish that very day. If we had a pre-existing ad budget the advantage would be clearer but the challenge would be bigger—how do we get our words to line up with reality? We've done a good job of having our brand line up with reality – we've struggled with the second part of the equation – getting the word out. When employees see our message out there in the market, it will be easier to connect the dots. We will have employees ask, "Where does 'How can we help?' line up with what I do every day?" and that will help people connect the brand with results.

Chamberlin (Tacoma Art Museum):

The hardest thing has been, as a visual institution, to determine the intersection between our brand and that of each exhibition. Each show has its own look and feel, so how do we align our institution with a look and feel of an exhibition and yet remain true to both of them?

Gemperle (Shurgard):

At first blush, *Expect More* seems awfully vague. Expect more what? More money? More service? More problems?

The challenge is to break down *Expect More* into something tangible for every level of the organization. As I mentioned above, we succeeded at creating specific proof points for our store teams, so we know what *Expect More* means at our stores.

But what exactly does it mean for my department? Or our teams who buy and build stores? Or the receptionist at the main office? Or our Chairman and CEO?

Every person in our company, whether he or she works at a store or not, does provide service to someone else. Our task at hand, then, is to determine how each of us can provide *Expect More* service to whomever that might be. In so doing, we'll learn to expect more of ourselves and each other – and how can we not be a better company for that?

How did your organization get sponsorship for living your brand?

Valandra (GA):

It was the director's idea and he asked me to go out and discover how to do it – he explained it was what we needed to do to bring everyone into a single focus. He had a positive brand experience in another organization.

The support was there at the top from the beginning – I think he heard people telling him the same things over and over – we had divisions who were part of GA in name but they operated as separate organizations.

Gemperle (Shurgard):

We included many different team members – across all disciplines – in the process. In our company, just like most others, support from the top is essential. But if our store managers don't buy into a program, it won't happen – guaranteed. So as we were creating our brand promise, we traveled to several different markets and met with store teams. We talked about the meaning of a brand, why it's important, what ours might be, if we even need one. We talked even further about different brand promises, and how comfortable they felt promising certain things to customers. The promise has to be at least a little lofty to be meaningful – and the loftier the promise, the greater the risk. What kinds of risks were they willing to take on in order to set ourselves apart from our competitors, and gain an edge in the minds and hearts of our customers?

Ferguson (Microsoft):

We have sponsorship right from the top. Steve Ballmer our CEO. He wants to know how our work relates to our mission/ values / tenets / brand. It is at a reflex level with him. Also our VP of HR, Ken DiPietro thinks of our brand holistically.

Also our brand team (which sits in corporate marketing) has done a good job of articulating what our brand can be. They set things up well for us so we can work toward living it in our group. They have also worked with us to give leaders who do have the natural inclination to use our brand as a guide; tools to help them do so. They served up brand templates.

Gier (IDX Carecast):

I knew we needed to do a thorough assessment of our current brand perception to find out how best to position ourselves in the marketplace, but we didn't have any good market data. There wasn't any research, especially within our customer base or, if there was, the right questions were not being asked. We had to start by asking the basic but important question 'what makes us unique?' Because "brand" was viewed more as a marketing gimmick at best, I had to make brand relevant to the leadership team and individual departments by selling the benefits gained by all core areas of our business including development, customer service, operations and so on. For instance, the business argument for operations is that they are responsible for implementing software and providing ongoing customer support once it is installed. The business benefit is that if we are aligned internally around what our customers value in service, this will have a direct impact on customer satisfaction. If customers are satisfied, they will continue to purchase our services, not to mention pay for services rendered on a timely basis. So, in this case there is a monetary benefit.

Kessler (HNE):

This effort came from a strategic plan. We had not done one for some time and when we did the planning process, it became obvious to us if we had a brand, we couldn't really identify what it was. We also couldn't articulate what our unique advantage in the marketplace was. We consciously identified this as an area of focus within our strategic planning process. This showed people why we needed to work on it and implicitly suggested benefits we would get from spending money on it. This has not gone as quickly as we would have liked – we have not translated our work directly into increased market awareness.

Chamberlin (Tacoma Art Museum):

Part of it was the circumstance at the time: We were moving from an old to a new building and knew it was important to get off on the right foot. Because first impressions make a difference, we needed to have our ducks in a row by grand opening, to know who we were, and to know what was valuable about us that we didn't want to lose in the move.

Another way we got sponsorship was to involve key people including both skeptics and supporters. By having them be part of the process, we got everyone to buy in and made the brand an easier sell to all our stakeholders.

Were there investments you made that you now think were mistakes? Investments you didn't make but should have?

Valandra (GA):

No, I don't think we've made any investments that haven't paid off—financially, we got a good deal with Parker LePla; the web site usability study was also very successful.

Gier (IDX Carecast):

No investments were a mistake. However we could have made additional investments in training our employees around the brand so brand would become more second nature. Based on our most current brand audit we are seeing that integration of our brand into employee decision making needs to become more automatic and routine. Soon after the brand was launched we did some brand training with our employees but we didn't have the resource capacity to continue it. Also, I think we underestimated the impact and power of brand training – especially among our employees. Most of brand efforts have been external rather than internal – when you are strapped for resources the external sell is easier than the internal sell to management. Our initial training was successful – we spent a considerable amount of time working with individual departments to understand where and how they touched the brand. We then created action plans for each department to teach them how to apply the brand in their daily work. We also coached employees on how to be on brand so brand-based action would be automatic in daily decision making. We did this by showing relevancy to the brand and their contributions to it in their daily decisions. Employees appreciated this degree of customized training – making brand real for each area of our business.

Kessler (HNE):

We haven't succeeded in having a day-to-day brand manager. A lot of what we've done has been by committee and volunteer effort. That is a big part of why things are going slower than I would like. If we had someone whose job was to do this we would have had a lot more progress – it's been okay. In reality there are advantages to having the committee – a lot of people on the committee have become brand ambassadors and champions and taken this idea and run with it. That wouldn't have happened if there was a single brand person responsible for moving things forward.

Ferguson (Microsoft):

Investments that did not pay off – I can't think of any right now.

Our leaders are not always ready for the investments we want to make, so we hold off. On the horizon, all HR tools, systems and solutions will have a unified and consistent interface that will communicate and support our brand. Our systems will enable people to do their work. Investments here will go a long way to living our brand. Sponsorship of course has to be there.

Where we had false starts, I now see the reasons. For example we looked at some of our training materials in isolation and should have waited to look at all HR materials.

Brandon (CVMN):

We invested in a database and a tool that we thought would help all our federation members. However our members have different funders, different data needs, different technology, etc. Since we are not just in the data business, this was a very hard partnership investment to execute effectively on. We could not please everyone in the amount of time and resources we had to invest here. We've since revised our plan and approach, distilling our data needs down to the minimum needed to tell our collective story well.

Chamberlin (Tacoma Art Museum):

I don't think we made any investments that were mistakes. The one thing we didn't do was really push finding that marriage of our visual brand and each exhibitions' brand; we still struggle with that. That may not be easy to solve. We need some strong visual association with the museum that can brand all our exhibitions as well.

Gemperle (Shurgard):

To be honest, I don't think we took enough risk. We wanted to be absolutely, positively certain we could live up to our four proof point promises before we published them. The good news is that we have lived up to them. But if we came up with a promise or two that might be more of a stretch for us, even with a little risk, the wedge between us and our competitors would be just a little deeper.

Did you encounter resistance to making alignment changes? What were they? How did you resolve them?

Fukai (GA):

Resistance comes in the form of what Steve Valandra refers to as the 'flavor of the month' or others view of the brand as a slogan or a logo – all of the things integrated branding is not. We are working with the brand team to get things on the ground and actually motivating employees in a way that causes change. We were in danger of having too much of a linear process going on – if it takes too long – customers don't see anything that is different other than our words. Another issue is that in government it's all about process – in the private sector it's about moving things quickly. We have to find the right balance of honoring the process and moving the ball quickly which gets back to my struggle of wanting to say, 'let's do it'. I could write a list right now of how to do what needs to be done, but this would not get accepted and would create extra work on the other end.

Gier (IDX Carecast):

It started first with a successful internal launch. Employees were the first ones we reached out to in order to generate excitement and enthusiasm around our new brand. As part of the launch, we created a video of testimonials from customers on how they were already living the brand. We wanted to help employees visualize what brand is to our organization and show its application across all areas of our business – particularly its impact on customer success. We then developed a brand training program to teach employees how to apply brand in their respective areas. Prior to the training, we worked with managers to understand where they touched the customer experience, how they contributed to customer satisfaction. As the brand team we took the attitude when visiting other departments that 'we are visiting your world. We don't understand your total operations, but we want to give you the tools to have an impact on making better decisions based on brand.' We'd learn about their processes and then offer enough suggestions to get them thinking about how to ask themselves the right questions in order to make different decisions that are on brand. We helped employees summarize the work they do, where they touch the brand, recommend changes and how they would support our brand. We left it up to them to do the actual work. This helped them live the brand and apply a new way of thinking to their challenges.

For example, in operations there are several touch points for our customers – as the customer goes through the implementation process there are handoffs within the organization as the customer transitions from implementation to support. The message we heard from customers is that we were inconsistent in the way we communicate to customers, employees didn't communicate with one another and the handoffs were very rough. We worked with teams to better streamline that. We asked questions like: 'Where are the breakdowns? Who needs to be included on customer communication lists so that employees are better informed?' and 'How do we tie that back to making improvements?' At that time there were a number of values we rolled out – making it easier to link our brand to specific departmental actions.

Brandon (CVMN):
Yes. There has been resistance to operating the way we do, but I believe it is a healthy and necessary tension to be a dynamic organization.

At the board level, we had some resistance when board members wanted to see more new sites without necessarily investing in the sustainability of already-existing partner sites. We had to revisit our mission and the importance of partnerships. It helped to share specific information with the board from our sites, so they could see what was needed in order to sustain delivery of CVM to people in crisis and transition, which is, of course, our mission.

We also have encountered resistance from our site partners if we try to standardize service delivery procedures. We have decided to push these types of issues to the local level, focusing on three basic standards at the national level: 1) the voicemail must be free to the end user, 2) it must be accessible across the community and from a broad range of agency types, and 3) only visual monitoring of voicemail activity is permissible.

There is ongoing tension between how directive and flexible to be in our partnerships; in order to learn more, we conduct site visits, have partner sites on our board of directors, and evaluate our MOA performance annually.

Chamberlin (Tacoma Art Museum):

Some people just don't like change so we went into the process expecting some resistance. For the curators, using the brand tools meant a new way of thinking about exhibitions – it made them look at our customers and review how they explained the art in a new way. There is a dynamic tension between the communications person and the curator's point of view, and it's a sensitive thing for the communications person to try and tell the curator how to do their job from a brand perspective.

The curators had ways of communicating that weren't necessarily on brand, due to how much they invested in studying the art and their fear that we would dumb it down through our branding. But once they understood it was about getting people to understand the art better and that there are different ways to promote things, they saw the benefit of being consistent.

Gemperle (Shurgard):

Once we agreed that expect more was what we wanted to deliver, then focus was the issue, not resistance. Since we hire the kinds of people who are able to deliver on expect more, we are all aligned because it's how we naturally think about our business.

The greater challenge for us has been to define how we deliver our brand promise internally. How can the human resources team, for example, deliver more than expected to our accounting department? Our payroll team? Our asset management group? What does that look like? We're still evolving our internal response and are marshalling the resources to address how we live our brand internally.

What advice would you give to a new brand manager? (Unique insights)

Valandra (GA):

First be patient – the changes will not happen quickly – I thought we could move this faster but as we got more into it we realized we can't move too quickly. If we did, we would pass over some important steps along the way and we would fail.

Second, understand that there will be resistance from more than just a few people – even in the face of valid research.

Gier (IDX Carecast):

To clearly understand the definition of brand within their organization. While external markets are important, brand managers need to understand its application across all organizational entities. They also need to be able to create focused action plans – so that the compass is relevant to the entire organization. This is not to say that advertising is not important – but that it is just one medium. We found that when all entities – such as development, HR and executive leadership – are in alignment, they have a huge impact on the ultimate effectiveness of our brand in the marketplace.

One area you have not focused on in these questions is monitoring your brand. What is different today is not what will be different in three to five years. If you don't monitor effectiveness your brand will look like every other one and you will lose your competitive edge.

Ferguson (Microsoft):

They must see the job as a driver of change. They will be making the brand real in an integrated way. Expect that it is a change process and they will need to bring people along with them. It is somewhat intuitive how our brand fits into an IT company. They will need to leverage obvious synergies in our brand.

What they do ultimately needs to be "owned" by the business. We can construct it, but they have to own it for it to become fully integrated and real. For example: Our CEO took an interest in culture alignment and charged other executives to think about cultural evolution to support our business needs and our brand. He demonstrated some direct conviction here.

HR and marketing need to partner really, really closely. It is ESSENTIAL. They need to stay connected and in agreement.

Never isolate yourself from your customer (Microsoft employees and leaders) when you are trying to do your work. What they do has to be authentic to employees. You have to be right next to employees to know this, otherwise it won't be authentic.

Gemperle (Shurgard):

The process of establishing the brand takes a lot of thought. Research is really important. Does the brand promise connect with the customer in an emotional way? Is it relevant and meaningful? Are we making the brand clear enough to employees so they know how to live it? Is it aspirational enough – but still achievable? Can we not only live it, but live *up* to it?

Kessler (HNE):

Two parts: First, you want to connect the brand to the underlying strategy of the company – how does the brand relate to your corporate strategy? If you can't answer that question you need to run and not walk to whoever you report to and say we need to deal with this! The second part is to constantly have your eye on how brand relates to the daily work of the company on an ongoing basis. If you can't make that connection, people will begin to see it as a project or activity and not part of the corporate culture or daily business.

Chamberlin (Tacoma Art Museum):

The most important thing was to make sure the staff could all relate and talk about the brand and know all the tools and how to use them. Accomplishing this made my job much easier. It's also important to keep staff continually invested, that is, keep them tied in as time goes on beyond the initial roll out. We tried to make it fun, too, so that living the brand was a positive thing versus a drag.

Did you run into key tipping points that made it successful and what were they?

Valandra (GA):

Communicating over and over and over is the biggest one. One of the most effective ways is email. We've also had quarterly reports where all the divisions report in on the state of the agency. Branding is always a topic at our annual leadership meetings of all managers. Additionally, we have an in-house newsletter, with a regular brand column. Our executive director talks about our brand at his weekly management team meeting. I can't stress how important the communication and how you can't do it enough. If there is any void at any time, people will fill it in and begin to wonder if there is any forward movement at all or if this is just another management initiative that will fall apart.

A second tipping point is to develop job descriptions and evaluations that reinforce the brand promise. That is something that will take some time. If we had rushed, we would have missed those.

Our promise of essential operations partner requires us to get better at serving our customers across divisions in a coordinated way. The idea of creating an account manager by customer rather than by division is something we are testing right now. This was one of the key areas that our brand team has identified to explore more fully. Early on there was a lot of resistance from the management team to the account manager idea. They were already shooting it down when it was just being floated out there as an idea. There is a sub group within our brand team that is looking at the account manager role. They are asking for volunteers from the programs to give them insights as to both the possibilities and the pitfalls of such a role. Without our executive director mentioning this idea repeatedly to the management team, it probably wouldn't have happened. In the end it came down to the director saying this is something we were going to look at.

Ferguson (Microsoft):

We are in the perfect storm of readiness. Microsoft leaders are really signed up for the brand. We are through that work. Now it is so much easier to think and talk in terms of the brand.

Gier (IDX Carecast):

Our initial brand efforts were not widely accepted by long time employees who were resistant to this change. So for our launch to be successful, we knew early on that the co-founders of our product were key to a successful brand launch. Given their status and influence power within our organization, they had to come along internally – otherwise we would not have had alignment. This was the single most important tipping point. Also important was the fact we could demonstrate the brand as experienced by our customers. While the brand was new, the value built was already showing up tangibly with our customers, which made it real, as well as easy for our employees to understand. The only other tipping point was ensuring that the brand team was a multi-departmental process – comprised of every entity with our organization. This representation helped us to get over the perception that this was a marketing program. Other important factors were having leadership support and also making sure that the research had substance to it – selecting a firm that sees brand beyond logos, graphics and color.

One that understands there is more substance to your brand and that it is the heart of the organization. A lot of professionals go wrong by hiring design firms. They misunderstand what brand truly is versus a name and identity. If it is just a name and identity you are not going to get your employees aligned because there will be no compass to guide all areas of the business.

Kessler (HNE):
We first did this in the context of strategic planning and what we hoped to accomplish. Secondly, we got buy in from our CEO who thought this was a good idea and our senior management team said 'Yes, this makes sense.' Third, we found the people in the company who were interested in this and kept some of the momentum and interest going. Fourth, we've tried to keep the brand discussion tied to the focus on the day-to-day work and continue to show that connection – that's very difficult – that's the crux right now. We did a good job of explaining it in associate meetings but we must continue to show people how it applies to them.

Chamberlin (Tacoma Art Museum):
One key tipping point was to manifest the brand personality with visual objects – silly ones. People were given these objects, they would keep them on their desk and pass them around to others caught living the brand. This kept the brand top of mind for people. And if I asked staff people about the brand traits, they would relate to the objects and feed that back. This in turn really helped drive the brand personality traits home.

Were there any key people or roles that helped the process?

Valandra (GA):
The director and deputy director being part of the brand team has been a huge benefit. The deputy director has been responsible for strategic planning and all division-level plans. It's his job to make sure branding is a focus and a priority for assistant directors and program managers. People here know that the deputy director is getting orders from the director. Having this top level support and a brand team that is representative of everyone across the agency are two key roles that help with brand success. And we've added to that brand team – the program manager for employee service, the HR people, and the guy

who is our legislative liaison. He knows who is affected by any changes we make.

Gier (IDX Carecast):

The leadership and brand teams were very important. Our leaders were participants in our program launch and gave formal presentations on the importance of this change. We also knew we would not have 100% of employees on board at first. We were committed to working with those individuals and sooner or later they would come along. We believed if we could get 75% of our employees on board, we would have a foundation for future success. Certainly today a majority are, and we can see that direct impact by how our employees are making decisions and telling us stories about how they are using the brand.

We knew we would have to go through changes as we developed the brand – branding was a significant change and we had also gone through a name change and had gone from a small startup to a large major international corporation – many people thought the brand efforts had taken the last thread of their heritage and torn it away. We approached the two co-founders of this operating unit and engaged them early on in the process, as part of the process. The success of the launch would be contingent on their buy in – whether they were a part of the brand.

Gemperle (Shurgard)

Brand manager isn't a position – it's a culture and a frame of mind at Shurgard. Essential in the development and integration of the brand was our marketing team, but it can sure stop there if nobody else climbs aboard. It worked like an assembly line, HR joined in helping with the integration into training, communication and rewards and our operations team brought it full circle through service delivery on the promise.

Chamberlin (Tacoma Art Museum):

Having that brand manager is absolutely essential, otherwise the brand will disappear. It's also important to have the leader buy into the brand, make it important, put it on agendas, and bring it up as a filter for all decisions. I can't push it up as the brand manager, it has to come from the top down to be effective.

Do you cultivate brand champions? How?

Gemperle (Shurgard)

We do create brand champions. Our most effective champions are our store managers who deliver expect more service to their customers. We celebrated 10 store managers in the past year by flying them in from all over the country to our annual shareholders meeting where we presented them with expect more awards. We also have other various forms of expect more recognition throughout our organization, creating heroes among our employees for living up to our brand promise.

Valandra (GA):

I don't think we do that all that well. I think it is something we are aware of but haven't put a big effort into yet.

Gier (IDX Carecast):

We incorporate the brand into the new hire orientation. We do a presentation about our product and our brand attributes, what our customers value and introduce the brand to each new employee in this way. While that is one component of cultivating brand champions, there is a lot more we can do which is around additional training. We are also talking about creating a brand website, creating an award system for employees who demonstrate they are living the brand, and also working brand living into our performance goals.

Brandon (CVMN):

Yes. In a number of structural ways. We have federation members (those we partner with) on our board of directors. We also have board term limits.

Our board participates in our annual conference for federation members.

Also pursuing and valuing partnerships is institutionalized in our Memorandum of Agreement and our application process, so those that we work with are already used to valuing partnerships.

In our hiring process we look for people who are broad thinkers and we include many of our partners in the interview process. For example: our technology manager position remained open for longer than anticipated – until we could get enough of the site managers and staff to agree they could partner effectively with the new hire.

Chamberlin (Tacoma Art Museum):

Absolutely. The central brand concept of "mind-stretching" really hit home with our educators, so they took it really far. It is the concept that was in mind when the Open Art Studio, a hands-on artmaking room for visitors, was designed to make personal connections to the art on view. For the staff, we also created brand-based rewards that paid people off with candy bars when they did actions on-brand.

Was this a rewarding process for you?

Valandra (GA):

Yes, for sure! I just learned a hell of a lot more about things in general and it has given me a better focus and a reason for that focus on what I am trying to do here. It comes down to answering the question of 'What's in it for me?' From a personal standpoint, the answer is to keep my job in the future by understanding what we at GA could do better than the private sector or much less expensively. If we can better serve our agencies but we don't do the things that demonstrate that or promote that, we will be out of jobs.

Developing focus among all employees about improving our services doesn't mean we have to completely revamp everything. It can be done in little ways such as by answering phones or by who we decide to communicate with on certain initiatives. A GA division came up with a contract for State employees where the State realizes a 30% savings. But they went through this contracting process without properly informing a large business association. And out of 1,800 possible stakeholders they only contacted 60. Once the contract was awarded, everyone came out of the woodwork – we've had workers and legislators calling on this— we didn't do the proper communications upfront and we had to do a lot of damage control. If we had done a better job of communicating – then instead of seeing GA as a hindrance to their activities, State employees would view us as their essential operations partner.

I have learned a lot and I went on a great trip to a brand conference in Chicago and listened to all these big corporations like FedEx and their brand experiences. The problems they've encountered along the way are just the same as ours and I also found out that just because we are a government agency, doesn't mean we are behind the curve. Most of the private sector companies attending were way behind us! They hadn't done the research, had no brand team, and didn't know how to go about properly explaining what they were trying to do. They were having communication problems because they hadn't done anything to base their brand promise on, nor had they put together the proper group of people to promote it. They were looking for the lesson plan – first you do this and then this and this. I realized we had the steps and we were going through them properly.

Gier (IDX Carecast):

Absolutely! My background is marketing and I am very passionate about my profession and work. But unless I have something of value to market there is no substance to what I do on a daily basis. I don't have direction or that compass to guide competitive marketing strategies. I can come up with great marketing programs and use all the marketing tools but it is not very satisfying. In addition, leading the brand development process allowed me to step away from my marketing role and focus more on the lifeline of our business. And today, as we conclude our first brand audit, seeing the impact our brand has made on customer loyalty and satisfaction is very rewarding and validating. This speaks to the importance of the brand and the contribution it makes for the organization

Ferguson (Microsoft):

Absolutely! It has been great to see the impact on employees. It is rewarding to enable our leaders to be more successful in their capabilities. I think our customers will benefit from that.

Kessler (HNE):

Yes, absolutely. Going through the process is incredibly rewarding. It is a tremendous lens. It helps you look at your organization in ways you weren't likely to have tried otherwise. You really do see what is there and what's missing about the company in an understandable and comprehensive way. You see it holographically – each of the pieces of information shows you the whole picture.

Brandon (CVMN):

Yes! I feel like I've received an MBA without paying tuition. It is incredibly rewarding. It is such a challenge on many levels. A board member told me that it is a unique opportunity to grow as much as I have in the time that I've been here.

Such fantastic things come of embracing the partnership tension between the national office needs and the federation member needs. I find it really rewarding.

I'm fortunate to have been around long enough to see the integration of our mission, strategy, work practices, values and decisions, etc. The alignment we've developed on our brand value has helped us become a much stronger and more compelling organization.

Chamberlin (Tacoma Art Museum):

Yes, the brand process started a conversation and gave us some answers we didn't have before. Having the shared vocabulary with board and staff to talk about some things is invaluable. We couldn't have said why we were different from other visual art institutions before, now each person can. And because the research and facilitation came from outside the organization, that made it easier for the staff to buy into the results. When you hire a non-partisan entity to help define your brand, it makes it feel more valid to people involved in the process.

The word "brand" carries a lot of meanings. How do you refer to your organization's "brand" (some call it values, some call it vision, some call it customer experience)?

Valandra (GA):

The word "brand" kept coming up as a nebulous term and a lot of people were suspicious of it. We did away with that. We said it is 'the promise that you keep' instead. We call it the GA promise – that resonates with people here. It's all about what our promise is and how to honor it and what people can do to help that along. A lot of people needed it explained which gives us an opportunity to achieve greater understanding and usage.

Brandon (CVMN):

What you're talking about is our values. We value partnerships as the way we achieve our mission.

Gemperle (Shurgard):

Let's face it – Shurgard is not a sexy brand and storage is not a sexy business. Our brand is not ubiquitous like Nike, Nordstrom, Crest or FedEx and our brand isn't yet strong enough to stand on its own. Still, we provide a valuable service and we're a truly great place to work. We're proud of the brand we have. We call it our brand promise and values, and even though we may never be the kind of product that commands that compelling brand we'll work hard to make it a meaningful promise to the people who use us, work with and for us, and invest in us.

Kessler (HNE):

Calling it the brand has been a challenge in some ways for people who associate brand with just advertising and image, and not the substance. That is why we were excited about the tagline, 'How can we help?' It enables us to talk internally about the brand without saying the word brand. It also redirects people who think they already know it all to more concrete action.

What should MBA schools teach about branding and its real application inside an organization? (beyond communications branding?)

Valandra (GA):

Focusing on the realities of what branding is. That it needs to be research-based, employing appropriate and valid research upfront. Everything builds from that. People can identify the 'flavor of the month' if there isn't a foundation of valid research that applies to them. With good research, they can start to see what it is all about. An outside perspective is the key. We couldn't have done the research ourselves. To have a third party such as Parker LePla come in gives it a lot more weight than if it was done in-house.

I'd probably also tell business schools to teach guidance counseling, a focus on the customer and an understanding that it is something that won't be done quickly.

Gier (IDX Carecast):

Do MBA schools even teach anything about brand? Number one they should teach it as a business strategy. That the compass drives the business strategy for the organization – if you don't have a pulse on what's important to customers even the written business plan will not result in much, because you have missed the point. If you don't know the unique value you bring to the marketplace, I don't know how you can compete and have a sustainable business.

In addition, the curriculum needs to incorporate courses on how to build a brand, and its application across all disciplines. This would make the brand manager's life much easier because executives would get this context as part of the core curriculum being taught to our future leaders.

Ferguson (Microsoft):

Change management! And, a little bit of organization development.

In my MBA we never covered the internal aspects of branding. This is starting to emerge – but the programs need more.

There needs to be more on *employee value propositions.* Where it takes the brand and puts it in terms of what you need to give to employees – in order to get the right things from them. There should be more case studies here.

I'd like to know more about what is different when you are integrating your brand internally vs. externally. Example: With segmented business does the brand show up differently to different employees?

I'd also like to see more on linkage to corporate culture. More culture theory.

Kessler (HNE):

I've never been to a business school. But I think the phrase you use at Parker LePla is essential, 'the promise that you keep.' It is easy to forget in the nuts and bolts of the business that it is really the promises you do – or don't keep – that make the difference. There are dozens of companies that I can think of who have gotten into trouble because they forgot that – being reminded that that's really why you are there in the first place. You won't be in business very long if you keep breaking your promises. Brand is about looking at the whole. It is a really useful way to bring your attention back to the business. It is the gestalt of the business. A way to look at the whole enterprise without getting caught up in the details.

Brandon (CVMN):

Listen to people as much as you can and communicate effectively. Consider different forums, consider who to ask, consider how to ask, or just listen attentively. Sometimes it is good to argue to better understand how to partner with someone. And despite the wonders of email, sometimes it's really important to pick up the phone – or better yet – have a face to face.

Another very important skill is about how you communicate information – the presentation. Nuance becomes lost in bulleted lists, but we can't expect people to read paragraphs anymore. So how do you best synthesize the information and communicate it to others so that your audience truly comprehends the information, the context, and the critical decision or action to be taken? Communicating is not just sharing what you want, but how you want to share it.

What are the biggest challenges in prioritizing alignment activities?

Valandra (GA):

We knew we had to communicate with people. We felt like we had to do something to show that this was moving along. But until I saw the experience of the other organizations, I didn't understand as well the importance of focusing upfront on talking to all employees. Now we are doing that and getting the word out to as many people as possible, top to bottom. It was also challenging to narrow our work plan down to a few key things – manageable goals that will show results. Initially these include identifying employees who have been part of the discussion with the director, the web page suitability study, and getting at some of the things we talk about in our promise. For instance, speaking in language customers understand and focusing on our businesses where they make the most sense together rather than separating by division.

We are also developing a new logo. This is another aspect where it took a lot more time than I thought it would. We decided to hold off on implementation because our executives didn't want employees to think that the logo is what branding is all about. We wanted to get other things going to show them that this was about more concrete stuff – such as organization-wide account managers, and overall service guarantees are of greater importance to help build our promise next year.

It would help if there were somebody dedicated totally to this effort. A lot of this is on me but it is only part of my job. It takes up a lot of my time – it takes time away from some of the others things I would like to focus on.

The other point I want to make is that many of the brand books are based on consumer products. Our sales cycle is unique at 18-36 months. We are having to continuously build relationships, and maintain relationships with our prospects. It's important that you have a brand that is meaningful and helps to guide and sustain those relationships and keep us in the process. In addition to that there are a number of different touchpoints where you have customer service and operations involved in the process – that prospect has touched every person in our organization. Because of that brand alignment, it is very important for customers to know we are aligned and consistent. There can be just one thing that can destroy us – if just one goes wrong. Perhaps over a product demonstration that has gone bad or a poorly written proposal – you need everyone on board to understand what is unique and how we are to act throughout the process.

We've incorporated the brand into strategic imperatives and based performance on it. We may see a change going into 2005 based on this. We also rewrote the position descriptions and the type of people we were looking for.

Kessler (HNE):

To be able to connect brand work back to challenges in day-to-day business. Business is so challenging for everyone. The pressure to focus on what is immediately in front of your face is huge – unless you can remind people about the big picture in a compelling way, it's hard for them to care about it. You need to be able to tell them, 'This is how it will help with the problems you are facing right now.'

Brandon (CVMN):

As a non-profit, we need to balance our mission with our resources – they call it managing the double bottom line. We look for the biggest bang for the buck that leverages real impact, not just a quick fix, and we need to maintain our integrity. There's typically too much to do, so sometimes it is really hard to determine what the priority is and I'll be the first to admit that I rely on my staff to help me! We remind each other of the organization's purpose, and the clearer that gets; the easier it gets to make decisions.

NOTES

[1] See Chapter 1 for more references.

GLOSSARY OF TERMS

Alignment The process of making all company actions and communications consistent with brand tool direction.

Associations Shortcuts to brand meaning and the most memorable landmark for telling the world about your brand. Examples: the AFLAC duck, the Intel Inside four-tone jingle, and the Nike swoosh.

Brand The sum total of customer experience. It includes all of your company's actions, communications and customer interactions. It results from your brand promise, strategic role, tools, culture, brand assets, practices and communications.

Brand assets Brand assets result from any company activities that benefit customers, such as unique customer experience, unique company approach, company reputation, industry leadership position, quality control systems, employee experience/training, company culture, employee compensation and rewards, and delivery systems.

Brand-based due diligence Capturing the most value from any merger, acquisition or company sale through analyzing and integrating company brand tools, cultures and brand assets.

Brand equity The value your brand has in the target customer's mind. High equity brands translate into bottom line benefits because their customers will pay more for their products, tend not to shop around and are influential in getting others to buy their products.

Brand equity pyramid A scale that measures customer and employee relationship strength that also correlates to company brand equity.

Brand plan The brand strategy broken down into work items and deliverables.

Brand promise The sum total of all the brand tools.

Brand report card   An at-a-glance view of significant brand equity and customer experience measurements that can be used for reporting and continuous improvement.

Brand strategy   The action plan for aligning and enhancing company actions with its brand to improve customer experience over time. The strategy is part of the corporate strategic planning process.

Brand structure   The relationship between the company's umbrella brand and sub-brands and other unbranded services. This differs from an organizational structure that defines how job functions are related to each other. A brand and its related products and services can be delivered from a variety of organizational structures.

Brand tools   The set of concepts, including mission, values, story, principle, personality, and associations, that collectively define the brand promise.

Communications branding   Where all communications are aligned with the company's brand tools – the lowest of the three branding levels. (See customer touchpoint and integrated branding).

Conveyor   Any action or communication based on the brand tools.

Corporate culture   Shared values, approach to decisions, personality traits and cultural norms.

Cultural norms   Behavioral and language shortcuts that allow employees to successfully take actions and make decisions. Can describe the 'way we do things' within an organization. In this book, also called rules of the road.

Customer (as used in this book)   May mean your clients, funders, donors, constituents, dealers, partners, or even the general public. A customer is anyone whom the organization sells to, sells with or services.

Customer experience   The sum total of experiences your customer has with your company, including product use, communications, sales, service, word of mouth discussion, etc.

Customer touchpoint branding   The second level of branding where all communications and all departmental activities that come in contact with the customer are aligned with the company brand tools. (See communications branding and integrated branding.)

Integrated branding A consistent set of individual and group company actions and communications that is based on what the company does well and what customers consider important. The deepest level of brand alignment. (See communications branding and customer touchpoint branding.)

Integrated brand model A model displaying the brand tools used by leaders and employees inside brand-driven companies to live their brand. These tools include mission, values, story, principle, personality and associations.

Integrated brand process The series of activities leading to a company living its integrated brand. These activities include in-depth research, analysis, facilitated consensus meetings, brand strategy, roll out to employees and customers and continuous improvement.

Landmarks   Company practices and brand assets that give employees and customers more context around the company brand.

Leader (as used in this book) Anyone who has the responsibility to guide others in a direction they deem successful. There are leaders at all levels and focused on all types of work and deliverables.

Living the integrated brand   The actions an entire company takes to execute against its brand promise.

Mission   One of the brand tools. Describes what a company does, the business it is in.

Off-brand Implies an action or message that is not consistent with (and perhaps conflicts with) a company's brand tools and strategic role.

On-brand   Implies an action or message that is consistent with a company's brand tools and strategic role.

Personality   One of the brand tools.   Your brand's public face – usually experienced in the tone and manner of your communications and marketing materials.

Practices   Group activities that are necessary to conduct business.   They can be inter- or intra-departmental.

Principle   One of the brand tools.   A company's unique approach to its business, used as a compass by employees for making decisions and communicating.   A differentiator that provides direction for guiding 'on-brand' activities.

Return on brand investment   Measurement that connects brand equity increases/ decreases with investment in integrated branding strategies and activities.

Rules of the road   Cultural norms that shape employee behavior within an organization.

Sponsor   The individual(s) who has the power to legitimize a work item or deliverable and demonstrate approval through communicating decisions, prioritization, allocation of resources, reward and redirection.

Story   One of the brand tools.   What individuals within a company say to others about their history and purpose.   Describes brand concepts in the context of past actions.

Strategic role   Answers the question of 'what part do you want to play in your best customers' lives?'   The strategic role keeps companies open to new trends in meeting customer needs by taking the long-term focus off of specific products or services.

Sustainable business   The ability to retain a healthy market share and margins over many years.

Values   One of the brand tools.   Cherished beliefs (often unwritten) that influence how individuals work and which are followed even in difficult situations.   One input into the formation of corporate cultures.

Verbal branding The use of language that consistently conveys the personality of the company.

Visual branding A corporate identity, typically consisting of a logo and business paper design, but which may also include graphic templates and illustration and photographic style treatments.

INDEX

202, 224, 239, 258, 273, 288, 311

Extension limits, evaluate brand, 298

External vii, 4, 6, 21, 30, 47, 48, 57, 59, 97, 103, 185, 195, 198, 207, 215, 262, 265, 287, 320, 324, 336, 341

audience landmarks, vii, 4, 6, 21, 30, 47, 48, 57, 59, 103, 185, 195, 198, 207, 215, 287, 97, 262, 265, 320, 324, 336, 341

measurement, 83

F

'Family', 9

Facility design and location, 192

FedEx 5, 11, 190, 193, 194, 204, 254, 347, 349

football weekend, 56, 79, 190

living the brand, 64, 212, 271, 346

redesign of in support of brand equity 194, 231

success in branding customer experience, vii, ix, 13, 22, 24, 33, 39, 65, 71, 105, 140, 159, 227, 235, 244, 245, 247, 305, 338, 355

Financial services company debacle in branding as 'marketing only' campaign, 11

Flexibility, company, 157, 160, 307

Followers, effective leaders have, 180

Follow the leader culture type, 128, 129, 130

Ford Motor Co. and Firestone/Bridgestone crisis, mismanagement of, 198

Fresh, brand strategy that keeps thing, 239

Functionally designed organizations, 160, 161

Functional form, illustration of, 161

G

General Motors, Saturn brand, 28, 91

Glossary, 355

Group actions, aligning, 55, 57

H

Harlem Globe Trotters, 234

Harley-Davidson 8–9, 107–108

'family', 9, 13, 45, 112, 122, 190, 191, 231, 250, 262, 264, 278

tactics to communicate brand destination, 107

Harmonious culture, 128, 143, 143–144

Healthcare v, viii, 43, 70, 275–289, 315–316, 321, 325, 371

branding, state of, 225, 230, 263, 266, 276, 316, 317, 322, 324, 347

journey viii, 1, 3, 15, 17, 39, 41, 42, 45, 50, 55, 58, 127, 130, 149, 150, 167, 168, 181, 201, 223, 227, 243, 261, 293

High relationship brands, 255

Home Depot, 91

HR leader log, 15, 17, 25, 37, 52, 74, 75, 82, 92, 108, 123, 124, 125, 129, 130, 146, 147, 164, 167, 177, 180, 182, 202, 224, 239, 240, 258, 273, 288, 311, 357

Hybrid 160, 162

culture, 56, 85, 109, 113, 126–128, 135, 137, 140, 141, 146, 148, 159, 166, 186, 204, 226, 272, 293, 299, 312

matrix structure, 162–163

I

IBM, 11, 96

and brand communication process, 96

Ikea, 11

In-office visuals, 105

ABOUT THE AUTHOR

F. Joseph LePla has 26 years' experience in integrated branding, marketing and business consulting. He works with executive teams to help them tie their brands to customers' experiences that generate higher ROIs. He co-founded Parker LePla, an integrated branding business consultancy, with Lynn Parker in 1994, and has since grown it into a multi-million dollar agency serving national and international clients in a variety of industries including business-to-business, high technology, healthcare, real estate/resort, government, retail/food and not for profit. Clients have included Group Health, IDX, Blue Cross and Blue Shield, Microsoft, Imation, Weyerhauser, Apple Computer, Attachmate, Hewlett Packard, Tektronix, Avanade, Bastyr University and Newhall Land and Farming.

In the early 1990s, he created the concept and coined the term "integrated branding" in conjunction with Lynn Parker. He co-authored the best selling *Integrated Branding: Becoming Brand Driven Through Company-wide Action*. He is also a contributing author to *Cracking the New E-conomy*, a compendium of practical advice for high-tech start-ups.

Susan Voeller Davis is a leadership and organizational development consultant, trainer, coach and public speaker. She is founder and principal consultant at Leadership Designs (www.leadershipdesigns. com) a consultancy based in Seattle Washington. For nearly 15 years, she has developed executives and leaders at all levels, and helped organizations re-align around strategic shifts, mergers and acquisitions. She also helps companies new and old create or change corporate cultures to adapt to fast moving markets. She has extensive experience with Microsoft and other companies such as Corbis, Avanade, QPass, and Getty Images. Susan holds a Bachelor of Science degree in management and marketing from University of Oregon. Her masters degree is in Applied Behavioral Science from the Leadership Institute of Seattle, Bastyr University. Previous to co-authoring this book, Susan has published articles on leadership and organization alignment for use by her corporate clients.

Lynn M. Parker is co-founder of Parker LePla. Lynn is one of the early practitioners of technology PR. She has worked with many industry pioneers, including Apple, Intel, Microsoft, Tektronix and

Hewlett-Packard. Lynn has been instrumental in creating Parker LePla's approach to integrated branding, and is co-author with Joe LePla of *Integrated Branding: Becoming Brand Driven Through Company-wide Action* (Quorum Books, 1999). Lynn is also an award-winning copywriter, counting ads, brochures, and articles among her credits. Before founding Parker LePla, Lynn was creative strategies director at Floathe Johnson, in Kirkland, WA, senior writer at Regis McKenna in Palo Alto, CA, and reporter at the San Jose Mercury News. She has served on the international and local boards of directors for the World Entrepreneurs Organization, is a mentor to MBA students at the University of Washington, and is president of the board of The Pomegranate Center.

Printed in the United States
221610BV00001B/23/A

9 781425 937089